Sofia 01 | 2021

MW00761240

IAMBLICHUS
of Syrian Chalcis's

THE LIFE OF PYTHAGORAS

VOLUME ONE
Biographies

CHAPTER I
IMPORTANCE OF THE SUBJECT

Since wise people are in the habit of invoking the divinities at the beginning of any philosophic consideration, this is all the more necessary on studying that one which is justly named after the divine Pythagoras. Inasmuch as it emanated from the divinities it could not be apprehended without their inspiration and assistance. Besides, its beauty and majesty so surpasses human capacity, that it cannot be comprehended in one glance. Gradually only can some details of it be mastered when, under divine guidance we approach the subject with a quiet mind. Having therefore invoked the divine guidance, and adapted ourselves and our style to the divine circumstances, we shall acquiesce in all the suggestions that come to us. Therefore we shall not begin with any excuses for the long neglect of this sect, nor by any explanations about its having been concealed by foreign disciplines, or mystic symbols, nor insist that it has been obscured by false and spurious writings, nor make apologies for any special hindrances to its progress. For us it is sufficient that this is the will of the Gods, which all enable us to undertake tasks even more arduous than these. Having thus acknowledged our primary submission to the divinities, our secondary devotion shall be to the prince and father of this philosophy as a leader. We shall, however have to begin by a study of his descent and nationality.

CHAPTER II
YOUTH, EDUCATION, TRAVELS

It is reported that Ancaeus, who dwelt in Cephallenian Samos, was descended from Jupiter, the fame of which honorable descent might have been derived from his virtue, or from a certain magnanimity; in any case, he surpassed the remainder of the Cephallenians in wisdom and renown. This Ancaeus was, by the Pythian oracle, bidden form a colony from Arcadia and Thessaly; and besides leading some inhabitants of Athens, Epidaurus, and Chalcis, he was to render habitable an island, which, from the virtue of the soil and vegetation was to be called Blackleaved, while the city was to be called Samos, after Same, in Cephallenia. The oracle ran thus: "I bid you, Ancaeus, to colonise the maritime island of Same, and to call it Phyllas." That the colony originated from these places is proved first from the divinities, and their sacrifices, which were imported by the inhabitants, second by the relationships of the families, and third by their Samian gatherings.

From the family and alliance of this Ancaeus, founder of the colony, were therefore descended Pythagoras's parents Mnesarchus and Pythais. That Pythagoras was the son of Apollo is a legend due to a certain Samian poet, who thus described the popular recognition of the nobility of his birth. Sang he,

"Pythais, the fairest of the Samian race
From the embraces of the God Apollo
Bore Pythagoras, the friend of Jove."

It might be worth while to relate the circumstances of the prevalence of this report. Mnesarchus had gone to Delphi on a business trip, leaving his wife without any signs of pregnancy. He enquired of the oracle about the event of his return voyage to Syria, and he was informed that his trip would be lucrative, and most conformable to his wishes; but that his wife was now with child, and would present him with a son who would surpass all who had ever lived in beauty and wisdom, and that he would be of the greatest benefit to the human race in everything pertaining to human achievements. But when Mnesarchus realized that the God, without waiting for any question about a son, had by an oracle informed him that he would possess an illustrious prerogative, and a truly divine gift, he immediately changed his wife's former name Parthenis to one reminiscent of the Delphic prophet and her son, naming her Pythais, and the infant, who was soon after born at Sidon in Phoenicia, Pythagoras, by this name commemorating that such an offspring had been promised him by the Pythian Apollo. The assertions of Epimenides, Eudoxus and Xenocrates, that Apollo having at that time already had actual connexion with Parthenis, causing her pregnancy, had regularized that fact by predicting the birth of Pythagoras, are by no means to be admitted. No one will deny that the soul of Pythagoras was sent to mankind from Apollo's domain, having either been one of his attendants, or more intimate associates, which may be inferred both from his birth, and his versatile wisdom.

After Mnesarchus had returned from Syria to Samos, with great wealth derived from a favorable sea-voyage, he built a temple to Apollo, with the inscription of Pythius. He took care that his son should enjoy the best possible education, studying under Creophilus, then under Phorecydos the Syrian, and then under almost all who presided over sacred concerns, to whom he especially recommended his son, that he might be as expert as possible in divinity. Thus by education and good fortune he became the most beautiful and godlike of all those who have been celebrated in the annals of history.

After his father's death, though he was still but a youth, his aspect was so venerable, and his habits so temperate that he was honored and even reverenced by elderly men, attracting the attention of all who saw and heard him speak, creating the most profound impression. That is the reason that many plausibly asserted that he was a child of the divinity. Enjoying the privilege of such a renown, of an education so thorough from infancy, and of so impressive a natural appearance he showed that he deserved all these advantages by deserving them, by the adornment of piety and discipline, by exquisite habits, by firmness of soul, and by a body duly subjected to the mandates of reason. An inimitable quiet and serenity marked all his words and actions, soaring above all laughter, emulation, contention, or any other irregularity or eccentricity; his influence at Samos was that of some beneficent divinity. His great renown, while yet a youth, reached not only men as illustrious for their wisdom as Thales at Miletus, and Bias at Prione, but also extended to the neighboring cities. He was celebrated everywhere as the "long-haired Samian," and by the multitude was given credit for being under divine inspiration.

When he had attained his eighteenth year, there arose the tyranny of Policrates; and Pythagoras foresaw that under such a government his studies might be impeded, as they engrossed the whole of his attention. So by night he privately departed with one Hermodamas, - who was surnamed Creophilus, and was the grandson of the host, friend and general preceptor of the poet Homer, - going to Phorecydes, to Anaximander the natural philosopher, and to Thales at Miletu. He successively associated with each of those philosophers in a manner such that they all loved him, admired his natural endowments, and admitted him to the best of their doctrines, Thales especially, on gladly admitting him to the intimacies of his confidence, admired the great difference between him and other young men, who were in every accomplishment surpassed by Pythagoras. After increasing the reputation Pythagoras had already acquired, by communicating to him the utmost he was able to impart to him, Thales, laying stress on his advanced age and the infirmities of his body, advised him to go to Egypt, to get in touch with the priests of Memphis and Jupiter. Thales confessed that the instruction of these priests was the source of his own reputation for wisdom, while neither his own endowments nor achievements equaled those which were so evident in Pythagoras. Thales insisted that, in view of all this, if Pythagoras should study with those priests, he was certain of becoming the wisest and most divine of men.

CHAPTER III
JOURNEY TO EGYPT

Pythagoras had benefited by the instruction of Thales in many respects, but his greatest lesson had been to learn the value of saving time, which led him to abstain entirely from wine and animal food, avoiding greediness, confining himself to nutriments of easy preparation and digestion. As a result, his sleep was short, his soul pure and vigilant, and the general health of his body was invariable.

Enjoying such advantages, therefore, he sailed to Sidon, which he knew to be his native country, and because it was on his way to Egypt. In Phoenicia he conversed with the prophets who were the descendants of Moschus the physiologist, and with many others, as well as with the local hierephants. He was also initiated into all the mysteries of Byblus and Tyre, and in the sacred functions performed in many parts of Syria. He was led to all this not from any hankering after superstition as might easily be supposed, but rather from a desire of and love for contemplation, and from an anxiety to miss nothing of the mysteries of the divinities which deserved to be learned. After gaining all he could from the Phoenician mysteries, he found that they had originated from the sacred rites of Egypt, forming as it were an Egyptian colony. This led him to hope that in Egypt itself he might find monuments of erudition still more genuine, beautiful, and divine. Therefore following the advice of his teacher Thales, he left, as soon as possible, through the agency of some Egyptian sailors, who very opportunely happened to land on the Phoenician coast under Mount Carmel, in the temple on the peak of which Pythagoras for the most part dwelt in solitude.

He was gladly received by the sailors who intended to make a great profit by selling him into slavery. But they changed their mind in his favor during the voyage, when they perceived the chastened venerability of the mode of life he had undertaken. They began to reflect that there was something supernatural in the youth's modesty, and in the manner in which he had unexpectedly appeared to them on their landing, when from the summit of Mount Carmel, which they know to be more sacred than other mountains, and quite inaccessible to the vulgar, he had leisurely descended without looking back, avoiding all delay from precipices or difficult rocks and that when he came to the boat, he said nothing more than, "Are you bound for Egypt?" And farther that, on their answering affirmatively, he had got aboard, and had, during the whole trip sat silent where he would be least likely to inconvenience them at their tasks. For two nights and three days Pythagoras had remained in the same unmoved position, without food, drink, or sleep, except that, unnoticed by the sailors, he might have dozed while sitting upright. Moreover the sailors considered that, contrary to their expectations, their voyage had proceeded without interruptions, as if some deity had been on board. From all these circumstances they concluded that a very divinity had passed over with them from Syria into Egypt.

Addressing Pythagoras and each other with a gentleness and propriety that was unwonted, they completed the remainder of their voyage through a halcyon sea, and at length happily landed on the Egyptian coast. Reverently the sailors here assisted him to disembark; and after they had seen him safe onto a firm beach, they raised before him a temporary altar, heaped on it the now abundant fruits of trees, as if these were the first-fruits of their freight, presented then to him and departed hastily to their destination. Pythagoras, however, whose body had become emaciated through the severity of so long a fast, did not refuse the sailors' help in landing, and as soon as they had left partook of as much of the fruits as was requisite to restore his physical vigor. Then he went inland, in entire safety preserving his wonted tranquillity and modesty.

CHAPTER IV
STUDIES IN EGYPT AND BABYLONIA

Here in Egypt he frequented all the temples with the greatest diligence, and most studious research, during which time he won the esteem and admiration of all the priests and prophets with whom he associated. Having most solicitously familiarized himself with every detail, he did not, nevertheless, neglect any contemporary celebrity, whether sage renowned for wisdom, or peculiarly performed mystery; he did not fail to visit any place where he thought he might discover something worthwhile. That is how he visited all of the Egyptian priests, acquiring all the wisdom each possessed. He thus passed twenty-two years in the sanctuaries of temples, studying astronomy and geometry, and being initiated in no casual or superficial manner in all the mysteries of the Gods. At length, however, he was taken captive by the soldiers of Cambyses, and carried off to Babylon. Here he was overjoyed to associate with the Magi, who instructed him in their venerable knowledge, and in the most perfect worship of the Gods. Through their assistance, likewise, he studied and completed arithmetic, music, and all the other sciences. After twelve years, about the fifty-sixth year of his age, he returned to Samos.

CHAPTER V
TRAVELS IN GREECE;
SETTLEMENT AT CROTONA

On his return to Samos he was recognized by some of the older inhabitants, who found that he had gained in beauty and wisdom, and achieved a divine graciousness; wherefore they admired him all the more. He was officially invited to benefit all men by imparting his knowledge publicly. To this he was not averse; but the method of teaching he wished to introduce was the symbolical one, in a manner similar to that in which he had been instructed in Egypt. This mode of teaching, however did not please the Simians, whose attention lacked perseverance. Not one proved genuinely desirous of those mathematical disciplines which he was so anxious to introduce among the Greeks; and soon he was left entirely alone. This however did not embitter him to the point of neglecting or despising Samos. Because it was his home town; he desired to give his fellow-citizens a taste of the sweetness of the mathematical disciplines, in spite of their refusal to learn. To overcome this he devised and executed the following stratagem. In the gymnasium he happened to observe the unusually skillful and masterful ball-playing of a youth who was greatly devoted to physical culture, but impecunious and in difficult circumstances. Pythagoras wondered whether this youth if supplied with the necessaries of life, and freed from the anxiety of supplying them, could be induced to study with him. Pythagoras therefore called the youth, as he was leaving the bath, and made him the proposition to furnish him the means to continue his physical training, on the condition that he would study with him easily and gradually, but continuously so as to avoid confusion and distraction, certain discipline which he claimed to have learned from the Barbarians in his youth, but which were now beginning to desert him in consequence of the inroads of the forgetfulness of old age. Moved by hopes of financial support, the youth took up the proposition without delay. Pythagoras then introduced him to the rudiments of arithmetic and geometry, illustrating them objectively on an abacus, paying him three *oboli* as fee for the learning of every figure. This was continued for a long time, the youth being incited to the study of geometry by the desire for honor, with diligence, and in the best order. But when the sage observed that the youth had become so captivated by the logic, ingeniousness and style of those demonstrations to which he had been led in an orderly way, that he would no longer neglect their pursuit merely because of the sufferings of poverty, Pythagoras pretended poverty, and consequent inability to continue the payment of the three *oboli* fee. On hearing this, the youth replied, that even without the fee he could go on learning and receiving this instruction. Then Pythagoras said, "But even I myself am lacking the means to procure food!"As he would have to work to earn his living, he ought not to be distracted by the abacus and other trifling occupations. The youth, however, loath to discontinue his studies, replied, "In the future, it is I who will provide for you, and repay your kindness in a way resembling that of the stork; for in my turn, I will give you three *oboli* for every figure. From this time on he was so captivated by these disciplines, that, of all the Samians, he alone elected to leave home to follow Pythagoras, being a namesake of his, though differing in patronymie, being the son of Eratocles. It is probably to him that should be ascribed three books on Athletics, in which he recommends a diet of flesh, instead of dry figs, which of course would hardly have been written by the Mnesarchian Pythagoras.

About this time Pythagoras went to Delos where he was much admired as he approached the so-called bloodless altar of Father Apollo, and worshipped it. Then Pythagoras visited all the oracles. He dwelt for some time in Crete and Sparta, to learn their laws; and on acquiring proficiency therein he returned home to complete his former omissions. On his arrival in Samos, he first established a school, which is even now called, the Semicircle of Pythagoras, in which the Samians now consult about public affairs, feeling the fitness of dispensing justice and promoting profit in the place constructed by him who promoted the welfare of all mankind. Outside of the city he formed a cave adapted to the practices of his philosophy, in which he spent the greater part of day and night, ever busied with scientific research, and meditating as did Minos, the son of Jupiter. Indeed he surpassed those who later practised his disciplines chiefly in this, that they advertised themselves for the knowledge of theorems of minute importance, while Pythagoras unfolded a complete science of the celestial orbs, founding it on arithmetical and geometrical demonstrations. Still more than for all this, he is to be admired for what he accomplished later. His philosophy now gained great importance, and his fame spread to all Greece so that the best students visited Samoa on his account, to share in his erudition. But his fellow-citizens insisted on employing him in all their embassies, and compelled him to take part in the administration of public affairs. Pythagoras began to realise the impossibility of complying with the claims of his country while remaining at home to advance his philosophy; and observing that all earlier philosophers had passed their life in foreign countries, he determined to resign all political occupations. Besides, according to contemporary testimony, he disgusted at the Samarians scorn for education.

Therefore he went to Italy, conceiving that his real fatherland must be the country containing the greatest number of most scholarly men. Such was the success of his journey that on his arrival at Crotona, the noblest city in Italy, that he gathered as many as six-hundred followers, who by his discourses were moved, not only to philosophical study, but to an amicable sharing of their worldly goods, whence they derived the names of *Cenobites*.

CHAPTER VI
THE PYTHAGOREAN COMMUNITY

The *Cenobites* were students that philosophized; but the greater part of his followers were called *Hearers*, of whom, according to Nicomachus there were two thousand that had been captivated by a single oration on his arrival in Italy. These, with their children, gathered into one immense auditory, called Auditorium, which was so great as to resemble a city, thus founding a place universally called Greater Greece. This great multitude of people, receiving from Pythagoras laws and mandates as so many divine precepts, without which they declined to engage in any occupation, dwelt together in the greatest general concord, estimated and celebrated by their neighbors as among the number of the blessed, who, as was already observed, shared all their possessions.

Such was their reverence for Pythagoras, that they ranked him with the Gods, as a genial beneficent divinity, while some celebrated him as the Pythian, others called him the Northern Apollo. Others considered him Paeon, others, one of the divinities that inhabit the moon; yet others considered that he was one of the Olympian Gods, who, in order to correct and improve terrestrial existence appeared to their contemporaries in human form, to extend to them the salutary light of philosophy and felicity. He never indeed came, nor, for that matter of that, ever will come to mankind a greater good than that which was imparted to the Greeks through this Pythagoras. Hence, even now, the nick-name of "long-haired Samian" is still applied to the most venerable among men.

In his treatise on the Pythagoric Philosophy, Aristotle relates that among the principal arcana of the Pythagoreans was preserved this distinction among rational animals: Gods, men, and beings like Pythagoras. Well indeed may they have done so, inasmuch as he introduced so just and apt a generalization as Gods, heroes and demons; of the world, of the manifold notions of the spheres and stars, their oppositions, eclipses, inequalities, eccentricities and epicycles; of all the natures contained in heaven and earth, together with the intermediate ones, whether apparent or occult. Nor was there, in all this variety of information, anything contrary to the phenomena, or to the conceptions of the mind. Besides all this, Pythagoras unfolded to the Greeks all the disciplines, theories and researches that would purify the intellect from the blindness introduced by studies of a different kind, so as to enable it to perceive the true principles and causes of the universe.

In addition, the best polity, popular concord, community of possessions among friends, worship of the Gods, piety to the dead, legislation, erudition, silence, abstinence from eating the flesh of animals, continence, temperance, sagacity, divinity, and in one word, whatever is anxiously desired by the scholarly, was brought to light by Pythagoras. It was, on account of all this, as we have already observed, that Pythagoras was so much admired.

CHAPTER VII
ITALIAN POLITICAL ACHIEVEMENTS

Now we must relate how he traveled, what places he first visited, and what discourses he made, on what subjects, and to whom addressed; for this would illustrate his contemporary relations. His first task, on arriving in Italy and Sicily, was to inspire with a love of liberty those cities which he understood had more or less recently oppressed each other with slavery. Then, by means of his auditors, he liberated and restored to independence Crotona, Sybaris, Catanes, Rhegium, Himaera, Agrigentum, Tauromenas and some other cities. Through Charondas the Catanaean, and Zaleucus the Locrian, he established laws which caused the cities to flourish, and become models for others in their proximity. Partisanship, discord and sedition, and that for several generations, he entirely rooted out, as history testifies, from all the Italian and Sicilian lands, which at that time were disturbed by inner and outer contentions. Everywhere, in private and in public, he would repeat, as an *epitome* of his own opinions, and as a persuasive oracle of divinity, that by any means so ever; stratagem, fire, or sword, we should amputate from the body, disease; from the soul ignorance; from the belly, luxury; from a city, sedition; from a household, discord; and from all things so ever, lack of moderation; through which he brought home to his disciples the quintessence of all teachings, and that with a most paternal affection. For the sake of accuracy, we may state that the year of his arrival in Italy was that one of the Olympic victory in the stadium of Eryxidas of Chalcis, in the sixty-second Olympiad. He became conspicuous and celebrated as soon as he arrived, just as formerly he achieved instant recognition at Delos, when he performed his adorations at the bloodless altar of Father Apollo.

CHAPTER VIII
INTUITION, REVERENCE, TEMPERANCE, and STUDIOUSNESS

One day, during a trip from Sybaris to Crotona, by the sea-shore, he happened to meet some fishermen engaged in drawing up from the deep their heavily-laden fish-nets. He told them he knew the exact number of the fish they had caught. The surprised fishermen declared that if he was right they would do anything he said. He then ordered them, after counting the fish accurately, to return them alive to the sea, and what is more wonderful, while he stood on the shore, not one of them died, though they had remained out of their natural element quite a little while. Pythagoras then paid the fisher-men the price of their fish, and departed for Crotona. The fishermen divulged the occurrence, and on discovering his name from some children, spread it abroad publicly. Everybody wanted to see the stranger, which was easy enough to do. They were deeply impressed on beholding his countenance, which indeed betrayed his real nature.

A few days later, on entering in the gymnasium, he was surrounded by a crowd of young men, and he embraced this opportunity to address them, exhorting them to attend to their elders, pointing out to them the general preeminence of the early over the late. He instanced that the East was more important than the West, the morning than the evening, the beginning than the end, growth than decay; natives than strangers, city-planners than city-builders; and in general that Gods were more worthy of honor than, divinities, divinities than semi-divinities, and heroes than men; and that among these the authors of birth in importance excelled their progeny. All this, however, he said only to prove by indiction, that children should honor their parents to whom, he asserted, they were as much indebted for gratitude as would be a dead man to him who should bring him back to life, and light. He continued to observe that it was no more than just to avoid paining, and to love preeminently those who had benefited us first and most. Prior to the children's birth, these are benefited by their parents exclusively, being the springs of their offspring's righteous conduct. In any case, it is impossible for children to ere by not allowing themselves to be outdistanced in reciprocation of benefits, towards their parents. Besides, since from our parents we learn to honor divinity, no doubt the Gods will pardon those who honor their parents no less than those who honor the Gods, (thus making common cause with them). Homer even applied the paternal name to the King of the Gods, calling lim the father of Gods and men. Many other mythologists informed us that the chiefs of the Gods even were anxious to claim for themselves that superlative affection which, through marriage, binds children to their parents. That is why (the Orphic theologians) introduced among the Gods the terms father and mother, Jupiter begetting Minerva, while Juno produced Vulcan, the nature of which offspring is contrary so as to unite the most remote through friendship. As this argument about the immortals proved convincing to the Crotonians, Pythagoras continued to enforce voluntary obedience to the parental wishes, by the example of Hercules, who had been the founder of the Crotonian colony. Tradition indeed informed us that divinity had undertaken labors so great out of obedience to the commands of a senior, and that after his victories therein, he instituted the Olympic games in honor of his father. Their mutual association should never result in hostility to friends, but in transforming their own hostility into friendship. Their benevolent filial disposition should manifest as modesty, while their universal philanthropy should take the form of fraternal consideration and affection.

Temperance was the next topic of his discourses. Since the desires are most flourishing during youth, this is the time when control must be effective. While temperance alone is universal in its application to all ages, boy, virgin, woman, or the aged, yet this special virtue is particularly applicable to youth. Moreover, this virtue alone applied universally to all goods, those of body and soul, preserving both the health, and studiousness. This may be proved conversely. When the Greeks and Barbarians warred about Troy, each of them feel into the most dreadful calamities, both during the War, and the return home, and all this through the incontinence of a single individual. Moreover, the divinity ordained that the punishment of this single injustice should last over a thousand and ten years, by an oracle predicting the capture of Troy, and ordering that annually the Locrians should send virgins into the Temple of Minerva in Troy.

Cultivation of learning was the next topic Pythagoras urged upon the young men. He invited them to observe how absurd it would be to rate the reasoning power as the chief of their faculties, and indeed consult about all other things by its means, and yet bestow no time or labor on its exercise. Attention to the body might be compared to unworthy friends, and is liable to rapid failure; while erudition lasts till death, and for some procures post-mortem renown, and may be likened to good, reliable friends. Pythagoras continued to draw illustrations from history and philosophy, demonstrating that erudition enables a naturally excellent disposition to share in the achievements of the leaders of the race. For others share in their discoveries by erudition.

Erudition (possesses four great advantages over all other goods). First, some advantages, such as strength, beauty, health and fortitude, cannot be exercised except by the cooperation of somebody else. Moreover, wealth, dominion, and many other goods do not remain with him who imparts them to somebody else. Third, some kinds of goods cannot be possessed by some men, but all are susceptible of instruction, according to the individual choice. Moreover, an instructed man will naturally, and without any impudence, be led to take part in the administration of the affairs of his home country, (as does not occur with more wealth). One great advantage of erudition is that it may be imparted to another person without in the least diminishing the store of the giver. For it is education which makes the difference between a man and a wild beast, a Greek and a Barbarian, a free man and a slave, and a philosopher from a boor. In short, erudition is so great an advantage over those who do not possess it, that in one whole city and during one whole Olympiad seven men only were found to be eminent winners in racing, and that in the whole habitable globe those that excelled in wisdom amounted to no more than seven. But in subsequent times it was generally agreed that Pythagoras alone surpassed all others in philosophy; for instead of calling himself a sage, he called himself a philosopher.

CHAPTER IX
COMMUNITY AND CHASTITY

What Pythagoras said to the youths in the Gymnasium, these reported to their elders. Hereupon these latter, a thousand strong, called him into the senate-house, praised him for what he had said to their sons, and desired him to unfold to the public administration any thoughts advantageous to the Crotonians, which he might have.

His first advice was to build a temple to the Muses, which would preserve the already existing concord. He observed to them that all of these divinities were grouped together by their common name, that they subsisted only in conjunction with each other, that they specially rejoiced in social honors, and that (in spite of all changes) the choir of the Muses subsisted always one and the same. They comprehended symphony, harmony, rhythm, and all things breeding concord. Not only to beautiful theorems does their power extend, but to the general symphonius harmony.

(Justice) was the next desideratum. Their common country was not to be victimized selfishly, but to be received as a common deposit from the multitude of citizens. They should therefore govern it in a manner such that, as an hereditary possession they might transmit it into their posterity. This could best be effected if the members of the administration realised their equality with the citizens, with the only supereminence of justice. It is from the common recognition that justice is required in every place, that were created the fables that Themis seated in the same order with Jupiter, and that Dice, or rightness, is seated by Pluto, and that Law is established in all cities, so that whoever is unjust in things required of him by his position in society, may concurrently appear unjust towards the whole world. Moreover, senators should not make use of any of the Gods for the purpose of an oath, inasmuch as their language should be such as to make them credible even without any oaths.

As to their domestic affairs, their government should be the object of deliberate choice. They should show genuine affection to their own offspring, remembering that these, from among all animals, were the only ones who could appreciate this affection. Their associations with their partners in life, their wives, should be such as to be mindful that while other compacts are engraved in tables and pillars, the uxorial ones are incarnated in children. They should moreover make an effort to win the affection of their children, not merely in a natural, involuntary manner, but through deliberate choice, which alone merits beneficence.

He further besought them to avoid connexion with any but their wives; lest, angered by their husbands' neglect and vice, these should not get even by adulterating the race. They should also consider that they received their wives from the Vestal hearth with libations, and brought them home in the presence of the Gods themselves as suppliants would have done. Also that by orderly conduct and temperance they should become model not only for their family, but also for their community.

Again, they should minimize public vice, lest offenders indulge in secret sins to escape the punishment of the laws, but should, rather be impelled to justice from reverence for beauty and propriety. Procrastination also was to be ended inasmuch as opportuneness was the best part of any deed. The separation of parents from their children Pythagoras considered the greatest of evils. While he who is able to discern what is advantageous to himself may be considered the best man, next to him in excellence should be ranked he who can see the utility in what happens to others; while the worst man was he who waited till he himself was afflicted before under standing where true advantage lies. Seekers of honor might well imitate racers, who do not injure their antagonists, but limit themselves to trying to achieve the victory themselves. Administrators of public affairs should not betray offense at being contradicted, but on the other hand benefit the tractable. Seekers of true glory should strive really to become what they wished to seem; for counsel is not as sacred as praise, the former being useful only among men, while the latter mostly referred to the divinities.

In closing, he reminded those that their city happened to have been founded by Hercules, at a time when, having been injured by Lacinius, he drove the oxen through Italy; when, rendering assistance to Croton by night, mistaking him for an enemy he slew him unintentionally. Wherefore Hercules promised that a city should be built over the sepulchre of Croton and from him derive the name Crotona, thus endowing him with immortality. Therefore, said Pythagoras to the rulers of the city, these should justly render thanks for the benefits they had received.

The Crotonians, on hearing his words built a temple to the Muses, and drove away their concubines, and requested Pythagoras to address the young men in the temple of Pyhian Apollo, and the women in the temple of Juno.

CHAPTER X
ADVICE TO YOUTHS

To boys Pythagoras, complying with their parents' request, gave the following advice. They should neither revile any one nor revenge themselves on those who did. They should devote themselves diligently to learning, which in Greek derives its name from their age. A youth who started out modestly would find it easy to preserve probity for the remainder of his life, which would be a difficult task for one who at that age was not well disposed; nay, for one who begins his course from a bad impulse to run well to the end is almost impossible.

Pythagoras pointed out that boys were most dear to the divinities; and he pointed out that, in times of great drought, cities would send boys as ambassadors to implore rain from the Gods, in the persuasion that divinity is especially attentive to children, although such as are permitted to take part in sacred ceremonies continuously hardly ever arrive at perfect purification. That is also the reason why the most philanthropic of the Gods, Apollo and Love, are, in pictures, universally represented as having the ages of boys. It is similarly recognized that some of the games in which conquerors are crowned were instituted for the behoof of boys; the Pythian, in consequence of the serpent Python having been slain by a boy, and the Nemean and Istimian, because of the death of Archemerus and Nelicerta.

Moreover, while the city of Crotona, was building, Apollo promised to the founder that he would give him a progeny, if he brought a colony into Italy, inferring therefrom that Apollo presided over their development, and that inasmuch as all the divinities protected their age, it was no more than fair that they should render themselves worthy of their friendship. He added that they should practise hearing, so that they might learn to speak. Further, that as soon as they had entered on the path along which they intended to proceed for the remainder of their existence, they should imitate their predecessors, never contradicting those who were their seniors. For later on, when they themselves will have grown, they will justly expect not to be injured by their future juniors. Because of these moral teachings, Pythagoras deserved no longer to be called by his patronymic, but that all men should call him divine.

CHAPTER XI
ADVICE TO WOMEN

To the women Pythagoras spoke as follows, about sacrifices. To begin with, inasmuch as it was no more than natural that they would wish that some other person who intended to pray for them should be worthy, nay, excellent, because the Gods attend to those particularly, so also it is advisable that they themselves should most highly esteem equity and modesty, so that the divinities may be the more inclined to grant their requests.

Further, they should offer to the divinities such things as they themselves have with their own hands produced, such as cakes, honey-combs, [to-ers?] and perfumes, and should bring them to the altars without the assistance of servants.

They should not worship divinities with blood and dead bodies, nor offer so many things at one time that it might seem they meant never to sacrifice again.

Concerning their association with men, they, should remember that their female nature had by their parents been granted the license to love their husbands more excessively than even the authors of their existence. Consequently they should take care neither to oppose their husbands, nor consider that they have subjected their husbands should these latter yield to them in any detail.

It was in the same assembly that Pythagoras is said to have made the celebrated suggestion that, after a woman has had connexion with her husband, it is holy for her to perform sacred rites on the same day, which would be inadmissible, had the connection been with any man other than her husband.

He also advised the women that their conversation should always be cheerful, and to endeavor that others may speak good things of them. He further admonished them to care for their good reputation, and to try not to justify the fable-writer who accused three women of using a single eye in common, so great is their mutual willingness to accommodate each other with the loan of garments and ornaments, without a witness, when some one of them has special need thereof, returning them without arguments or litigation.

Further Pythagoras observed that (Mercury) who is called the wisest of all, who arranged the human voice, and in short, was the inventor of names, whether he was a God (in Jupiter, the supermundane gods, the liberated gods, or the planet Mercury), or a divinity (the Mercurial order of demons), or a certain divine man (the Egyptian Theuth, or in special animals such as the ibis, ape, or dogs), perceiving that the female sex was most given to devotion, gave to each of their ages the name of one divinity. So an unmarried woman was called Core, or Proserpine, a bride Nympha, a matron, Mother; and a grandmother, in the Doric dialect, *Maia*. Consequently, the oracles at Dodona and Delphi are brought to light by a woman.

By this praise of female piety Pythagoras is said to have effected so great a change in popular female attire, that the women no longer dared to dress up in costly raiment, consecrating thousands of their garments in the temple of Juno.

This discourse had effect also on marital fidelity, to an extent such that in the Crotonan region connubial faithfulness became proverbial; (thus imitating) Ulysses who, rather than abandon Penelope, considered immortality well lost. Pythagoras encouraged the Crotonian women to emulate Ulysses, by exhibiting their probity to their husbands. In short, through these (social) discourses Pythagoras acquired great fame both in Crotona, and in the rest of Italy.

CHAPTER XII
WHY PYTHAGORAS CALLS HIMSELF A PHILOSOPHER

(From Heraclides Ponticus, vi. 3 Cicero.Tusc.v?)

Pythagoras is said to have been the first to call himself a philosopher, a world which heretofore had not been an appellation, but a description. He likened the entrance of men into the present life to the progression of a crowd to some public spectacle. There assemble men of all descriptions and views. One hastens to sell his wares for money and gain; another exhibits his bodily strength for renown; but the most liberal assemble to observe the landscape, the beautiful works of art, the specimens of valor, and the customary literary productions. So also in the present life men of manifold pursuits are assembled. Some are incensed by the desire of riches and luxury; others by the love of power and dominion, or by insane ambition for glory. But the purest and most genuine character is that of the man who devotes himself to the contemplation of the most beautiful things; and he may properly be called a philosopher.

Pythagoras adds that the survey of the whole haven, and of the stars that revolve therein, is indeed beautiful, when we consider their order which is derived from participation in the first and intelligible essence. But that first essence is the nature and number of reasons (or, productive principles), which pervades everything, and according to which all these (celestial) bodies are arranged elegantly, and adorned fittingly. -----veritable wisdom is a science conversant with the first beautiful objects (the intelligible property so called); which subsist in invariable sameness, being undecaying and divine, by the participation in which other things also may well be called beautiful. The desire for something like this is philosophy. Similarly beautiful is devotion to erudition; and this notion Pythagoras extended, order to effect the improvement of the human race.

CHAPTER XIII
HE SHARED ORPHEUS' CONTROL OVER ANIMALS

According to credible historians, his words possessed an admonitory quality that prevailed even with animals, which confirms that, in intelligent men learning tames beasts even wild or irrational. The Daunian bear, who had severely injured the inhabitants, was by Pythagoras detained, long stroking it gently, feeding it on maize and acorns, and after compelling it by an oath to leave alone living beings, he sent it away. It hid itself in the mountains and forest, and was never since known to injure any irrational animal.

At Tarentum he saw an ox feeding in a pasture, where he ate green beans. He advised the herdsman to abstain from this food to tell the ox to abstain from this food. The herdsman laughed at him, remarking he did not know the language of oxen; but that if Pythagoras did, he had better tell him so himself. Pythagoras approached the ox's ear and whispered into it for a long time, hereafter the ox not only refrained from them, but even never tasted them. This ox lived a long while at Tarentum, near the temple of Juno, and was fed on human food by visitors, till very old, considered sacred. Once happening to be talking to his intimates about birds, symbols and prodigies, and observed that all these are messengers of the Gods, sent by them to men truly dear to them, when he brought down an eagle flying over Olympia, which he gently stroked and dismissed.

Through such and similar occurrences, Pythagoras demonstrated that he possessed the same dominion as Orpheus over savage animals, and that he allured and detained them by the power of his voice.

CHAPTER XIV
PYTHAGORAS'S PREEXISTENCE

Pythagoras used to make the very best possible approach to men by teaching them what would prepare them to learn the truth in other matters. For by the clearest and surest indications he would remind many of his intimates of the former life lived by their soul before it was bound to their body. He would demonstrate by indubitable arguments that he had once been Eiuphorbus, son of Panthus, conqueror of Patroclus. He would especially praise the following funeral Homeric verses pertaining to himself, which he would sing to the lyre most elegantly, frequently repeating them.

"The shining circlets of his golden hair,
Which even the Graces might be proud to wear,
Instarred with gems and gold, bestrew the shore
With dust dishonored, and deformed with gore.
As the young olive, in some sylvan scene,
Crowned by fresh fountains with eternal green,
Lifts the gay head, in snowy flowerets fair,
And plays and dances to the gentle air;
When lo, a whirlwind from high heaven invades
The tender plant and withers all its shades;
It lies uprooted from its genial bed,
A lovely ruin now defaced and dead; Thus young, thus beautiful Euphorbus lay,
While the fierce Spartan tore his arms away."

Homer Iliad, 17, Pope.

We shall however omit the reports about the shield of this Phrygian Euphorbus, which, among other Trojan spoils, was dedicated to the Argive Juno, as being too popular in nature. What Pythagoras, however, wished to indicate by all those particulars was that he knew the former lives he had lived which enabled him to begin providential attention to others, in which he reminded them of their former existences.

CHAPTER XV
PYTHAGORAS CURED BY MEDICINE AND MUSIC

Pythagoras conceived that the first attention that should be given to men should be addressed to the senses, as when one perceives beautiful figures and forms, or hears beautiful rhythms and melodies. Consequently he laid down that the first erudition was that which subsists through music's melodies and rhythms, and from these he obtained remedies of human manners and passions, and restored the pristine harmony of the faculties of the soul. Moreover, he devised medicines calculated to repress and cure the diseases of both bodies and souls. There is also, by heavens something which deserves to be mentioned above all: namely, that for his disciples he arranged and adjusted what might be called apparatus and massage, divinely contriving mingling of certain *diatonic, chromatic* and *enharmonic* melodies through which he easily switched and circulated the passions of the soul in a contrary direction, whenever they had accumulated recently, irrationally or clandestinely such as sorrow, rage, pity, over-emulation, fear, manifold desires, angers, appetites, pride, collapses, or spasms. Each of those he corrected by the use of virtue, attempering them through appropriate melodies, as if through some salutary medicine.

In the evening, likewise, when his disciples were retiring to sleep, he would thus liberate them from the day's perturbations and tumults, purifying their intellective powers from the influxive and effluxive waves of corporeal nature, quieting their sleep, and rendering their dreams pleasing and prophetic. But when they arose again in the morning, he would free them from the night's logginess, coma and torpor through certain peculiar chords and modulations, produced by either simply striking the lyre, or adapting the voice. Not through instrument or physical voice organs did Pythagoras effect this; but by the employment of a certain indescribable divinity, difficult of apprehension, through which he extended his power of hearing filing his intellect on the sublime *symphonies* of the world, he alone apparently hearing and grasping the universal harmony and consonance of the spheres, and the stars that are moved through them, producing a melody fuller and more intense than anything effected by mortal sounds. This melody was also the result of dissimilar and varying sounds, speeds, magnitudes and intervals arranged with reference to each other in a certain musical ratio, producing a convoluted motion most musical if gentle.

Irrigated therefore with this melody, his intellect ordered and exercised thereby, he would, to the best of his ability exhibit certain symbols of these things to his disciples, especially through imitations thereof through instruments or the physical organs of voice. For he conceived that, of all the inhabitants of earth, by him alone were these mundane sounds understood and heard, as if coming from the central spring and root of nature. He therefore thought himself worthy to be taught, and to learn something about the celestial orbs, and to be assimilated to them by desire and imitation, inasmuch as his body alone had been well enough thereto conformed by the divinity who had given birth to him. As to other men, he thought they should be satisfied with looking to him and the gifts he possessed, and in being benefited and corrected through images and examples, in consequence of their inability truly to comprehend the first and genuine archetypes of things. Just as to those who are unable to look intently at the sun we contrive to show its eclipses in either the reflections of still water, or in melted pitch, or some smoked glass, well burnished brazen mirror we spare the weakness of their eyes devising a method of representing light that is reflective, though less intense than its archetype, to those who are interested in this sort of a thing. This peculiar organization of 'Pythagoras's body, far finer than that of any other man, seems to be what Empodocles was obscurely driving at in his enigmatical verses:

"Among the Pythagoreans was a man transcendent in knowledge;
Who possessed the most ample stores of intellectual wealth,
And in most eminent degree assisted in the works of' the wise.
When he extended all the powers of his intellect,
He easily beheld everything,
As far as ten or twenty ages of the human race!"

These words "transcendent," he beheld every detail of all beings, "and the wealth of intellect," and so on, describe as accurately as at all possible his peculiar, and exceptionally accurate method of hearing, seeing and understanding.

CHAPTER XVI
PYTHAGOREAN ASCETICISM

Music therefore performed this Pythagorean adjustment. But another kind of purification of the discursive reason, and also of the whole soul, through various studies, was effected (by asceticism). He had a general notion that disciplines and studies should imply some form of labor; and therefore, like a legislator, he decreed trials of the most varied nature, punishments, and restraints by fire and sword, for innate intemperance, or an ineradicable desire for possession, which the depraved could neither suffer nor sustain. Moreover, his intimates were ordered to abstain from all animal food, and any other that are hostile to the reasoning power by impeding its genuine energies. On them he like-wise enjoined suppression of speech, and perfect silence, exercising them for years at a time in the subjugation of the tongue, while strenuously and assiduously investigating and ruminating over the most difficult theorems. Hence also he ordered them to abstain from wine, to be sparing in the their food, to sleep little, and to cultivate an unstudied contempt of, and hostility to fame, wealth, and the like; unfeignedly to reverence those to whom reverence is due, genuinely to exercise democratic assimilation and heartiness towards their fellows in age, and towards their juniors courtesy, encouragement, without envy.

Moreover Pythagoras is generally acknowledged to have been the inventor and legislator of friendship, under its many various forms, such as universal amity of all towards all, of God towards men through their pity and scientific theories, or the mutual interrelation of teachings, or universally of the soul towards the body and of the rational to the rational part, through philosophy and its underlying theories; or whether it be that of men towards each other, or citizens indeed through sound legislation, but of strangers through a correct physiology; or of the husband to the wife or brothers and kindred, through unperverted communion; or whether, in short, it be of all things towards all, and still farther, of certain irrational animals through justice, and a physical connexion and association; or whether it be the pacification and conciliation of the body which of itself is mortal, and of its latent conflicting powers, through health and a temperate diet conformable to this, in imitation of the salubrious condition of the mundane elements.

In short, Pythagoras procured his disciples the most appropriate converse with the Gods, both waking and sleeping; something which never occurs in a soul disturbed by anger, pain, or pleasure, and surely, all the more, by any base desire, or defiled by ignorance, which is the most noxious and unholy of all the rest. By all these inventions, therefore, he divinely purified and healed the soul, resuscitating and saving it diving part, and directing to the intelligible its divine eye, which, as Plato says, is more worth saving than ten thousand corporeal eyes; for when it is strengthened and clarified by appropriate aids, when we look through this, we perceive the truth about all beings. In this particular respect, therefore, Pythagoras purified the discursive power of the soul. This is the (practical) form that erudition took with him, and such are the objects of his interest.

CHAPTER XVII
TESTS OF PYTHAGOREAN INITIATION

As he therefore thus prepared his disciples for culture, he did not immediately receive as an associate any who came to him for that purpose until he had tested them and examined them judiciously. To begin with he inquired about their relation to their parents and kinsfolk. Next he surveyed their laughter, speech or silence, as to whether it was unreasonable; further, about their desires, their associates, their conversation, how they employed their leisure, and what were the subjects of their joy or grief. He observed their form, their gait, and the whole motions of their body. He considered their frame's natural indications physiognomically, rating them as visible exponents of the invisible tendencies of the soul. After subjecting a candidate to such trials, he allowed him to be neglected for three years, still covertly observing his disposition towards stability, and genuine studiousness, and whether he was sufficiently averse to glory, and ready to despise popular honors.

After, this the candidate was compelled to observe silence for five years, so as to have made definite experiments in continence of speech, inasmuch as the subjugation of the tongue is the most difficult of all victories, as has indeed been unfolded by those who have instituted the mysteries. During this probation, however, the property of each was disposed of in common, being committed to trustees, who were called politicians, economizers or legislators. Of these probationers, after the quinquennial silence, those who by modest dignity had won his approval as worthy to share in his doctrines, then became *esoterics*, and within the veil both heard and saw Pythagoras. Prior to this they participated in his words through the hearing alone, without seeing him who remained within the veil, and themselves offering to him a specimen of their manners. If rejected, they were given the double of the wealth they had brought, but the *auditors* raised to him a tomb, as if they were dead; the disciples being generally called *auditors*.

Should these later happen to meet the rejected candidate, they would treat him as a stronger, declaring that he whom they had by education modeled had died, inasmuch as the object of these disciplines had been to be turned out good and honest men.

Those who were slow in the acquisition of knowledge were considered to be badly organized or, we may say, deficient, and sterile.

If, however, after Pythagoras had studied them physiognomically, their gait, motions and state of health, he conceived good hopes of them; and if, after the five years' silence, and the emotions and initiations from so many disciplines together with the ablutions of the soul, and so many and so great purifications produced by such various theorems, through which sagacity and sanctity is ingrained into the soul...................if, after all this even, someone was found to be still sluggish and dull, they would raise to such a candidate within the school a pillar or monument, such as was said to have been done to Perialus the Thurian, and Cylon the prince of the Sybarites, who were rejected, they expelled him from the auditorium, loading him down with silver and gold. This wealth had by them been deposited in common, in the care of certain custodians, aptly called *Economics*. Should any of the Pythagoreans later meet with the reject, they did not recognize him whom they accounted dead. Hence also Lysis, blaming a certain Hipparchus for having revealed the Pythagorean doctrines to the profane, and to such as accepted them without disciplines or theory, said:

"It is reported that you philosophise indiscriminately and publicly, which is opposed to the customs of Pythagoras. With assiduity you did indeed learn them, O Hipparchus; but you have not preserved them. My dear fellow, you have tasted Sicilian tit-bits, which you should not have repeated. If you give them up, I shall be delighted; but if you do not, you will to me be dead. For it would be pious to recall the human and divine precepts of Pythagoras, and not to communicate the treasures of wisdom to those who have not purified their souls, even in a dream. It is unlawful to give away things obtained with labors so great, and with assiduity so diligent to the first person you meet, quite as much as to divulge the mysteries of the Eleusynian goddesses to the profane. Either thing would be unjust and impious. We should consider how long a time was needed to efface the stains that had insinuated themselves in our breasts, before we became worthy to receive the doctrines of Pythagoras. Unless the dyers previously purified the garments in which they wish the desired colors to be fixed, the dye would either fade, or be washed away entirely. Similarly, that divine man prepared the souls of lovers of philosophy, so that they might not disappoint him in any of those beautiful qualities which he hoped they would possess. He did not impart spurious doctrines, nor stratagems, in which most of the Sophists, who are at leisure for no good purpose, entangle young men; but his knowledge of things human and divine was scientific. These Sophists, however, use his doctrines as a mere pretext commit dreadful atrocities, sweeping the youths away as in a dragnet, most disgracefully, making their auditors become rash nuisances. They infuse theorems and divine doctrines into hearts whose manners are confused and agitated, just as if pure, clear water should be poured into a deep well full of mud, which would stir up the sediment and destroy the clearness of the water. Such a mutual misfortune occurs between such teachers and disciples. The intellect and heart of those whose initiation has not proceeded by disciplines, are surrounded lay thickets dense and thorny, which obscure the mild, tranquil and reasoning power of the soul, and impede the development and elevation of the intellective part. These thickets are produced by intemperance and avarice, both of which are prolific. Intemperance produces lawless marriages, lusts, intoxications, unnatural enjoyments, and passionate impulsions which drive headlong into pits and abysses. The unbridling of desires has removed the barriers against incest with even mothers or daughters, am just as a tyrant would violate city regulations, or country's laws, with their hands bound behind them, like slaves, they have been dragged to the depths of degradation. On the other hand, avarice produces rapine, robbery, parricide, sacrilege, sorcery, and kindred evils. Such being the case, these surrounding thickets, infested with passions, will have to be cleared out with systematic disciplines, as if with fire and sword; and when the reason will have been liberated from so many and great evils, we are in a position to offer to it, and implant within it something useful and good."

So great and necessary was the attention which, according to Pythagoras, should be paid to disciplines as introductions to philosophy.

Moreover, inasmuch as he devoted so much care to the examination of the mental attitudes of prospective disciples, he insisted that the teaching and communication of his doctrines should be distinguished by great honor.

CHAPTER XVIII
ORGANIZATION OF THE PYTHAGOREAN SCHOOL

The next step to set forth how, after admission to discipleship followed distribution into several classes according to individual merit. As the disciples were naturally dissimilar, it was impracticable for them to participate in all things equally, nor would it have been fair for some to share in the deepest revelations, while others might get excluded therefrom, or others from everything; such discriminations, being unjust. While he communicated some suitable of his discourses to all, he sought to benefit everybody, preserving the proportion of justice, by making every man's merit the index of the extent of his teachings. He carried this method so far as to call some *Pythagoreans*, and others *Pythagorists*, just as we discriminate poets from poetasters. According to this distinction of names, some of his disciples he considered genuine, and to be the models of the others. The Pythagoreans' possessions were to be shared in common inasmuch as they were to live together, while the Pythagorists should continue to manage their own property, though by assembling frequently they might all be at leisure to pursue the same activities. These two modes of life which originated from Pythagoras, was transmitted to his successors. Among the Pythagoreans there were also two forms of philosophy, pursued by two classes, the *Hearers* and the *Students*. The latter were universally recognized as Pythagoreans by all the rest, though the *Students* did not admit as much for the *Hearers*, insisting that these derived their instructions not from Pythagoras, but from Hippasus, who was variously described as either a Crotonian or Metapontine.

The philosophy of the *Hearers* consisted in lectures without demonstrations or conferences or arguments merely directing something to be done in a certain way, unquestioningly preserving them as so many divine dogmas, non-discussible, and which they promised not to reveal, esteeming as most wise who more than others retained them. Of the lectures there were three kinds; the first merely announced certain facts; others expressed what it was especially, and the third, what should, or should not be done about it. The objective lectures studied such questions as, What are the islands of the Blessed? What are the sun and moon? What is the oracle at Delphi? What is the *Tetractys*? What is harmony? What was the real nature of the Sirens? Ñ The subjective lectures studied the especial nature of an object, such as, What is the most just thing? To sacrifice. What is the wisest thing? The next wisest is the naming of power. What is the wisest human thing? Medicine what is the most beautiful? Harmony. What is the most powerful? Mental decision. What is the most excellent? Felicity. Which is the most unquestioned proposition? That all men are depraved. That is why Pythagoras was said to have praised the Salaminian poet Hippodomas, for singing:

"Tell, O ye Gods, the source from whence ye came,
And ye, O Men, how evil ye became."

Such were these subjective lectures, which taught the distinctive nature of everything.

This sort of study really constitutes the wisdom of the so-called seven sages. For these also did not investigate what was good simply, but especially, nor what is difficult, but what is particularly so, ---- namely, for a man to know himself. So also they considered not what was easy, but what was most so, namely, to continue following out your habits Such studies resembled, and followed the sages, who however preceded Pythagoras.

The practice lectures, which studied what should or should not be done, considered questions such as: That it is necessary to beget children, inasmuch as we must leave after us successors who may worship the divinities. Again, that we should put on first the shoe on the right foot. That it is not proper to parade on the public streets, nor to dip into a sprinkling vessel, nor to wash in a public bath. For in all these cases the cleanliness of the agents is uncertain. Other such problems were, Do not assist a man in laying down a burden, which encourages him to loiter, but to assist him in undertaking something. Do not hope to beget children from a woman who is rich. Speak not about Pythagoric affairs without light. Perform libations to the Gods from the handle of the cup, to make the omen auspicious and to avoid drinking from the same part (from which the liquor was poured out?) Wear not the image of a God on a ring, for fear of defiling it, as such resemblances should be protected in a house. Use no woman ill, for she is a suppliant; wherefore, indeed, we bring her from the Vestal hearth, and take her by the right hand. Nor is it proper to sacrifice a white cock, who also is a suppliant, being sacred to the moon and announces the hours.- To him who asks for counsel, give none but the best, for counsel is a sacrament. The most laborious path is the test, just as the pleasurable one is mostly the worst, inasmuch as we entered into the present life for the sake of education, which best proceeds by chastening. It is proper to sacrifice, and to take off ones shoes on entering into a temple. In going to a temple, one should not turn out of the way; for divinity should not be worshipped carelessly. It is well to sustain, and show wounds, if they are in the breast, but not if they are behind. - The soul of man incarnates in the bodies of all animals, except in those which it is lawful to kill; hence we should eat none but those whom it is proper to slay. Such were subjects of these ethical lectures.

The most extended lectures, however, were those concerning sacrifices, both at the time when migrating from the preset life, and at other times; also about the proper manner of sepulture.

Of some of these propositions the reason is designed; such as for instance that we must beget children to leave successors to worship the Gods. But no justification is assigned for the others, although in some cases they are implied proximately or remotely, such as that bread is not to be broken, because it contributes to the judgment in Hades. Such merely probable reasons, that are additional, are not Pythagoric, but were devised by non-Pythagoreans who wished to add weight to the statement. Thus, for instance, in respect to the last statement, that bread is not to be broken, some add the reason that we should not (unnecessarily) distribute what has been assembled, inasmuch as in barbaric times a whole friendly group would together pounce upon a single piece. Others again explain that precept on the grounds that it is inauspicious, at the beginning of an undertaking, to make an omen of fracture or diminution. Moreover, all these precepts are based on one single underlying principle, the end of divinity, so that the whole of every life may result in following God, which is besides that principle and doctrine of philosophy. For it is absurd to search for good in any direction other than the Gods. Those who do so resemble a man who, in a country governed by a king, should do honor to one of his fellow-citizens who is a magistrate, while neglecting him who is the ruler of all of them. Indeed, this is what the Pythagoreans thought of people who searched for good elsewhere than from God. For since He exists, as the lord of all things, it must be self-evident that good must be requested of Him alone. For even men impart good to those they love and enjoy, and do the opposite to those they dislike. Such indeed was the wisdom of those precepts.

There, was, however, a certain Aegean named Hippomedon, one of the Pythagorean *Hearers*, who insisted that Pythagoras himself gave the reasons for, and demonstrations of these precepts himself; but that in consequence of their being delivered to many, some of whom were slow, the demonstrations were removed, leaving the bare propositions. The

Pythagorean *Students*, however, insist that the reasons and demonstrations were added by Pythagoras himself, explaining the difference arose as follows. According to them, Pythagoras, hailed from Ionia and Samos, to Italy then flourishing under the tyranny of Polycrates, and he attracted as associates the very most prominent men of the city. But the more elderly of these who were busied with politics, and therefore had no leisure, needed the discourses of Pythagoras dissociated from reasonings, as they would have found it difficult to follow his meanings through disciplines and demonstrations, while nevertheless Pythagoras realized that they would be benefited by knowing what ought to be done, even though lacking the underlying reason, just as physicians' patients obtain their health without hearing the reasons of every detail of the treatment. But Pythagoras conversed through disciplines and demonstrations with the younger associates, who were able both to act and learn. Such then are the differing explanations of the *Hearers* and *Students*.

As to Hippasus, however, they acknowledge that he was one of the Pythagoreans, but that he met the doom of the impious in the sea in consequence of having divulged and explained the method of squaring the circle, by twelve pentagons; but nevertheless he obtained the renown of having made the discovery. In reality, however, this just as everything else pertaining to geometry, was the invention of that man as they referred to Pythagoras. But the Pythagoreans say that geometry was divulged under the following circumstances: A certain Pythagorean happened to lose his fortune to recoup which he was permitted to teach that science, which, by Pythagoras was called History.

So much then concerning the difference of each mode of philosophizing, and the classes of Pythagoras's disciples. For those who heard him either within or without the veil, and those who heard him accompanied with seeing, or without seeing him, and who are classified as internal or external auditors, were none other than these. Under these can be classified the Political, Economic, and Legislative Pythagoreans.

CHAPTER XIX
ABARIS THE SCYTHIAN

Generally, however, it should be known, that Pythagoras discovered many paths of erudition, but that he communicated to each only that part of wisdom which was appropriate to the recipient's nature and power, of which the following is an appropriate striking illustration. When Abaris the Scythian came from the Hyperboreans, he was already of an advanced age, and unskilled and uninitiated in the Greek learning. Pythagoras did not compel him to wade through introductory theorems, the period of silence, and long ausculation, not to mention other trials, but considered him to be fit for an immediate listener to his doctrines, and instructed him in the shortest way, in his treatise on Nature, and one On the God This Hyperborean Abaris was elderly, and most wise in sacred concerns, being a priest of the Apollo there worshipped. At that time he was returning from Greece to his country, in order to consecrate the gold which he had collected to the God in his temple among the Hyperboreans. As therefore he was passing through Italy, he saw Pythagoras, and identified him as the God of whom he was the priest.

Believing that Pythagoras resembled to no man, but was none other than the God himself, Apollo, both from the venerable associations he saw around him, and from those the priest already knew, he paid him homage by giving him a sacred dart. This dart he had taken with him when he had left his temple, as an implement that would stand him in good stead in the difficulties that might befall him in so long a journey. For in passing through inaccessible places, such as rivers, lakes, marshes, mountains and the like, it carried him, and by it he was said to have performed lustrations and expelled winds and pestilences from the cities that requested him to liberate from such evils. For instance, it was said that Lacedemon, after having been by him purified, was no longer infected with pestilence, which formerly had been endemic, through the miasmatic nature of the ground, in the suffocating heat produced by the overhanging mountain Taygetus, just as happens with Cnossus in Crete. Many other similar circumstances were reported of Abaris.

Pythagoras, however, accepted the dart, without expressing any amazement at the novelty of the thing, nor asking why the dart was presented to him, as if he really was a god. Then he took Abaris aside, and showed him his golden thigh, as an indication that he was not wholly mistaken (in his estimate of his real nature). Then Pythagoras described to him several details of his distant Hyperborean temple, as proof of deserving being considered divine. Pythagoras also added that he came (into the regions of mortality) to remedy and improve the condition of the human race, having assumed human form lest men disturbed by the novelty of his transcendency should avoid the discipline he advised. He advised Abaris to stay with him, to aid him in correcting (the manners and morals) of those they might meet, and to share the common resources of himself and associates, whose reason led them to practice the precept that the possessions of friends are common. So Abaris stayed with him, and was compendiously taught physiology and theology; and instead of living by the entrails of beasts, he revealed to him the art of prognosticating by numbers conceiving this to be a method purer, more divine and more kindred to the celestial numbers of the Gods. Also he taught Abaris other studies for which he was fit.

Returning however to the purpose of the present treatise, Pythagoras endeavored to correct and amend different persons according to their individual abilities. Unfortunately most of these particulars have neither been publicly transmitted nor is it easy to describe that which has been transmitted to us concerning him.

CHAPTER XX
PSYCHOLOGICAL REQUIREMENTS

We must now set forth a few of the most celebrated points of the Pythagoric discipline, and landmarks of their distinctive studies.

When Pythagoras tested a novice, he considered the latter's ability to hold his counsel, "*ochemuthein*" being his technical term for this. Namely, whether they could reserve and preserve what they had heard and learned. Next, he examined their modesty, for he was much more anxious that they should be silent, than that they should speak. Further, he tested every other quality, for instance, whether they were astonished by the energies of any immoderate desire or passion. His examination of their affectability by desire or anger, their contentiousness or ambition, their inclination to friendship or discord, was by no means superficial. If then after an accurate survey these novices were approved as of worthy manners, he then directed his attention to their facility in learning, and their memory. He examined their ability to follow what was said, with rapidity and perspicuity; and then, whether they were impelled to the disciplines taught them by temperance and love. For he laid stress on natural gentleness. This he called culture. Ferocity he considered hostile to such a kind of education. For savage manners are attended by impudence, shamelessness, intemperance, sloth, stupidity, licentiousness, disgrace, and the like, while their opposite attend mildness and gentleness.

These things then he considered in making trial of those that came to him, and in these the Learners were exercised. Those that were adapted to receive the goods of the wisdom he possessed he admitted to discipleship; endeavoring to elevate them to scientific knowledge; but if he perceived that any novice was unadapted to them, he expelled him as a stranger and a barbarian. (In the original, the XX th chapter continues until after the second next paragraph.)

CHAPTER XXI
DAILY PROGRAM

The studies which he delivered to his associates, were as follows; for those who committed themselves to the guidance of his doctrine acted thus. They took solitary morning walks to places which happened to be appropriately quiet, to temples or groves, or other suitable places. They thought it inadvisable to converse with anyone until they had gained inner serenity, focusing their reasoning powers; they considered it turbulent to mingle in a crowd as soon as they rose from bed; and that is the reason why these Pythagoreans always selected the most sacred spots to walk. After their morning walk they associated with each other, especially in temples, or, if this was not possible, in similar places. This time was employed in the discussion of disciplines and doctrines, and in the correction of manners.

(Chapter XX) After an association so holy, they turned their attention to the health of the body. Most of them were rubbed down, and raced; fewer wrestled, in gardens or groves; others in leaping with leaden weights on their hands, or in oratorical gesticulations, with a view to the strengthening of the body, studiously selecting for this purpose opposite exercises. They lunched on bread and honey, or on the honey-comb, avoiding wine. Afterwards, they held receptions to guests and strangers, conformably to the mandates of the laws, which was restricted to this time of day.

In the afternoon, they once more betook themselves to walking, yet not alone, as in the morning walk, but in parties of two or three, rehearsing the disciplines they had learned, and, exercising themselves in attractive studies. After the walk, they patronized the bath; and after whose ablution they gathered in the common dining-room, which accommodated no more than a group of ten. Then were performed libations and sacrifices with fumigations and incense. Then followed supper, which closed before the setting of the sun. They ate herbs, raw and boiled, maize, wine, and every food eatable with bread. Of any animals lawful to immolate, they ate the flesh, but they rarely partook of fish, which was not useful to them for certain causes animals not naturally noxious were, neither to be injured, nor slain. This supper was followed by libations, succeeded by readings. The youngest read what the eldest advised, and as they suggested.

When they were about to depart, the cupbearer poured out a libation for them, after which the eldest would announce precepts, such as the following: That a mild and fruitful plant should neither be injured nor corrupted, nor any harmless animal. Further, that we should speak piously, and form suitable conceptions of divine, tutelary and heroic beings, and similarly of parents and benefactors. Also, that we should aid, and not obstruct the enforcement of laws. Whereafter, all separated, to go home. They wore a white garment, that was pure. They also lay on white and pure beds, the coverlets of which, were made of linen, not wool. They did not hunt, not undertake any similar exercise. Such were the precepts daily delivered to the disciples of Pythagoras, in respect to eating and living.

CHAPTER XXII
FRIENDSHIP

Tradition tells of another kind of teaching by Pythagorean maxims pertaining to human opinions and practices, some examples of which may here be mentioned. It advised to remove strife from untrue friendship. If possible, this was to apply to all friendship; but at all events to that towards parents, elders, and benefactors. Existing friendships with such as these would not be preserved (but destroyed) by rivalry, contention, anger and subsequent graver passions. The scars and ulcers which their advice sometimes cause should be minimized as much as possible, which will be effected if especially the younger of the two should learn how to yield, and subdue his angry emotions. On the other hand, the so-called '*paedartases*," or corrections and admonitions of the elder towards the younger, should be made with much suavity of manners, and great caution; also with much solicitude and tact, which makes the reproof all the more graceful and useful.

Faith should never be separated from friendship, whether seriously or in jest. Existing friendship cannot survive the insinuation of deceit between professors of friendship.

Nor should friendship be affected by misfortune or other human vicissitude; and the only rejection of friendship which is commendable is that which follows definite and incurable vice.

Such is an example of the Pythagorean hortatory maxims, which extended to all the virtues, and the whole of life.

CHAPTER XXIII
USE OF PARABLES OF INSTRUCTION

Pythagoras considered most necessary the use of parables in instruction. Most of the Greeks had adopted it, as the most ancient; and it had been both preferentially and in principle employed by the Egyptians, who had developed it in the most varied manner. In harmony with this it will be found that Pythagoras attended to it sedulously, if from the Pythagoric symbols we unfold their significance and arcane intentions, developing their content of rectitude and truth, liberating them from their enigmatic form. When, according to straightforward and uniform tradition they are accommodated to the sublime intelligence of these philosophers, they deify beyond human conception.

Those who came from this school, not only the most ancient Pythagoreans, but also those who during his old age were still young, such as Philolaos, and Eurytus, Charendas and Zaleucus, Brysson and the elder Archytas, Aristaeus, Lysis and Empdocles, Zamoixis and Epimanides, Milo and Leucippus, Alcmaeon and Hippasus, and Thymaridas were all of that age, a multitude of savants, incomparably excellent, --- all these adopted this mode of teaching, both in their conversations, and commentaries and annotations. Their writings also, and all the books which they published, most of which have been preserved, to our times, were not composed in popular or vulgar diction, or in a manner usual to all other writers, so as to be immediately understood, but in a way such as to be not easily apprehended by their readers. For they adopted Pythagoras's law of reserve, in an arcane manner concealing divine mysteries from the uninitiated, obscuring their writings and mutual conversations.

The result is that they who presents theses symbols without unfolding their meaning by a unsuitable exposition, runs the danger of exposing them to the charge of being ridiculous and inane, trifling and garrulous. When however they expounded according to these symbols, and made clear and obvious even to the crowds, then they will be found analogous to prophetic sayings such as the oracles of the Pythian Apollo. Their admirable meaning will inspire those who unite intellect and scholarliness.

It might be well to mention a few of them, explain this mode of discipline.

Not negligently enter into a temple or adore carelessly, even if only at the doors.

Sacrifice and adore unshod.

Shunning public roads, walk in unfrequented paths.

Not without light speak about Pythagoric affairs.

Such is a sketch of the symbolic mode of teaching adopted by Pythagoras.

CHAPTER XXIV
DIETARY SUGGESTIONS

Since food, used properly and regularly, greatly contributes to the best discipline, it may be interesting to consider Pythagoras's precepts on the subject. Forbidden was generally all food causing flatulence or indigestion, while he recommended the contrary kind of food, that preserve and are astringent. Wherefore he recommended the nutritious qualities of millet. Rejected was all food foreign to the Gods, as withdrawing us from communion with them. On the other hand, he forbade to his disciples all food that was sacred, as too honorable to subserve common utility. He exhorted his disciples to abstain from such things as were an impediment to prophecy or to the purity and chastity to the soul, or to the habit of temperance, and virtue. Lastly, he rejected all things that were an impediment to sanctity and disturbed or obscured the other purities of the soul, and the phantasms which occur in sleep. Such were the general regulations about food.

Specially, however, the most contemplative of the philosophers, who had arrived at the summit of philosophic attainments, were forbidden superfluous, food such as wine, or unjustifiable food such as was animated; and not to sacrifice animals to the Gods, nor by any means to injure animals, but to observe most solicitous justice towards them. He himself lived after this manner, abstaining from animal food, and adoring altars undefiled with blood. He was likewise careful to prevent others from destroying animals of a nature kindred to ours, and rather corrected and instructed savage animals, than injured them as punishment. Further, he ordered abstaining from animal food even to politicians; for as they desired to act justly to the highest degree, they must certainly not injure any kindred animals. How indeed could they persuade others to act justly, if they themselves were detected in an insatiable avidity in devouring animals allied to us. These are conjoined to us by a fraternal alliance through the communion of life, and the same elements, and the commingling of these.

Eating of the flesh of certain animals was however permitted to those whose life was not entirely purified, philosophic and sacred; but even for these was appointed a definite time of abstinence. Besides, these were not to eat the heart, nor the brain, which entirely forbidden to all Pythagoreans. For these organs are predominant and as it were ladders and seats of wisdom and life. Food other than animal was by him also considered sacred, on account of the nature of divine reason.

Thus his disciples were to abstain from mallows, because this plant is the first messenger and signal of the sympathy of celestial with terrestrial natures. Moreover, the fish melanurus was interdicted because sacred to the terrestrial gods. Likewise, the erythinus. Beans also on account of many causes also were interdicted, physical, psychic and sacred.

Many other similar precepts were enjoined in the attempt to lead men to virtue through their food.

CHAPTER XXV
MUSIC AND POETRY

Pythagoras was likewise of opinion that music, if properly used, greatly contributed to health. For he was wont to use it in no careless way, but as a purification. Indeed, he restricted this word to signify music used as medicine.

About the vernal season he used a melody in this manner. In the middle was placed a person who played on the lyre, and seated around him in a circle were those able to sing. Then the lyrist in the centre struck up and the singers raised certain paeans, through which they were evidently so overjoyed that their manners became elegant and orderly. This music instead of medicines was also used at certain other times.

Certain melodies were devised as remedies against the passions of the soul, as also against despondency and gnashing of the teeth, which were invented by Pythagoras as specifics. Further, he employed other melodies against anger and rage, and all other aberrations of the soul. Another kind of modulation was invented against desires. He likewise used dancing, which was accompanied by the lyre, instead of the pipe, which he conceived to have an influence towards insolence, being theatrical, and by no means liberal. For the purpose of correcting the soul, he also used select verses of Homer and Hesiod.

It is related among the deeds of Pythagoras that once, through a spondaic song, he extinguished the rage of a Tauromanian lad, who after feasting by night, intended to burn the vestibule of the house of his mistress, on seeing her issuing from the house of a rival. (To this rash attempt the lad had been inflamed, by a Phrygian song, which however Pythagoras at once suppressed.) As Pythagoras was astronomizing he happened to meet this Phrygian piper at an unseasonable time of night, and persuaded him to change his Phrygian song for a spondaic one; through which the fury of the lad being immediately repressed, he retired home in an orderly manner, although but a little while since he had stupidly insulted Pythagoras as on meeting him, would bear no admonition, and could not be restrained.

Here is another instance. Anchitus, the host of Empedocles, had as judge, condemned to death the father of a youth, who rushed on Anchitus with drawn sword, intending to slay him. Empedocles changed the youth's intention by singing, to his lyre, that verse of Homer (Od,4):

"Nepenthe, without gall, o'er every ill
Oblivion spreads; -"

thus saving his host Anchitus from death, and the youth from committing murder. It is said that from that time on the youth became one of the most faithful disciples of Pythagoras.

The Pythagoreans distinguished three states of mind, called *exartysis*, or readiness; *synarmoge*, or fitness, and *epaphe*, or contact, which converted the soul to contrary passions, and these could be produced by certain appropriate songs.

When they retired, they purified their reasoning powers from the noises and perturbations to which they had been exposed during the day, by certain odes and hymns which produced tranquil sleep, and few, but good dreams. But when they arose from slumbers, they again liberated themselves from the dazedness and torpor of sleep by songs of another kind. Sometimes the passions of the soul and certain diseases were, as they said, genuinely lured by enchantments, by musical sounds alone, without words. This is indeed probably the origin of the general use of this word *epode*.

Thus therefore, through music Pythagoras produced the most beneficial correction of manners and lives.

CHAPTER XXVI
THEORETICAL MUSIC (from Nicomachus)

While describing Pythagoras's wisdom in instructing his disciples, we must not fail to note that he invented the harmonic science and ratios. But to explain this we must go a little backwards in time.

Once as he was intently considering music, and reasoning with himself whether it would be possible to devise some instrumental assistance to the sense of hearing, so as to systematize it, as sight is made precise by the compass rule, and [telescope], or touch is made reckonable by balance and measures, - so thinking of these things Pythagoras happened to pass by a brazier's shop, where providentially he heard the hammers beating out a piece of iron on the anvil, producing sounds that harmonized, except one. But he recognized in these sounds, the concord of the octave, the fifth, and the fourth. He saw that the sound between the fourth and the fifth, taken by itself, was a dissonance, and yet completed the greater sound among them. Delighted, therefore, to find that the thing he was anxious to discover had by divine assistance succeeded, he went into the smithy, and by various experiments discovered that the difference of sound arose from the magnitude of the hammers, but not from the force of the strokes, nor from the shape of the hammers, nor from the change of position of the beaten iron. Having then accurately examined the weights and the swing of the hammers, he returned home, and fixed one stake diagonally to the walls, lest some difference should arise from there being several of them, or from some difference in the material of the stakes. From this stake he then suspended four gut-strings, of similar materials, size, thickness and twist. A weight was suspended from the bottom of each. When the strings were equal in length, he struck two of them simultaneously, he reproduced the former intervals, forming different pairs.

He discovered that the string stretched by the greatest weight, when compared with that stretched by the smallest weight, the interval of an octave. The weight of the first was twelve pounds, and that of the latter six. Being therefore in a double ratio, it formed the octave, which was made plain by the weights themselves. Then he found that the string from which the greater weight was suspended compared with that from which was suspended the weight next to the smallest, and which weight was eight pounds, produced the interval known as the fifth. Hence he discovered that this interval is in a ratio of one and a half to one, or three to two, in which ratio the weights also were to each other. The he found that the string stretched by the greatest weight produced, when compared with that which was next to it, in weight, namely, nine pounds, the interval called the fourth, analogous to the weights. This ratio, therefore, he discovered to be in the ratio of one and a third to one, or four to three; while that of the from string from which a weight of nine pounds was suspended to the string which had the smallest weight, again in a ratio of three to two, which is 9 to 6. In like manner, the string next to that from which the small weight was suspended, was to that which had the smallest weight, in the ratio of 4 to 3 (being 8 to 6) but to the string which had the greatest weight, in a ratio of 3 to 2, being 12 to 8. Hence that which is between the fifth and fourth, and by which the fifth exceeds the fourth is proved to be as nine is to eight. But either way it may be proved that the octave is a system consisting of the fifth in conjunction with fourth, just as the double ratio consists of three to two, and four to three; as for instance 12, 8 and 6; or, conversely of the fourth and the fifth, as in the double ratio of four to three and three to two, as for instance, 12, 9 and 6 therefore, and in this order, having confirmed both his hand and hearing to the suspended weights, and having established according to them the ratio of the proportions, by an easy artifice he transferred the common suspension of the strings from the diagonal stake to the head of the instrument which he called "chordotenon," or string-stretcher. Then by the aid of pegs he produced a tension of the strings analogous to that effected by the weights. Employing this method, therefore, as a basis, and as it were an infallible rule, he afterward extended the experiment to other instruments, namely, the striking of pans, to pipes and [r----], to monochords, triangles, and the like in all of which he found the same ratio of numbers to obtain. Then he named the sound which participates in the number 6, tonic; that which participates of the number 8, and is four to three, sub-dominant; that which participates of the number 9, and is one tone higher then the sub-dominant, he called, dominant, and 9 to 8; but that which participates of the number 12, octave.

Then he filled up the middle spaces with analogous sounds in diatonic order, and formed an octochord from symmetric numbers; from the double, the three to two, the four to three, and from the difference of these, the 8 to 9. Thus he discovered the harmonic progression, which tends by a certain physical necessity from the lowest to the most acute sound, diatonically. Later, from the diatonic he progressed to the chromatic and enharmonic orders, as we shall later show when we treat of music. This diatonic scale however, seems to have the following progression, a semi-tone, a tone, and a tone; and this is the fourth, being a system consisting of two tones, and of what is called a semi-tone. Afterwards, adding another tone, we produce the fifth, which is a system consisting of three tones and a semi-tone. Next to this is the system of a semi-tone, a tone, and a tone, forming another fourth, that is, another four to three ratio. Thus in the more ancient octave indeed, all the sounds from the lowest pitch which are with respect to each other fourths, produce everywhere with each other fourths; the semi-tone, by transition, receiving the first, middle and third place, according to that tetrachord. Now in the Pythagoric octave, however, which by conjunction is a system of the tetrachord and pentachord, but if disjoined is a system of two tetrachords separated from each other, the progression is from the gravest to the most acute sound. Hence all sounds that by their distance from each other are fifths, with each other produce the interval of the fifth; the semi-tone successively proceeding into four places, the first, second, third, and fourth.

This is the way in which music is said to have been discovered by Pythagoras. Having reduced it to a system, he delivered it to his disciples to utilize it to produce things as beautiful as possible.

(This story of the smithy is an ancient error, as pieces of iron give the same note whether struck by heavy or light hammers. Pythagoras may therefore have brought the discovery with him from Egypt, though he may also have developed the further details mentioned in this chapter.)

CHAPTER XXVII
MUTUAL POLITICAL ASSISTANCE

Many deeds of the Pythagoreans in the political sphere are deservedly praised. At one time the Crotonians were in the habit of making funerals and interments too sumptuous. Thereupon one of them said to the people that once he had heard Pythagoras converse about divine natures, during which he had observed that the Olympian divinities attended to the dispositions of the sacrificers, and not to the multitude of the offerings. The terrestrial gods, on the contrary, as being interested in less important matters, rejoiced in lamentations and banquets, libations, delicacies, and obsequial pomp; and as proof thereof, the divinity of Hades is called Pluto from his wish to receive. Those that honor him slenderly (he does not much care for), and permits to stay quite a little while; but he hastens to draw down those disposed to spend profusely on funeral solemnities, that he may obtain the honors offered in commemoration the dead. The result was that the Crotonians that heard this advice were persuaded that if they conducted themselves moderately in misfortunes, they would be promoting their own salvation, but would die prematurely if immoderate in such expenses. A certain difference arose about an affair in which there was no witness. [Pythagoras on] A Pythagorean was made arbitrator; and he led both litigants to a certain monument, announcing that the man buried was exceedingly equitable. The one prayed that he might receive much reward for this good life, while the other declared that the defunct was no better-off for his opponent's prayers. The Pythagorean condemned the latter, confirming that he who praised the dead man for his worth had earned credibility.

In a cause of great moment, this Pythagorean decided that one of the two who has agreed to settle that affair by arbitration, should pay four talents, while the other should receive two. Then from him who had received two he took three, and gave them to the other, so that each had been mulcted one talent (the text is confused).

Two persons had fraudulently deposited a garment with a woman who belonged to a court of justice, and told her that she was not to give it to either of them unless both were present. Later, with intent to defraud, one claimed and got the common deposit, saying he had the consent of the other party. The other one turned informer and related the compact made at the beginning to the magistrates. A certain

Pythagorean, however, as arbitrator, decided that the woman was guiltless, construing the claimed assent as constructive presence.

Two persons, who had seemed to be great friends, but who had gotten to suspect each other through calumnies of a sycophant, who told the one the other had taken undue liberties with his wife. A Pythagorean happened to enter the smithy where the injured party was finding fault with the blacksmith for not having sufficiently sharpened a sword he had brought him for that purpose. The Pythagorean suspecting the use to which the sword was be put said, "The sword is sharper than all things except calumny." This caused the prospective avenger to consider that he should not rashly sin against his friend who was within on an invitation (for the purpose of killing him).

A stranger in the temple of Aesculapius accidentally dropped his belt, on which were gold ornaments. When he tried to pick it up, he was informed that the temple-regulations forbad picking up anything on the floor. He was indignant, and a Pythagorean advised him to remove the golden ornaments which were not touching the floor leaving the belt which was. (Text corrupt).

During a public spectacle, some cranes flew over the theatre. One sailor said to his companion, "Do you see the witnesses?" A Pythagorean near by hailed them into a court presided over by a thousand magistrates, where, being examined they confessed to having thrown certain boys into the sea, who, on drowning had called on the cranes, flying above them, to witness to the deed. This story is mistakenly located elsewhere, but it really happened at Crotona.

Certain recent disciples of Pythagoras were at variance with each other, and the junior came to the senior, declaring there was no reason to refer the matter to an arbitrator, inasmuch as all they needed to do was to dismiss their anger. The elder agreed, but regretted he had not been the first to make that proposition. We might relate here the story of Damon and Phinthias, of Plato and Archytas, and of Clinias and Prorus. At present however we shall limit ourselves to that of Eubulus the Messenian, who, when sailing homeward, was taken captive by the Tyrrhenians, where he was recognized by a Pythagorean named Nausithus, who redeemed him from the pirates, and sent him home in safety.

When the Carthaginians were about to send five thousand soldiers into a desert island, the Carthaginian Miltiades saw among them the Argive Pythagorean Possiden. Approaching him, and without revealing his intentions, he advised him to return home with all possible haste.

He placed him in a ship then sailing near the shore, supplied him with the travel necessaries, and thus saved him from the impending danger.

He who would try to relate all the fine deeds that beautified the mutual relations of the Pythagoreans would find the task exceeding space and patience. I shall therefore pass on to show that some of the Pythagoreans were competent administrators, adapted to rule. Many were custodians of the laws, and ruled over certain Italian cities, infolding to them, and advising them to adopt the most salutary measures, while themselves refusing all pay. Though greatly calumniated, their probity and the desire of the citizens prevailed to make them administrators. At this time the best governed states seem to have been in Italy and Sicily. One of the best legislators, Chatondas the Catanean, was a Pythagorean, and so were the celebrated Locrian legislators Zaleucus and Timares. Pythagoreans also were those Rheginic polities, called the Gymnasiarchic, named after Theocles. Excelling in studies and manners which were then adopted by their fellow-citizens, were Phytius, Theocles, Elecaon and Aristocrates. Indeed, it is said that Pythagoras was the originator of all political erudition, when he said that nothing existent pure, inasmuch as earth participates of fire, fire of air, and air of water, and water of spirit. Likewise the beautiful participates in the deformed, the just of the unjust, and so on; so that from this principle human impulse may (by proper direction) be turned in either direction. He also said that there were two motions, one of the body which is irrational, and one of the soul, which is the result of deliberate choice. He also said polities might be likened to three lines whose extremities join, forming a (triangle containing) one right angle (the lines being as 4, 3 and 2); so that one of them is as 4 to 3, another as 5 to 2, and the other (3) is the arithmetical medium between 2 and 4. Now when, by reasoning, we study the mutual relations of these lines, and the places under them, we shall find that they represent the best image of a polity. Plato plagiarized, for in his Republic he clearly says, "That the result of the 4 to 3 ratio, conjoined with the 5 ratio, produce two harmonies." (This means that) he cultivated the moderation of the passions, and the middle path between extremes, rendering happy the life of his disciples by relating them to ideals of the good.

We are also told that he persuaded the Crotonians to give up associations with courtesans and prostitutes. Crotonian wives came to Deine, the wife of the Pythagorean Brontinus, who was a wise and splendid woman, the author of the maxim that it was proper for women to sacrifice on the same day they had risen from the embraces of their husbands, ---(which some ascribe to Pythagoras' wife Theano), --- and entreated to persuade Pythagoras to discourse to them on their continence as due to their husbands. This she did, and Pythagoras accordingly made an address to the Crotonians, which successfully ended the then prevalent incontinence.

When ambassadors came from Sybaris to Crotona to demand the (return of) the exiles, and Pythagoras, seeing one of the ambassadors who with his own hand had slain one of Pythagoras's friends, made no answer whatever. But when this man insisted on an explanation and addressed Pythagoras, the latter said it was unlawful to converse with murderers. This induced many to believe he was Apollo.

All these stories, together with what we mentioned above about the destruction of tyrants, and the democratization of the cities of Italy and Sicily, and many other circumstances, are eloquent of the benefits conferred on mankind by Pythagoras, in political respects.

CHAPTER XXVIII
DIVINITY OF PYTHAGORAS

Henceforward we shall confine ourselves to the works flowing from Pythagoras's virtues. As usual, we shall begin from the divinities, endeavoring to exhibit his piety, and marvelous deeds. Of his piety, let this be a specimen: that he knew what his soul was, whence it came into the body, and also its former lives, of this giving the most evident indications. Again, once passing over the river Nessus along with many associates, he addressed the river, which, in a distinct and clear voice, in the hearing of all his associates, answered, "Hail, Pythagoras!"

Further, all his biographers insist that during the same day he was present in Metapontum in Italy, and at Tauromenium in Sicily, discoursing with his disciples in both places, although these cities are separate, both by land and sea by many stadia, the traveling over which consumes many days. It is also a matter of common report that showed his golden thigh to the Hyperborean Abaris, who said that he resembled the Apollo worshipped among the Hyperboreans, and of whom Abaris was the priest; and that he had done this so that he was not deceived therin.

A myriad of other more admirable and divine particulars are likewise unanimously and uniformly related of *the man*, such as infallible predictions of earthquakes, rapid expulsions of pestilences, and hurricanes, instantaneous cessations of hail, tranquilizations of the waves of rivers and seas, in order that his disciples might the more easily pass over them. The power of effecting miracles of this kind was achieved by Empedocles of Agrigentum, Epimenides the Cretan, and Abaris the Hyperborean, and these persons performed them in many places. Their deeds were so manifest that Empedocles was surnamed a wind-stiller, Epimenides an expiator, and Abaris an air-walker, because, carried on the dart given him by the Hyperborean Apollo, he passed over rivers, and seas and inaccessible places like one carried on air. Many think that Pythagoras did the same thing, when in the same day he discoursed with his disciples at Metapontum and Tauromenium. It is also said that he predicted there would be an earthquake from the water of a well which he had tasted; and that a ship was sailing with a prosperous wind, would be submerged in the sea. These are sufficient proofs of his piety.

Pitching my thoughts on a higher key, I wish to exhibit the principle of the worship of the Gods, established by Pythagoras and his disciples:

that the mark aimed at by all plans, whether to do or not to do, is consent with the divinity.

The principle of their piety, and indeed their whole life is arranged with a view to follow God. Their philosophy explicitly asserts that men act ridiculously in searching for good from any source other than God; and that in respect the conduct of most men resembles that of a man who, in a country governed by a king should reverence one of the city magistrates, neglecting him who is the ruler of all of them. Since God exists as the lord of all things, it is evident and acknowledged that good must be requested of him. All men impart good to those they love, and admire, and the contrary to those they dislike. Evidently we should do those things in which God delights. Not easy, however, is it for a man to know which these are, unless he obtains this knowledge from one who has heard God, or has heard God himself, or procures it through divine art. Hence also the Pythagoreans were studious of divination, which is an interpretation of the benevolence of the Gods. That such an employment is worth while will be admitted by one who believes in the Gods; but he who thinks that either of these is folly will also be of opinion that both are foolish. Many of the precepts of the Pythagoreans derived from the mysteries.

Pythagoras should be received as referring not to a mere man, but to a super-man. This is also what is meant by their maxim, *that man, bird, ar[--] another th[---] thing are bipeds*, thereby referring to Pythagoras. Such, therefore, on account of his piety, was Pythagoras; and such he was truly thought to be.

Oaths were religiously observed by the Pythagoreans, who were mindful of that precept of theirs,

"As duly by law, thy homage pay first to the immortal Gods;
Then to thy oath, and last to the heroes illustrious."

For instance: A Pythagorean was in court, and asked to take an oath. Rather than to disobey this principle, although the oath would have been a religiously permitted one, he preferred to pay to the defendant a fine of three talents.

Pythagoras taught that no occurrence happened by chance or luck, but rather conformably to divine Providence, and especially so to good and pious men. This is well illustrated by a story from Androcides's treatise on Pythagoric symbols about the Tarentine Pythagorean Thymaridas. He was happening to be sailing away from his country, his friends were all present to bid him farewell, and to embrace him. He had already embarked when someone cried to him, "O Thyramidas, I pray that the Gods may shape all your circumstances accord into your wishes!" But he retorted, "Predict me better things; namely, that what may happen to me may be conformable to the will of the Gods !" For he thought it more scientific and prudent not to resist or grumble against divine providence.

If asked about the source whence these men derived so much piety, we must acknowledge that the Pythagorean number-theology was clearly fore-shadowed, to some extent, in the Orphic writings. Nor is it to be doubted that when Pythagoras composed his treatise *Concerning the Gods*, he received assistance from Orpheus, wherefore indeed that theological treatise is sub-titled, the learned and trustworthy Pythagoreans assert, *by Telauges*; taken from the commentaries left by Pythagoras himself to his daughter, Damo, Telauges's sister, and which, after her death, were said to have been given to Bitale, Damo's daughter and to Telauges, the son of Pythagoras and husband of Bitale, when he was of mature age for he was at Pythagoras's death left very young with his mother Theano. Now who can judge who it was that delivered what there is said of the Gods from the Sacred Discourse, or Treatise on the Gods, which bears both titles. For we read:

"Pythagoras, the son of Mnesarchus was instructed in what pertains to the Gods when he celebrated orgies in the Thracian Libethra, being therein initiated by Aglaophemus; and that Orpheus, the son of Calliope, having learned wisdom from his mother in the mountain Pangaeus, said that the eternal essence of number is the most providential principle of the universe, of heaven and earth, and of the intermediate nature; and farther still, that it is the root of the permanency of divine natures, of Gods, and divinities."

From this it is evident that he learned from the Orphic writers that the essence of the Gods is defined by number. "Through the same numbers also, he produced a wonderful prognostication and worship of the Gods, both of which are particularly allied to numbers."

As conviction is best produced by an objective fact, the above principle may be proved as follows. When Abaris performed sacred rites according to his customs, he procured a foreknowledge of events, which is studiously cultivated by all the Barbarians, by sacrificing animals, especially birds; for they think that the entrails of such animals are particularly adapted to this purpose. Pythagoras, however, not wishing to suppress his ardent pursuit of the truth, but to guide it into a safer way, without blood and slaughter, and also because he thought that a cock was sacred to the sun, "furnished him with a consummate knowledge of all truth, through arithmetical science." From piety, also, he derived faith concerning the Gods. For Pythagoras always insisted that nothing marvelous concerning Gods or divine teachings should be disbelieved, inasmuch as the Gods are competent to effect anything. But the divine teachings in which we must believe are those delivered by Pythagoras. The Pythagoreans therefore assumed and believed what they taught (on the priori ground that) they were not the offspring of false opinion. Hence Eurytus the Crotonian, the disciple of Philolaus, said that a shepherd feeding his sheep near Philolaus's tomb had heard someone singing. But the person to whom this was related did not at all question this, merely asking what kind of harmony it was. Pythagoras himself also, being asked by a certain person the significance of the converse with his defunct father in sleep, answered that it meant nothing. For neither is anything portended by your speaking with me, said he.

Pythagoras wore clean white garments, and used clean white coverlets, avoiding the woolen ones. This custom he enjoined on his disciples. In speaking of super-human natures, he used honorable appellations, and words of good omen, on every occasion mentioning and reverencing the Gods; so, while at supper, he performed libations to the divinities, and taught his disciples , daily to celebrate the super-human beings with hymns. He attended likewise to rumors and omens, prophecies and lots, and in short to all unexpected circumstances. Moreover, he sacrificed to the Gods with millet, cakes, honeycombs, and fumigations. But he did not sacrifice animals, nor did any of the contemplative philosophers. His other disciples, however, the Hearers and the Politicians, were by him ordered to sacrifice animals such as cock, or a lamb, or some other young animal, but not frequently; but they were prohibited from sacrificing oxen.

Another indication of the honor he paid the Gods was his teaching that his disciples must never use the names of the divinities uselessly in swearing. For instance, Syllus, one of the Crotonian Pythagoreans, paid a fine rather than swear, though he could have done so without violating the truth. Just as the Pythagoreans abstained from using the names of the Gods, also, through reverence, they were unwilling to name Pythagoras, indicating him whom they meant by the invention of the *Tetraktys*. Such is the form of an oath ascribed to them:

"I swear by the discoverer of the *Tetraktys*, which is the spring of all our wisdom; The perennial fount and root of Nature."

In short, Pythagoras imitated the Orphic mode of writing, and (pious) disposition, the way they honored the Gods representing; them images and in brass not resembling our (human form), but the divine receptacle (of the sphere), because they comprehend and provide for all things, being of a nature and form similar to the universe.

But his divine philosophy and worship was compound, having learned much from the Orphic followers, but much also from the Egyptian priests, the Chaldeans and Magi, the mysteries of Eleusis, Imbrus, Samothracia, and Delos and even the Celtic and Iberian. It is also said that Pythagoras's Sacred Discourse is current among the Latins, not being read to or by all, but only by those who are disposed to learn, the best things, avoiding all that is base.

He ordered that libations should be made thrice, observing that Apollo delivered oracles from the tripod, the *triad* being the first number. Sacrifices to Venus were to be made on the sixth day, because this number is the first to partake of every number and when divided in every possible way, receives the power of the numbers subtracted, and those that remain. Sacrifices to Hercules, however, should be made on the eighth day, of the month, counting from the beginning, commemorating his birth in the seventh month.

He ordained that those who entered into a temple should be clothed in a clean garment, in which no one had slept; because sleep, just as and brack and brown, indicates sluggishness, while cleanliness is a sign, of equality and justice in reasoning.

If blood should be found unintentionally spilled in a temple, there should be made a lustration, either in a golden vessel, or with sea-water; gold being the most beautiful of all things and the measure of exchange of everything else; while the latter was derived from the principle of moistness, the food of the first and more common matter. Also, children should not be brought forth in a temple; where the divine part of the soul should not be bound to the body. On a festal day neither should the hair be cut, nor the nails pared; as it was unworthy to disturb the worship of the Gods, to attend to our own advantage. Nor should lice be killed in a temple, as divine power should not participate in anything superfluous or degrading.

The Gods should be honored with cedar, laurel, cypress, oak and myrtle; nor should the body be purified with these, nor any of them be cut with the teeth.

He also ordered that what is boiled should not be roasted, signifying hereby that mildness has no need of anger.

The bodies of the dead he did not suffer to be burned, herein following the Magi, being unwilling that anything (so) divine (as fire) should be mingled with mortal nature. He thought it holy for the dead to be carried out in white garments; thereby obscurely prefiguring the simple and first nature, according to number, and the principle of all things.

Above all, he ordained that an oath should be taken religiously; since that which is behind (the futurity of punishment) is long.

He said it was much more holy to be a man injured than to kill a man; for judgment is pronounced in Hades, where the soul and its essence, and the first nature of things is correctly appraised.

He ordered that coffins should not be made of cypress, either because the scepter of Jupiter was made of this wood, or for some other mystic reason. Libations were to be performed before the altar of Jupiter the Savior, of Hercules, and the Dioscuri; thus celebrating Jupiter as the presiding cause and leader of the meal; Hercules as the power of Nature, and the Dioscuri, as the symphony of all things. Libations should not be offered with closed eyes, as nothing beautiful should be undertaken with bashfulness and shame. When it thundered, one ought to touch the earth, in remembrance of the generation of things.

Temples should be entered from places on the right hand; and left from the left hand; for the right hand is the principle of what is called the odd number, and is divine; while the left hand is a symbol of the even number, and of dissolution.

Such are many of the injunctions he is said to have adopted in the pursuance of piety. Other particulars which have been omitted may be inferred from what has been given. Hence the subject be closed.

CHAPTER XXIX
SCIENCES AND MAXIMS

The Pythagoreans' Commentaries best express his wisdom; being accurate, concise, savoring of the ancient elegance of style, and deducing the conclusions exquisitely. They contain the most condensed conceptions, and are diversified in form and matter. The are both accurate and eloquent, full of clear and indubitable arguments, accompanied by scientific demonstration, in syllogistic form; as indeed will be discovered by any careful reader.

In his writings, Pythagoras, from a supernal source, delivers the science of intelligible natures and Gods.

Afterwards, he teaches the whole of physics, completely unfolding ethics and logic. Then come various discipline and other excellent sciences. There is nothing pertaining to human knowledge which is not discussed in these encyclopedic writings. If therefore it is acknowledged that of the (Pythagoric) writings which are now in circulation, some were written by Pythagoras himself, while others consist of what he was heard to say, and on this account are anonymous, though of Pythagoric origin; - if all this be so, it is evident that he was abundantly skilled in all wisdom.

It is said that while he was in Egypt he very much applied himself to geometry. For Egyptian life bristles with geometric problem; since, from remote periods, when the Gods were fabulously said to have reigned in Egypt, on account of the rising and falling of the Nile, the skillful have been compelled to measure all the Egyptian land which they cultivated; wherefrom indeed the science's name, geometry, was derived. Besides, the Egyptians studied the theories of the celestial orbs, in which Pythagoras also was skilled. All theorems about lines seem to have been derived from that country. All that relates to numbers and computation is said to have been discovered in Phoenicia.

The theorems about the heavenly bodies have by some been referred to the Egyptians and Chaldeans in common. Whatever Pythagoras received, however, he developed further, he arranged them for learners, and personally demonstrated them with perspicuity and elegance. He was the first to give a name to *philosophy*, describing it as a desire for and love of wisdom, which latter he defined as the science of objectified truth. Beings he defined as immaterial and eternal natures, alone possessing a power that is efficacious, as are incorporeal essences. The rest of things are beings only figuratively, and considered such only through the participation of real beings; such are corporeal and material forms, which arise and decay without ever truly existing. Now wisdom is the science of things which are truly beings; but not of the mere figurative entities. Corporeal natures are neither the objects of science, nor admit of a stable knowledge, since they are infinite, and by science incomprehensible, and when compared with universals resemble non-beings, and are in a genuine sense non-definable. Indeed it is impossible to conceive that there should be a science of things not naturally the objects of science; nor could a science of non-existent things prove attractive to anyone. Far more desirable will be things which are genuine beings, existing in invariable permanency, and always answering to their description. For the perception of objects existing only figuratively, never truly being what they seem to be, follows the apprehension of real beings, just as the knowledge of particulars is posterior to the science of universals. For, as said Archytas, he who properly knows universals, will also have a clear perception, of the nature of particulars, That is why beings are not alone, only-begotten, nor simple, but various and multiform. For those genuine beings are intelligible and incorporeal natures, while others are corporeal, falling under the perception of sense, communicate with that which is really existent only by participation. Concerning all these, Pythagoras formed sciences the most apposite, leaving nothing uninvestigated. Besides, he developed the master-sciences of method, common to all of them, such as logic, definitions, and analysis, as may be gathered from the Pythagoric commentaries.

To his intimates he was wont to utter symbolically oracular sentences, wherein the smallest number of words were pregnant with the most multifarious significance, not unlike certain oracles of the Pythian Apollo, or like nature herself in tiny seeds, the former exhibiting conceptions, and the latter effects innumerable in multitude, and difficult to understand. Such was Pythagoras's own maxim, "The beginning is the half of the whole." In this and similar utterances the most divine Pythagoras concealed the sparks of truth, as in a treasury, for those capable of being kindled thereby. In this brevity of diction he deposited an extension of theory most ample, and difficult to grasp, as in the maxim, "All things accord in number," which he frequently repeated to his disciples. Another one was, "Friendship is equality; Equality is friendship." He even used single words, such as "cosmos," or, adorned world; or, philosophy!Ó or further, "*Tetractys!*" All these and many other similar inventions were by Pythagoras devised for the benefit and amendment of his associates; and by those that understood them they were considered to be so worthy of veneration , and so divinely inspired, that those who dwelt in the common auditorium adopted this oath:

"I swear by the discoverer of the Tetraktys, which is the spring of all our wisdom;
The perennial founts and root of Nature."

This was the form of his so admirable wisdom.

Of the sciences honored by the Pythagoreans not the least were music, medicine and divination. [May be missing text]. . . .

Of medicine, the most emphasized part was dietetics; and they were most scrupulous in its exercise. First, they sought to understand the physical symptoms of equanimity, labor, eating and repose. They were nearly the first to make a business of the preparation of food, and to describe its methods. More frequently than their predecessors the Pythagoreans used poultices, however disapproving more of medicated ointments, which they chiefly limited to the cure of ulcerations. Most they disapproved of cuts and cauterizations. Some diseases they cured by incantations. Music, if used in a proper manner, was by Pythagoras supposed to contribute greatly to health. The Pythagoreans likewise employed select sentences of Homer and Hesiod for the amendment of souls.

The Pythagoreans were habitually silent and prompt to hear, and he won praise who listened (most effectively). But that which they had learned and heard was supposed to be retained and preserved in the memory. Indeed, this ability of learning and remembering determined the amount of disciplines and lectures, inasmuch as learning is the power by which knowledge is obtained, and remembering that by which it is preserved. Hence memory was greatly honored, abundantly exercised, and given much attention. In learning also it was understood that they were not to dismiss what they were taught, till its first rudiments had been entirely mastered. This was their method of recalling what they daily heard. No Pythagorean rose from his bed till he had first recollected the transactions of the day before; and he accomplished this by endeavoring to remember what he first said, or heard, or ordered done by his domestics before rising; or what was the second or third thing he had said, heard or commanded. The same method was employed for the remainder of the day. He would try to remember the identity of the first person he had met on leaving home, and who was the second; and with, whom he had discoursed first, second or third. So also he did with everything else, endeavoring to resume in his memory all the events of the whole day, and in the very same order in which each of them had occurred. If however, after rising there was enough leisure to do so, the Pythagoreans reminisced about day before yesterday. Thus they made it a point to exercise their memories systematically; considering that the ability of remembering was most important for experience, science and wisdom.

This Pythagorean school filled Italy with philosophers; and this place which before was unknown, was later, on account of Pythagoras called Greater Greece, which became most famous for is philosophers, poets and legislators. Indeed, the rhetorical arts, demonstrative reasonings and legislation was entirely transferred from Greece. As to physics, we might mention the principal physiologists, Empedocles and the Elean Parmenides. As to ethical maxims, this is Epicharmus, whose conceptions are used by all philosophers.

Thus much concerning the wisdom of Pythagoras, how in a certain respect he very much impelled all his *hearers* to its pursuit, so far as they were adapted to its participation, and how perfectly he delivered it.

CHAPTER XXX
JUSTICE AND POLITICS

How he cultivated and delivered justice to humanity we shall best understand if we trace it to its first principle, and ultimate cause. Also we must investigate the ultimate cause of injustice, which will show us how he avoided it, and what methods he adopted to make justice fructify in his soul.

The principle of justice is mutuality and equality, through which, in a way most nearly approximating union of body and soul, all men become cooperative, and distinguish the mine from the thine, as is also testified by Plato, who learned this from Pythagoras. Pythagoras effected this in the best possible manner by erasing from common life every thing private, while increasing everything held in common, so far as ultimate possessions, which after all are the causes of tumult and sedition (Among his disciples[),] everything, was common, and the same to all, no one possessing anything private. He himself indeed, who most approved of this communion, made use of common possessions in the most just manner; but disciples who changed their minds was given back his original contribution, with an addition, and left. Thus Pythagoras established justice in the best possible manner, beginning at its very first principle.

In the next place, justice is introduced by association with other people, while injustice is, produced by unsociability and neglect of other people. Wishing therefore to spread this sociability as far as possibility among men, he ordered his discipled to extend it to the most kindred animal races, considering these as their intimates and friends, which would forbid injuring, slaying, or eating any of them. He who recognizes the community of elements and life between men and animals will in much greater degree establish fellowship with those who share a kindred and rational soul. This also shows that Pythagoras prompted justice beginning from its very root principle. Since lack of money often compels men sometimes to act contrary to justice, he tried to avoid this by practising such economy that his necessary expenses might be liberal, and yet retain a just sufficiency. For as cities are only magnificent households, so the arrangement of domestic concerns is the principle of all good order in cities. For instance, it was said that he himself was the heir to the property of Alceus, who died after completing an embassy to the Lacedemonians; but that in spite of this Pythagoras was admired for his economy no less than for his philosophy. Also when he married, he so educated the daughter that was born to him, and who afterwards married the Crotonian Meno, that while unmarried she was a choir-leader, while as wife she held the first place among those who worshipped at altars. It is also said that the Metapontines preserved PythagorasÕs memory by turning his house into a temple of Ceres, and the street in which he lived into a museum.

Because injustice also frequently results from insolence, luxury, and lawlessness, he daily exhorted his disciples to support laws, and shun lawlessness. He considered luxury the first evil that usually glides into houses and cities; the second insolence, the third destruction.

Luxury therefore should by all possible means be ecluded and expelled; and that from birth men should be accustomed to live temperately, and in a manly manner. He also added the necessity of purification from bad language, whether it be piteous, or provocative, reviling, insolent or scurrilous.

Besides this household justice, he added another and most beautiful kind, the legislative, which both orders what to do and what not to do. Legislative justice is more beautiful that the judicial kind, resembling medicine which heals the diseased, but differs in this that it is preventive, planning the health of the soul from afar.

That is why the best of legislators graduated from the school of Pythagoras: first, Charondas the Catanean, and next Zaleucus and Timaratus, who legislated for the Locrians. Besides these were Theaetetus and Helicaon, Aristocrates and Phytius, who legislated for the Rhegini. All these aroused from the citizens honors comparable to those offered to divinities. For Pythagoras did not act like Heraclitus, who agreed to write laws for the Ephesians, but also petulantly added that in those laws he would order the citizens to hang themselves. What laws Pythagoras endeavored to establish were benevolent and scientific.

Nor need we specially admire those (above mentioned professional) legislators. Pythagoras had a slave by the name of Zamolxis, hailing from Thrace. After hearing Pythagoras's discourses, and obtaining his freedom, he returned to the Getae, and there, as has already been mentioned at the beginning of this work, exhorted the citizens to fortitude, persuading then that the soul is immortal. So much so is this that even at present all the Galatians and Trallians, and many others of the Barbarians, persuade their children that the soul cannot be destroyed, but survives death, so that the latter is not to be feared, so that (ordinary) danger is to be met with a firm and manly mind. For instructing the Getae in these things, and for having written laws for them, Zamolxis was by them considered as the greatest of the gods.

Further, Pythagoras conceived that the dominion of the divinities was most efficacious for establishing justice; and from this principle he deduced a hole polity, particular laws and a principle of justice. Thus his basic theology was that we should realize God's existence, and that his disposition towards the human race is such that he inspects and does not neglect it. This theology was very useful: for we require an inspection that we would not be disposed to resist, such as the inspective government of the divinity, for if divine nature is of this nature, it deserves the empire of the universe. For the Pythagoreans rightly taught that (the natural) man is an animal naturally insolent, and changeable in impulse, desire and passions. He therefore requires an extraordinary inspectionary government of this kind, which may produce some chastening and ordering. They therefore thought that any who recognize their changeableness should never be forgetful of piety towards and worship of divinity. Everyone should pay heed, beneath the divine nature, and that of genii, to his parents and the laws, and obey them unfeignedly and faithfully. In general, they thought it necessary to believe that there is no evil greater than anarchy; since the human race is not naturally adapted to salvation without some guidance. The Pythagoreans also considered it advisable to adhere to the customs and laws of their ancestors, even though somewhat inferior to other regulations. For it is unprofitable and not salutary to evade existing laws, or to be studious of innovation. Pythagoras, therefore, to evince that his life was conformable to his doctrines gave many other specimens of piety to the Gods.

It may be quite suitable to mention one of these, as an example of the rest. I will relate what Pythagoras said and did relative to the embassy from Sybaris to Crotona, relative to the return of the exiles. By order of the ambassadors, some of his associates had been slain, a part of them, indeed, by one of the ambassadors himself, while another one of them was the son of one of those who had excited the sedition, and had died of disease. When the Crotonians therefore were deliberating how they should act in this affair, Pythagoras told his disciples he was displeased that the Crotonians should be so much at odds over the matter, and that in his opinion the ambassadors should not even be permitted to lead victims to the altar, let alone drag thence the suppliant exiles. When the Sybarites came to him with their complaints, and the man who had slain some of his disciples with his own hands was

defending his conduct, Pythagoras declared he would make no answer
to (a murderer). Another (ambassador) accused him of asserting that he
was Apollo, because when in the past, some person had asked him
about a certain subject, why the thing was so; and he had retorted.
Would he think it sensible, when Apollo was delivering oracles to him,
to ask Apollo why he did so? Another one of the ambassadors derided
his school, wherein he taught the return of souls to this world saying
that, as Pythagoras was about to descend into Hades, the ambassador
would give Pythagoras an epistle to his father, and begged him to bring
back an answer, when he returned. Pythagoras responded that he was
not about to descend into the abode of the impious, where he clearly
knew that murderers were punished. As then the rest of the
ambassadors reviled him, Pythagoras, followed by many people, went to
the seashore, and sprinkled himself with water. After reviling the rest of
the ambassadors, one of the Crotonian counselors observed that he
understood they had defamed Pythagoras, whom not even a brute
would dare to blaspheme, though all animals should again utter the
same voice as men, as prehistoric fables relate. Pythagoras discovered
another method of restraining men from injustice: the fear of judgment.
He knew that this method could be taught, and that fear was often able
to suppress justice. He asserted therefore that it is much better to be
injured, than to kill a man; for judgment is dispensed in Hades, where
the soul and its essence and the first nature of beings, are accurately
appraised.

Desiring to exhibit among human unequal, indefinite and
unsytemmatical affairs the equality, definiteness and symmetry of
justice, and to show how it ought to be exercised, he likened justice to
(a right-angled) triangle, the only one among geometrical forms, which,
though, having an infinite diversity of adjustments of indeed unequal
parts (the length of the sides), yet has equal powers (the square on the
hypotenuse is equal to the squares on the other two sides).

Since all associations (imply relations with some other person) and
therefore entail justice, the Pythagoreans declared that there were two
kinds of associations, that differed: the seasonable, and the
unseasonable, according to age, merit, familiarity, philanthropy, and so
forth. For instance, the association of a younger person with an elderly
one is unseasonable, while that of two young persons is seasonable. No
kind of anger, threatening or boldness is becoming in a younger towards
an elderly man, all which unseasonable conduct should be cautiously
avoided. So also with respect to merit, for, towards a man who has

arrived at the true dignity of consummate virtue, neither unrestrained form of speech, nor any other of the above manners of conduct is seasonable.

Not unlike this was what he taught about the relations towards parents and benefactors. He said that the use of the opportune time was various. For of those who are angry or enraged, some are so seasonably, and some unseasonably. The same distinction obtains with desires, impulsions and passions, actions, dispositions, associations and meetings. He further observed that to a certain extent, the opportuneness is to be taught, and that also the unexpected might be analysed artificially; while none of the above qualifications obtain when applied universally, and simply. Nevertheless its results are very similar to those of opportuneness, namely elegance, propriety, congruence, and the like.

Reminding us that unity is the principle of the universe, being its principal element, so also is it in science, experiment, and growth. However two-foldness is most honorable in houses, cities, camps, and such like organizations. For in sciences we learn and judge not by any single hasty glance, but by a thorough examination of every detail. There is therefore grave danger of entire misapprehension of things, when the principle has been mistaken; for while the true principle remains unknown, no consequent conclusions can be final. The same situation obtains in things of another kind. Neither a city nor a house can be well organized unless each has an effective ruler who governs voluntary servants. For voluntariness is as necessary with the ruler to govern, as in the ruled to obey. So also must there be a concurrence of will between teacher and learner; for no satisfactory progress can be made while there obtains resistance on either side. Thus he demonstrated the beauty of being persuaded by rulers, and to be obedient to preceptors.

This was the greatest objective illustration of this argument. Pherecydes the Syrian had been his teacher, but now was afflicted with the morbus pedicularis, Pythagoras therefore went from Italy to Delos, to nurse him, tending him until he died, and piously performing whatever funeral rites were due to his former teacher. So diligent was he in discharge of his duties towards those from whom he had received instruction.

Pythagoras insisted strenuously with his disciples on the fulfillment of mutual agreements. (Here is an illustration). Lysis had once completed his worship in the temple of Juno, and was leaving as he met in the vestibule with Euryphamus the Syracusan, one of his fellow disciples, who was then entering into the temple. Euryphamus asked Lysis to wait for him, till he had finished his worship also. So Lysis sat down on a stone seat there situate, and waited. Euryphamus went in, finished his worship, but, having become absorbed in some profound considerations, forgot his appointment, and passed out of the temple by another gate. Lysis however continued to wait, without leaving his seat, the remainder of that day, and the following and also the greater part of the next day.

He might have staid there still longer, perhaps unless, the following day, in the auditorium, Euryphamus had heard that. LysisŌs associates were missing him. Recollecting his appointment, he hastened to Lysis, relieved him of the engagement, telling him the cause of his forgetfulness as follows: "Some God produced this oblivion in me, as a trial of your firmness in keeping your engagements."

Pythagoras also ordained abstinence from animal food, for many reasons, besides the chief one that it conduced to peaceableness. Those who are trained to abominate the slaughter of animals as iniquitous and unnatural will not think it much more unlawful to kill a man, or engage in war. For war promotes slaughter, and legalizes it, increasing it, and strengthening it. Pythagoras 's maxim "not to touch the balance above the beam" is in itself an exhortation to justice, demanding the cultivation of everything that is just, Ñ as will be shown when we study the Pythagorean symbols. In all these particulars, therefore, Pythagoras paid great attention to the practice of justice; and to its preachment to men, both in deeds and words.

CHAPTER XXXI
TEMPERANCE AND SELF-CONTROL

Temperance is our next topic, cultivated as it was by Pythagoras, and taught to his associates. The common precepts about it have already been detailed, in which we learned that everything irregular should be cut off with fire and sword. A similar precept is the abstaining from animal food, and also from such likely to produce intemperance, and lulling the vigilance and genuine energies of the reasoning powers. A further step in this direction is the precept to introduce, at a banquet, sumptuous fare, which is to be shortly sent away, and given to the servants, having been exhibited merely to chasten the desires. Another one was that none but courtesans should wear gold, not the free women. Further the practice of taciturnity, and even entire silence, for the purpose of governing the tongue. Next, intensive and continuous puzzling out of the most difficult speculations, for the sake of which wine, food and sleep would be minimized. Then would come genuine discrediting of notoriety, wealth, and the like; a sincere reverence towards those to whom reverence is due; joined with an unassumed democratic geniality towards one's equals in age, and towards the juniors guidance and counsel, free from envy, and everything similar which is to be deduced from temperance.

The temperance of the Pythagoreans, and how Pythagoras taught this virtue, may be learned from what Hippobotus and Neanthes narrate of Myllias and Timycha, who were Pythagoreans. It seems that Dionysius the tyrant could not obtain the friendship of any one of the Pythagoreans, though he did everything possible to accomplish that purpose; for they had noted, and condemned his monarchical leanings. He therefore sent a troop of thirty soldiers, under the command of Eurymenes the Syracusan, who was the brother of Dion, through (whose) treachery he hoped to take advantage of the Pythagoreans' usual annual migration to catch some of them; for they were in the habit of changing their abode at different seasons of the year, and they selected places suitable to such a migration. Therefore in Phalae, a rugged part of Tarentum, through which the Pythagoreans were scheduled to pass, Eurymenes insidiously concealed his troop; and when the unsuspecting Pythagoreans reached there about noon, the soldiers rushed upon them with shouts, after the manner of robbers. Disturbed and terrified at an attack so unexpected, at the superior number of their enemies, Ñ the Pythagoreans amounting to no more than ten, Ñ and

75

being unarmed against regularly equipped soldiery, the Pythagoreans saw that they would inevitably be taken captive, so they decided that their only safety lay in flight, which they did not consider inadmissible to virtue. For they knew that according to right reason, fortitude is the art of avoiding as well as enduring. So they would have escaped, and their pursuit would have been given up by Eurymenes's soldiers, who were heavily armed, had their flight not led them up against a field sown with beans, which were already flowering.

Unwilling to violate their principle not to touch beans, they stood still, and driven to desperation turned, and attacked their pursuers with stones and sticks, and whatever they found to hand, till they had wounded many, and slain some. But (numbers told), and all the Pythagoreans were slain by the spearmen, as none of them would suffer himself to be taken captive, preferring death, according to the Pythagorean teachings.

As Eurymenes and his soldiers had been sent for the express purpose of taking some of the Pythagoreans alive to Dionysius, they were much crest-fallen; and having thrown the corpses in a common sepulchre, and piled earth thereupon, they turned homewards. But as they were returning they met two of the Pythagoreans who had lagged behind. Myllias the Crotonian, and his Lacedemonian wife Timycha, who had not been able to keep up with the others, being in the sixth month of pregnancy. These therefore the soldiers gladly made captive, and led to the tyrant with every precaution, so as to insure their arrival alive. On learning what had happened, the tyrant was very much disheartened, and said to the two Pythagoreans, "You shall obtain from me honors of unusual dignity if you shall be willing to reign in partnership with me." All his offers, however, were by Myllias and Timycha rejected. Then said he, I will release you with a safe-guard if you will tell me one thing only. On Myllias asking what he wished to learn, Dionysius replied: "Tell me only why your companions chose to die rather than to tread on beans? But Myllis at once answered, "My companions did indeed prefer death to treading on beans; but I had rather do that than tell you the reason." Astonished at this answer, Dionysius ordered him removed forcibly, and Timycha tortured, for he thought that a pregnant woman, deprived of her husband, would weaken before the torments, and easily tell him all he wanted to know. The heroic woman, however, with her teeth bit her tongue until it was separated and spat it out at the tyrant, thus demonstrating that the offending member should be entirely cut off, even if her sex's weakness, vanquished by the torments, should be compelled to disclose something that should be reserved in silence. Such difficulties did they make to the admission of outside friendships, even though they happened to be royal.

Similar to these also were the precepts concerning silence, which tended to the practice of temperance; for of all continence, the subjugation of the tongue is the most difficult. The same virtue is illustrated by Pythagoras's persuading the Crotonians to relinquish all sacrilegious and questionable commerce with courtesans. Moreover Pythagoras restored to temperance a youth who had become wild with amatory passion, through music. Exhortations against lascivious insolence promote the same virtue. Such things were delivered to the Pythagoreans by Pythagoras himself, who was their cause.

They took such care of their bodies that they remained in the same condition, not being at one time lean, and at another stout, which changes they considered anomalous. With respect to their mind also, they managed to remain uniformly mildly joyful, and not at one time hilarious, and at another sad, which could be achieved only by expelling perturbations, despondency or rage.

It was a precept of theirs that no human casualties ought to be unexpected by the intelligent, expecting everything which it is not in their power to prevent. If however at any time any of them fell into a rage, or into despondency, he would withdraw from his associates' company, and seeking solitude, endeavor to digest and heal the passion.

Of the Pythagoreans it is also reported that none of them punished a servant or admonished a free man during angers but waited until he had recovered his wonted serenity. They used an especial word, *paidartan*, to signify such (self-controlled) rebukes, effecting this calming by silence and quiet. So Spintharus relates of Archytas the Tarentine that on returning after a certain time from the war against the Hessenians waged by the Tarentines, to inspect some land belonging to him, and finding that the bailiff and the other servants had not properly cultivated it, greatly neglecting it, he became enraged, and was so furious that he told his servants that it was well for them that he was angry, for otherwise, they would not have escaped the punishment due to so great an offense. A similar anecdote is related of Clinias, according to Spintharus; for he also was wont to defer all admonitions and punishments until his mind was restored to tranquillity. Of the Pythagoreans it is further related that they restrained themselves from all lamentation, weeping and the like; and that neither gain, desire, anger or ambition, or anything of the like, ever became the cause of dissension among them; all Pythagoreans being disposed towards each other as parents towards their offspring.

Another beautiful trait of theirs was that they gave credit to Pythagoras for everything, naming it after him, not claiming the glory of their own inventions, except very rarely. Few are there who acknowledged their own works.

Admirable too is the careful secrecy with which, they preserved the mystery of their writings. For during so many centuries, prior to the times of Philolaus, none of the Pythagorean commentaries appeared publicly. Philolaus first published those three celebrated books which, at the request of Plato, Dion of Syracuse is said to have bought for a hundred minae. For Philolaus had been overtaken by sudden severe poverty, and he capitalized the writings of which he was partaker through his alliance with the Pythagoreans.

As to the value of opinion, such were their views: A stupid man should defer to the opinion of any one, especially to that of the crowds. Only a very few are qualified to apprehend and opine rightly; for evidently this is limited to the intelligent, who are very few. To the crowds, such a qualification of course does not extend. But to despise the opinion of every one is also stupid; for such a person will remain unlearned and incorrigible. The unscientific should study that of which he is ignorant, or lacks scientific knowledge. A learner should also defer to the opinion of the scientific, and is able to teach. Generally, youths who wish to be saved should attend to the opinions of their elders, or of those who have lived well.

During the course of human life there are certain ages by them called *endedasmenae* which cannot be connected by the power of any chance person. Unless a man from his very birth is trained in a beautiful end upright manner, these ages antagonize each other. A well educated child, formed to temperance and fortitude, should devote a great part of his education to the stage of adolescence. Similarly, when the adolescent is trained to temperance and fortitude, he should focus his education on the next age of manhood. Nothing could be more absurd than the way in which the general public treats this subject . They fancy that boys should be orderly and temperate, abstaining from everything troublesome or indecorous, but as soon as they have arrived at the age of adolescence, they may do anything they please. In this age, therefore, there is a combination of both kinds of errors, puerile and virile. To speak plainly, they avoid anything that demands diligence and good order, while following anything that has the appearance of sport, intemperance and petulance, being familiar only with boyish affairs. Their desires should be developed from the boyish stage into the next one. In the meanwhile ambition and the rest of the more serious and turbulent inclinations and desires of the virile age prematurely invade adolescence; wherefore this adolescence demands the greatest care. In general, no man ought to be allowed to do whatever he pleases; but there is always need, of a certain inspection, or legal and cultured government, to which each of the citizens is responsible. For animals, when left to themselves, and neglected, rapidly degenerate into vice and depravity.

The Pythagoreans (who did not approve of men being intemperate), would often compel answers from, and puzzle (such intemperate people) by asking them why boys are generally trained to take food in an orderly and moderate manner, being compelled to learn that order and decency are beautiful, and their contraries, disorder and intemperance base, while drunkards and gormandizers are held in great disgrace. For if none of (these temperate) habits are to be continued on into the virile age, to accustom us, as boys, to such (temperate) habits, was useless. The same argument holds good in respect to other good habits to which children are trained, a reversal of training is not seen in the case of the education of other lower animals. From the very first a whelp and a colt are trained to, and learn those tricks which they are to exercise when they arrived at maturity. (The more liberal standard for man in the matter of morals is therefore not sustained by the common sense that trains children to temperance). The Pythagoreans are generally reported to have exhorted not only their intimates; but also whomsoever they happened to meet, to avoid pleasure as a danger demanding the utmost caution. More than anything else does this passion deceive us, and mislead us into error. They contended that it was wiser never to do anything whose end was pleasure, whose results are usually shameful and harmful. They asserted we should adopt as an end the beautiful, and fair, and do our duty. Only secondarily should we consider the useful and advantageous. In these matters there is no need to consider considerations of chance.

Of desire, the Pythagoreans said: That desire itself is a certain tendency, impulse and appetite of the soul, wishing to be filled with something or to enjoy the presence of something or to be disposed according to some sense-enjoyment. There are also contrary desires, of evacuation and repulsion, and to terminate some sensation. This passion is manifold, and is al most the most Protean of human experiences.

However, many human desires are artificially acquired, and self-prepared. That is why this passion demands the utmost care and watchfulness, and physical exercise that is more than casual. That when the body is empty it should desire food is no more than natural; and then it is just as natural that when it is full it should desire appropriate evacuation. But to desire superfluous food, or luxurious garment or coverlets, or residences, is artificial. The Pythagoreans applied this argument also to furniture, dishes, servants and cattle raised for butchering. Besides, human passions are never permanent, but are ever changing, even to infinity. That is why education of the youth should begin at the earliest moment possible, that the aspirations may be directed towards ends that are proper, avoiding those that are vain and unnecessary, so as to be undisturbed by, and remain pure from such undesirable passions; and may despise such as are objects of contempt because subjected to changeable desires. Yet it must be observed that senseless, harmful superfluous and insolent desires subsist in the souls of such individuals who are the most powerful; for there is nothing so absurd that soul of such boys, men and women would not lead them to perform.

Indeed, the variety of food eaten is beyond description. The kinds of fruits and roots which the human race eats is nothing less than infinite. The kinds of flesh eaten are innumerable; there is no terrestrial, aerial, or aquatic animal which has not been partaken of. Besides, in the preparation of these, the contrivances used are innumerable and they are seasoned with manifold mixtures of juices. Hence, according to the motions of the human soul, it is no more than natural that the human race should be so various as to be actually insane; for each kind of food that is introduced into the human body becomes the cause of a certain peculiar disposition.

(Quantity) is as important as quality, for sometimes a slight change in quantity produces a great change in quality, as with wine. First making men more cheerful, later it undermines morals and sanity. This difference is generally ignored in things in which the result is not so pronounced, although everything eaten is the cause of a certain peculiar disposition. Hence it requires great wisdom to know and perceive which quality and quantity of food to eat. This science, first unfolded by Apollo and Phaon, was later developed by Aesculapius and his followers.

About propagation, the Pythagoreans taught as follows. First, they prevented untimely birth. Not even among plants or animals is prematurity good. To produce good fruit there is need of maturation for a certain time to give strong and perfect bodies to fruits and seeds. Boys and girls should therefore be trained to work and exercise, with endurance, and that they should eat foods adapted to a life of labor and temperance, with endurance. There are many things in human life which it is better to learn at a late period in life, and this sex-life is one of them. It is therefore advisable that a boy should be educated so as not to begin sex-connection before the twentieth year, and even then rarely. This will take place if he holds high ideals of a good habit for the body. Body-hygiene and intemperance are not likely to subsist in the same individual. The Pythagoreans, praised the earlier Greek laws forbidding intercourse with a woman who is a mother, daughter or sister in a temple or other public place. It is advisable that there be many impediments to the practice of this energy. The Pythagoreans forbad entirely intercourse that was unnatural, or resulting from wanton insolence, allowing only the natural, the temperate, which occur in the course of chaste and recognized procreation of children.

Parents should make circumstantial provision for their offspring. The first precaution is a healthful and temperate life, not unseasonably filling himself with food, nor using foods which create bad body-habits, above all avoiding intoxication. The Pythagoreans thought that an evil, discordant, trouble-making character produced depraved sperma. They insisted that none but an indolent or inconsiderate person would attempt to produce an animal, and introduce it to existence, without most diligently providing for it a pleasing and even elegant ingress into his world. Lovers of dogs pay the utmost possible attention to the breeding of their puppies, knowing that goodness of the offspring depends on goodness of parents, at the right season, and in proper surroundings. Lovers of birds pay no less attention to the matter; procreators of generous animals therefore should by all possible means manage that their efforts be fruitful. It is therefore absurd for men to pay no attention to their own offspring, begetting casually and carelessly, and after birth, feed, and educate them negligently. This is the most powerful and manifest cause of the vice and depravity of the greater part of mankind, for the generality undertake procreation on impulse, like beasts.

Such were the Pythagoreans teachings about temperance, which they defended by word and practised in deed. They had originally received them from Pythagoras himself, as if they had been oracles delivered by the Pythian Apollo himself.

CHAPTER XXXII
FORTITUDE

Fortitude, the subject of this chapter, has already been illustrated, by the heroism of Timycha, and those Pythagoreans who preferred death, to transgression of Pythagoras's prohibition to touch beans, and other instances. Pythagoras himself showed it in the generous deeds he performed when traveling everywhere alone, undergoing heart-breaking labors and serious dangers, and in choosing to leave his country and living among strangers. Likewise when he dissolved tyrannies, ordered confused commonwealths, and emancipated cities. He ended illegalities, and impeded the activities of insolent and tyrannical men. As a leader, he showed himself benignant to the just and mild, but expelled rough and licentious men from his society, refusing even to answer them, resisting them with all his might, although he assisted the former.

Of these courageous deeds, as well as of many upright actions, many instances could be adduced; but the greatest of these is the prevailing freedom of speech he employed towards the tyrant Phalaris, the most cruel of them, who detained him in captivity. A Hyperborean sage named Abaris visited him, to convers with him on many topics, especially sacred ones, respecting statues and worship, the divine providence, natures terrestrial and celestial, and the like. Pythagoras, under divine inspiration, answered him boldly, sincerely and persuasively, so that he converted all listeners. This roused Phalaris's anger against Abaris, for praising Pythagoras and increased the tyrant's resentment against Pythagoras. Phalaris swore proudly as was his wont, and uttered blasphemies against the Gods themselves. Abaris however was grateful to him, and learned from him that all things are suspended from, and governed by the heavens; which he proved from many considerations, but especially from the potency of sacred rites. For teaching him these things, so far was Abaris from thinking Pythagoras an enchanter, that his reverence for him increased till he considered him a God. Phalaris tried to counteract this by discrediting divination, and publicly denying there was any efficacy of the sacraments performed in sacred rites. Abaris, however, guided the controversy towards such things as are granted by all men, seeking to persuade him of the existence of a divine providence, from circumstances that lie above human influence, such as immense wars, incurable diseases, the decay of fruits, incursions of pestilence, or the like, which are hard to endure, and are deplorable, arising from the beneficent (purifying) energy of the powers celestial and divine. Shamelessly and boldly Phalaris opposed all this. Then Pythagoras, suspecting that Phalaris intended to put him to death, but knowing he was not destined to die through Phalaris, retorted with great freedom of speech. Looking at Abaris, he said that from the heavens to aerial and terrestrial beings there was a certain descending communication. Then from instances generally known he showed that all things follow the heavens. Then he demonstrated the existence of an indisputable power of freedom of will, in the soul; proceeding further amply to discuss the perfect energy of reason and intellect. With his (usual) freedom of will he even (dared to) discuss tyranny, and all the prerogatives of fortune, concerning injustice and human avarice, solidly teaching that all these are of no value. Further, he gave Phalaris a divine admonition concerning the most excellent life, earnestly comparing it with the most depraved. He likewise clearly unfolded the manner of subsistence of the soul, its powers and passions; and, what was the most beautiful of all, demonstrated to him that the Gods are not the authors of evils, and that diseases and bodily calamities are the results of intemperance, at the same time finding fault with the poets and mythologists for the unadvisedness of many of their fables. Then he directly confuted Phalaris, and admonished him, experimentally demonstrating to him the power and magnitude of heaven, and by many arguments demonstrated to him that reason dictates that punishments should be legal. He demonstrated to him the difference between men and other animals, scientifically demonstrating the difference between internal and external speech. Then he expounded the nature of intellect, and the knowledge that is derived therefrom; with its ethical corollaries. Then he discoursed about the most beneficial of useful things adding the mildest possible implied admonitions, adding prohibitions of what ought not to be done. Most important of all, he unfolded to him the distinction between the productions of fate and intellect, and the difference between the results of destiny and fate. Then he reasoned about the divinities, and the immortality of the soul. All this, really, belongs to some other chapter, the present one's topic being the development of fortitude. For if, when situated in the midst of the most dreadful circumstances, Pythagoras philosophised with firmness of decision, if on all sides he resisted fortune, and repelled it, enduring its attacks strenuously, if he employed the greatest boldness of speech towards him who threatened his life, it must be evident that he entirely despised those things generally considered dreadful, rating them as unworthy of attention. If also he despised execution, when this appeared imminent, and was not moved by its imminence, it is evident that he was perfectly free from the fear of death, (and all possible torments).

But he did something still more generous, effecting the dissolution of the tyranny, restraining the tyrant when he was about to bring the most deplorable calamities on mankind, and liberating Sicily from the most cruel and imperious power. That it was Pythagoras who accomplished this, is evident from the oracles of Apollo, which had predicted that the dominion of Philaris would come to an end when his subjects would become better men, and cooperate; which also happened through the presence of Pythagoras, and his imparting to them instruction and good principles. The best proof of this may be found in the time when it happened. For on the very day that Phalaris condemned Pythagoras and Abaris to death, he himself by stratagem slain. Another argument for the truth of this are the adventures of Epimenides. He was a disciple of Pythagoras; and when certain persons planned to destroy him, he invoked the Furies and the avenging divinities, and thereby caused those who had attempted his life to destroy each other. In the same way Pythagoras, who assisted mankind, imitating both the manner and fortitude of Hercules for the benefit of men punished and occasioned the death of him who had behaved insolently and in a disorderly manner towards others; and this through the very oracles of Apollo, in the class of which divinity both he and Epimenides had naturally since birth belonged. This admirable and strenuous deed was the effect of his fortitude.

We shall present another example of preservation of lawful opinion; for following it out he did what to him seemed just and dictated by right reason without permitting himself to be diverted from his intention by pleasure, labor passion or danger. His disciples also preferred death to transgression of any precept of his. They preserved their manners unchanged under the most varying fortunes. Being involved in a myriad of calamities could not cause them to deviate from his rules. They never ceased exhorting each other to support the laws, to oppose lawlessness from birth to train themselves to a life of temperance and fortitude, so as to restrain and oppose luxury. They also used certain original melodies as remedies against the passions of the soul; against lamentation and despondency, which Pythagoras had invented, as affording the greatest relief in these maladies. Other melodies they employed against anger and rage, through which they could increase or diminish those passions, till they reduced them to moderation, and compatability with fortitude. The thought which afforded them the greatest support in generous endurance was the conviction that no human casualty should be unexpected by men of intellect, but that they must resign themselves to all vicissitudes beyond human control. Moreover, whenever overwhelmed by grief or anger, they immediately forsook the company of their associates, and in solitude endeavored to digest and heal the oppressing passion. They took it for granted that studies and disciplines implied labor, and that they must expect severe tests of different kinds and be restrained and punished even by fire and sword, so as to exorcise innate intemperance and greediness; for which purpose no labor or endurance should be spared. Further, to accomplish they un-selfishly abstained from animal food, and also some other kinds. This also was the cause of their slowing of speech and complete silence, as means to the entire subjugation of the tongue, which demanded year-long exercise of fortitude. In addition, their strenuous and. assiduous investigation and resolution of the most difficult theorems, their abstinence from wine, food and sleep, and their contempt of wealth and glory. Thus by many different means they trained themselves to fortitude.

But this is not all. They restrained themselves from lamentations and tears. They abstained from entreaty, supplication, and adulation as effeminate and abject (or humble). To the same practice of fortitude must be referred their peculiarity of absolute reserve among their arcana of the principal principles of their discipline, preserving them from being divulged to strangers, committing them unwritten to memory, and transmitting them orally to their successors as if they were the mysteries of the Gods. That is why nothing worth mentioning of their philosophy was ever made public and though it had been taught and learned for a long while, it was not known beyond their walls. Those outside who might call the profane, sometimes happened to be present; and under such circumstances the Pythagoreans would communicate only obscurely, though symbols, a vestige of which is retained by the celebrated precepts still in circulation, such as fire should not be poked with a sword, and other like ones, which taken literally, resemble old-wives' tales; but which, when properly unfolded, are to the recipients admirable and venerable.

That precept which, of all others, was of the greatest efficacy in the achievement of fortitude is that one which helps defend and liberate from the life-long bonds that retain the intellect in captivity, and without which no one can perceive or learn anything rational or genuine, whatever be the sense in activity. They said:

"Tis mind that sees all things, and hears them all; All else is deaf and blind."

The next most efficacious precept is that one which exhorts excessively to be studious of purifying the intellect, and by various methods adapting it through mathematical disciplines to receive something divinely beneficial, so as neither to fear a separation from the body, nor, when directed towards incorporeal natures, through their most refulgent splendor to be compelled to turn away the eyes, nor to be converted to those passions which fasten and even nail the soul to the body, and makes her rebellious to all those passions which are the progeny of procreation, degrading her to a lower level. The training of ascent through all these is the study of the most perfect fortitude. Such are important instances of the fortitude of Pythagoras and his followers.

CHAPTER XXXIII
UNIVERSAL FRIENDSHIP

Friendship of all things towards all was most clearly enforced by Pythagoras, God's friendship towards men he explained through piety and scientific cultivation; but that of teachings towards each other, and generally the soul to the body, of the rational towards the irrational part, through philosophy and its teachings. That of men towards each other; and of citizens, he justified through proper legislation; that of strangers, through the common possession of a body; that between man and wife, children brothers or kindred through the imperverted ties of nature. In short, he taught the friendship of all for all, and still further, of certain animals, through justice, and common physical experiences. But the pacification and conciliation of the body, which is mortal by itself, and of its latent immortal powers, he enforced through health, and a temperate diet suitable thereto, in imitation of the ever-healthy condition of the mundane elements. In all these, Pythagoras is recognized as the inventor and summarizer of them in a single name, that of friendship. So admirable was his friendship to his associates, that even now when people are extremely benevolent mutually people call them Pythagoreans, we should therefore narrate Pythagoras's discipline thereto related, and the precepts he taught, his disciples.

Pythagoreans therefore on the effacing of all rivalry and contention from true friendship, if not from all friendship; at least from parental friendship, and generally from all gratitude towards seniors and benefactors. To strive or contend with such, out of anger or some other passion, is not the way to preserve existing friendship. Scars and ulcers in friendship should be the least possible; and this will be the case if those that are friends know how to subdue their anger. If indeed both of them know this, or rather, the younger of the two, and who ranks in some of the above mentioned orders, (their friendship will be the more easily preserved). They also taught that corrections and admonitions, which they called "*paedartases*" should take place from the elder to the younger, and with much sumarity and caution; and likewise, that much careful and considerate attention should be manifested in admonitions. For thus they will be persuasive and helpful. They also said that confidence should never be separated from friendship whether in earnest, or in jest. Existing friendship cannot survive, when once falsehood insinuates itself into the habits of professed friends. According to them, friendship should not be abandoned en account of misfortune, or any other human vicissitude; the only permissible rejection of friend or friendship is the result of great and incorrigible vice. Hatred should not be entertained voluntarily against those who not perfectly bad, but when once formed, it should be strenuously and firmly maintained, unless its object should change his morals, so as to become a better man. Hostility should not consist in words, but in deeds. War is commendable and legitimate, when conducted in a manly manner.

No one should ever permit himself to become the cause of contention, and we should as far as possible avoid its source. In a friendship which is intended to be pure, the greater part of the things pertaining to it should be definite and legitimate. These should be properly distinguished and not be casual; and moreover our conversation should never grow casual or negligent, but remain orderly, modest and benevolent. So also with the remaining passions and dispositions.

We should not decline foreign friendships carelessly, but accept and guard them with the greatest care.

That the Pythagoreans preserved friendship towards each other for many ages may be inferred from what Aristoxenus in his treatise on the Pythagoric Life says he heard from Dionysius the tyrant of Sicily, when having been deposed he taught language at Corinth. Here in the words of Aristoxenus: "So far as they could these men avoided lamentations and tears, and the like; also adulation, entreaty, supplication and other emotions. Dionysius therefore, having fallen from his tyranny and come to Corinth, told us the detailed story about the Pythagoreans, Phintias and Damon, who were sponsors for each other's death. This is how it was: Certain intimates of his had often mentioned the Pythagoreans, defaming and reviling them, calling them arrogant and asserting that their gravity, their pretended fidelity, and stoicism, would disappear on falling in some calamity. Others contradicted this; and as contention arose on the subject, it was decided to settle the matter by an experiment. One man accused Phintias, before Dionysius, of having conspired with others against his life. Others corroborated the charges, which looked probable though Phintias was astonished at the accusation .When Dionysius had unequivocally said that he had verified the charges, and that Phintias must die, the latter replied that if Dionysius thought that this was necessary, he requested the delay of the remainder of the day, to settle the affairs of himself and Damon, as these two men lived together; and had all things in common; but as

Phintias was the elder, he mostly undertook the management of the household affairs. He therefore requested that Dionysius allow him to depart for this purpose, and that he would appoint Damon a his surety. Dionysius claimed surprise at such a request, and asked him if any man existed who would stand surety for the death of another. Phintias asserted that there was, and Damon was sent for; and on hearing what had happened, agreed to become the sponsor, and that he would remain there till Phintias's return. Dionysius declared astonishment at these circumstances, and they who had proposed the experiment derided Damon as the one who would be caught, sneering at him as the "vicarious stag;" when however sunset approached, Phintias came to die; at which all present were astonished and subdued. Dionysius, having embraced and kissed the men, requested that they would receive him as a third into their friendship. They however would by no means consent to anything of the kind, though he entreated them to comply with his request." These words are related by Aristoxenus who received them from Dionysius himself.

It is also said, that the Pythagoreans endeavored to perform the offices of friendship to those of their sect, though they were unknown, and had never seen each other; on receiving a sure indication of participation in the same doctrines; so that, judging from such friendly offices, it may be believed, as is generally reported, that worthy men, even though they should dwell in the remotest parts of the earth, are mutually friends, and this before they became known to, and salute each other.

The story runs that a certain Pythagorean, traveling through a long and solitary road on foot, came to an inn; and there from over-exertion, or other causes fell into a long and severe disease, as at length to want the necessaries of life. The inn-keeper however, whether from amity or benevolence, supplied him with everything requisite, sparing neither personal service, or expense. Feeling the end near, the Pythagorean wrote a certain symbol on a tablet, and desired the innkeeper, in event of his death, to hang the tablet near the road, and observe whether any traveler read the symbol. For that person, said he, will repay you what you have spent on me and will also thank you for your kindness. After the Pythagorean's death the innkeeper buried him and attended to the obsequies, without any expectation of being repaid, nor of receiving remuneration from anybody who might read the tablet. However, struck with the Pythagorean's request, he was induced to expose the writing in the public road. A long time thereafter a Pythagorean passed that way, and on understanding the symbol, found out who had placed the tablet there, and having also investigated every particular, paid the inn-keeper a much greater sum than he had disbursed.

It is also related that Clinias the Tarent when he Learned that the Cyranian Prorus, who was a zealous Pythagorean, was in danger of losing all his property, sailed to Cyrene, and having collected a sum of money, restored the affairs of Prorus to a better condition, though thereby diminished his own estate and risked the peril of the sea-voyage.

Similarly, Thestor Posidomiates, having from mere report heard that the Pythagorean Thymaridas Parius had fallen into poverty, from great wealth into abject poverty, is said to have sailed to Paros, and after having collected a large sum of money, and reinstated Thymaridas in affluence. These are beautiful instances of friendship.

But much more admirable than the above are examples were the Pythagorean's teachings respecting the communion of divine goods, the agreement of intellect, and their doctrines about the divine soul,........ They were ever exhorting each other not to tear apart the divine soul within them. The significance of their friendship both in words and deeds was effort to achieve a certain divine union, (or union with the divinity), or communion with the divine soul. Better than this, either what is uttered in words, or performed by, it is not possible to find. For I am of opinion that in this all the goods of friendship are united. In this, as a climax we have collected all the blessings of Pythagorean friendship; there is nothing left to say.

CHAPTER XXXIV
NON-MERCENARY SECRECY

Having thus, according to plan discussed Pythagoras and Pythagoreanism, we may be interested in scattered points which do not fall under any of the former topics.

(First, as to language). It is said that each Greek novice was ordered to use his native language, as they did not approve of the use of a foreign language. Foreigners joined the Pythagoreans: Messenians, Lucani, Picentini, and Romans. Metrodorus, the son of Thyrsus, who was the father of Epicharmus, who specialised in medicine, in explaining his father's writings to his brother, says that Epicharmus, and prior to him Pythagoras, conceived that the best dialect, and the most musical, was the Doric. The Ionic and Aeolic remind of chromatic progression, which however is still more evident in the Attic. The Doric, consisting of pronounced letters, is enharmonic.

The myths also bear witness to the antiquity of this dialect. Nereus was said to have married Doris, the daughter of Ocean; by whom he had fifty daughters, one of whom was the mother of Achilles. Metrodorus also says that some insist that Helen was the offspring of Deucalion, who was the son of Prometheus and Pyrrha the daughter of Epimetheus; and from him descended Dorus and Aeolus. Further he observes that from the Babylonian sacred rites he had learned that Helen was the offspring of Jupiter, and that the sons of Hellen were Dorus, Xuthus, and Aeolus; with which Herodotus also agrees. Accuracy in particulars so ancient is difficult for moderns, to enable them to decide which of the accounts is most trustworthy. But either of them claim that the Doric dialect is the most ancient, that the Aeolic, whose name derives it from Aeolus, is the next age, and that the third is the Ionic, derived from Ion, the son of Xuthus. Fourth is the Attic, formed from Creusa, the daughter of Erechtheus, who is three generations younger than the others; as it existed about the time of the Thracians and the rape of Orithyia, as is evident from the testimony of most histories. The Doric dialect was also used by the most ancient of the poets, Orpheus..... (repetition).

The Pythagoreans objected to those who offered disciplines for sale, who open their souls like the gates of an inn to every man that approaches them; and who, if they do not thus [have] buyers, diffuse themselves through cities, [so] in short, hire gymnasia, and require a reward from young men for those things that are without price.

Pythagoras indeed hid the meaning of much that was said by him, in order that those who were genuinely instructed might clearly partakers of it; but that others, as Homer says of Tantalus, might be pained in the midst of what they heard, in consequence of receiving no delight therefrom.

The Pythagoreans thought that those who teach for the sake of reward, that they show themselves worse than sculptors, or artists who perform [the] work sitting. For these, when someone orders [wood] to make a statue of Hermes, search for wood suited to receive the proper form; while those pretend that they can readily produce the works of virtue from every nature. The Pythagoreans likewise said that it is more necessary to pay attention to philosophy than to parents or agriculture; for no doubt it is owing to the latter that we live, but philosophers and preceptors are the causes of our living well, and becoming wise, on discovering the right mode of discipline and instruction.

Nor did they think fit either to speak or write in such a way such that their conceptions might be obvious to the first comer; for the very first thing Pythagoras is said to have taught is that, being purified from all intemperance, his disciples should preserve the doctrines they have heard in silence. It is accordingly reported that he who first divulged the theory of commensurable and incommensurable quantities to those unworthy to receive it was by the Pythagoreans so hated that they not only expelled him from their common association, and from living with him, but also for him constructed a tomb, as for one who had migrated from the human into another life. It is also reported that the Divine Power was so indignant with those who divulged the teachings of Pythagoras, that he perished at sea, as an impious person who divulged the method of inscribing in a sphere the dodecahedron, one of the five so-called solid figures, the composition of the icostagonus. But according to others, this is what happened to him who revealed the doctrine of rational and incommensurable quantities.

All Pythagoric discipline was symbolic, resembling riddles and puzzles, and consisting of maxims, in the style of the ancients. Likewise the truly divine Pythian oracles seem to be somewhat difficult of understanding and explanation; to those who carelessly receive the answers given. These are the indications about Pythagoras and the Pythagoreans collected from tradition.

CHAPTER XXXV
ATTACK ON PYTHAGOREANISM

There were however certain persons who were hostile to the Pythagoreans, and who rose against them. That stratagems were employed to destroy them, during Pythagoras's absence, is universally acknowledged; but the historians differ in their account of the journey which he then undertook. Some say that he went to Pherecydes the Syrian, and others, to Metapontum. Many causes of the stratagems are assigned. One of then, which is said to have originated from the men called Cylonians, is as follows: Cylon of Crotona was one of the most prominent citizens, in birth, renown and wealth, but in manners he was severe, turbulent, violent, tyrannical. His greatest desire was to become partner of the Pythagoric life, and he made application to Pythagoras who was no now advanced in age, but was rejected for the above causes. Consequently, he and his friends became violent enemies of the brotherhood. CeylonÕs ambition was so vehement and immoderate that with his associates, he persecuted the very last of the Pythagoreans. That is why Pythagoras moved to Metapontum, where he closed his existence.

Those who were called Cylonians continued to plot against the Pythagoreans, and to exhibit the most virulent malevolence. Nevertheless for a time this enmity was subdued by the Pythagoreans' probity, and also by the vote of the citizens, who entrusted the whole of the city affairs to their management.

At length, however, the Cylonians became so hostile to "*the men*," as they were called, that they set fire to Milo's residence, where were assembled all the Pythagoreans, holding a council of war. All were burnt, except two, Archippus and Lysis, who escaped through their bodily vigor. As no public notice was taken of this calamity, the Pythagoreans ceased to pay any further attention to public affairs, which was due to two causes: the cities's negligence, and through the loss of those men most qualified to govern. Both of the saved Pythagoreans were Tarentines, and Archippus returned home. Lysis resenting the public neglect went into Greece, residing in the Achian Peloponnesus. Stimulated by an ardent desire, he migrated to Thebes, where he had as disciple Epaminondas, who spoke of his teacher as his father. There Lysis died.

Except Archytas of Tarentum, the rest of the Pythagoreans departed from Italy, and dwelt together in Rhegium. The most celebrated were

Phantos, Echecrates, Polymnastus, and Diocrates, who were Phlyasians; and Xenophilus Chalcidensis of Thrace. But in course of time, as the administration of public affairs went from bad to worse, these Pythagoreans nevertheless preserved their pristine manners and disciplines; yet soon the sect began to fail, till they nobly perished. This is the account by Aristoxenus.

Nichomachus agrees with Aristoxenus, except that he dates the plot against the Pythagoreans during Pythagoras's journey to Delos, to nurse his preceptor Pherecydes the Syrian, who was then afflicted with the *morbus pedicularis*, and after his death performed the funeral rites. Then those who had been rejected by the Pythagoreans, and to whom monuments had been raised, as if they were dead, attacked them, and committed them all to the flames. Afterwards they were overwhelmed by the Italians with stones, and thrown out of the house unburied. Then science died in the breasts of its possessors, having by them been preserved as something mystic and incommunicable. Only such things as were difficult to be understood, and which were not expounded, were preserved in the memory of those who were outside of the sect, except a few things, which certain Pythagoreans, who at that time happened to be in foreign, lands, preserved as sparks of science very obscure, and of difficult investigation. These men being solitary, and dejected at this calamity, were scattered in different places retaining no longer public influence. They lived alone in solitary places, wherever they found any; each preferred association with himself to that with any other person.

Fearing however lest the name of philosophy should be entirely exterminated from among mankind, and that they should, on this account incur the indignation of the Gods, by suffering so great a gift of theirs to perish, they made an arrangement of certain commentaries and symbols, gathered the writings of the more ancient Pythagoreans, and of such things as they remembered. These relics each left at his death to his son, or daughter, or wife, with a strict injunction not to alienate from the family. This was carried out for some time and the relics were transmitted in succession to their posterity.

Since Apollonius dissents in a certain place regarding these particulars, and adds many things that we have not mentioned, we must record his account of the plot against the Pythagoreans. He says that from childhood Pythagoras had aroused envy. So long as he conversed with all that came to him, he was pleasing to all; but when he restricted his intercourse to his disciples the general peoples' good opinion of him was altered. They did indeed permit him to pay more attention to strangers than to themselves; but they were indignant at preferring some of their fellow-citizens before others; and they suspected that his disciples assembled with intentions hostile to themselves. In the next place, as the young men that were indignant with him were of high rank, and surpassed others in wealth, and, when they arrived at the proper age, not only, held the first honors in their own families, but also managed the affairs of the city in common, they, being more than three hundred in number, formed a large body, so that there remained but a small part of the city which was not devoted to their habits and pursuits.

Moreover so long as the Crotonians confined themselves to their own country, and Pythagoras dwelt among them, the original form of government continued; but the people had changed, and they were no longer satisfied with it; and were therefore seeking a pretext for a change. When they captured Sybaris, and the land was not divided by lot, according to the desire of the multitude, and Pythagoras gone, this veiled hatred against the Pythagoreans burst forth, and the populace forsook them. The leaders of this dissension were those that were nearest to the Pythagoreans, both by kindred and intercourse. These leaders, as well as the common folk were offended by the Pythagoreans' actions, which were unusual, and the people interpreted that peculiarity as a reflection on theirs. The Pythagoreans' kindred were indignant that they associated with none, their parents excepted; that they shared in common their possessions to the exclusion of their kindred, whom they treated as strangers. These personal motives turned the general opposition into active hostility. Hippasus, Diodorus and Theages united in insisting that the assembly and the magistracy should be opened to every citizen, and that the rulers should be responsible to elected representatives of the people. This was opposed by the Pythagoreans Alcimachus, Dimachus, Meton and Democides, and opposed changes in the inherited constitution. They were however defeated, and were formally accused in a popular as assembly by two orators, the aristocrat Cylon, and the plebeian Ninon. These two planned their speeches together, the first and longer one being made by Cylon, while Nino concluded by pretending that he had penetrated the Pythagorean mysteries, and that he had gathered and written out such particular as were calculated to criminate the Pythagoreans, and a scribe he gave to read a book which was entitled the Sacred Discourse.

Here is a specimen of what it contained: (This next paragraph is misplaced, but is put here as more suitable here than where it is the text, in front of the last one).

None of the Pythagoreans called Pythagoras by his name. While alive, they referred to him as the divine one; after his death, as "*that man*" just as Homer makes Eumaeus refer to Ulysses thus:

"Thou absent he may be, O guest, I fear
To name him; so great is my love and care."

Such were some of his precepts: They were to get up before sunrise, and never to wear a ring on which the image of God was engraved, lest that image be defiled by being worn at funerals, or other impure place. They were to adore the rising sun. Pythagoras ordered them never to do anything without previous deliberation and discussion; in the morning forming a plan of what was to be done later, and at night to review the day's actions, which served the double purpose of strengthening the memory, and considering their conduct. If any of their associates appointed them to meet them at some particular place and time they should stay there till he came, regardless of the length of time, for Pythagoreans should not speak carelessly, but remember what was said and regard order and method. At death they were not to blaspheme, but to die uttering propitious words, such as are used by those who sail out of the port into the Adriatic Sea. Friends are to be venerated in the same manner as Gods; but others are to be treated as brutes. This very sentiment is ascribed to Pythagoreans themselves, but in verse form such as:

"Like blessed Gods, his friends he e'er revered
But reckoned others as of no account."

Pythagoras considered that Homer deserved to be praised for calling a king the shepherd of the people which implied approval of aristocracy, in which the rulers are few, while the implication is that the rest of men are like cattle. Enmity was required to beans, because they were used in voting; inasmuch as the Pythagoreans selected office holders by appointment. To rule should be an object of desire, for it is better to be a bull for one day only, than for all one's life to be an ox. While other states' constitutions might be laudable, yet it would be advisable to use only that which is known to oneself.

In short, Ninon showed that their philosophy was a conspiracy against democracy: and advised the people to listen to the defendants, that they would never have been admitted into the assembly if the Pythagoreans' council had to depend for admission on the Session of a thousand men, that they should not allow speech to those who, had used their utmost to prevent speech by others.

The people must remember that when they raised their right hands to vote, or even count their votes, this their right hand was constructively rejected by the Pythagoreans, who were Aristocrats. It was also disgraceful that the Crotonian masses who had conquered thirty myriads of men at the river Tracis should be outweighed by a thousandth part of the same number through sedition in the city itself.

Through these calumnies Ninon so exasperated his hearers that a few days after a multitude assembled intending to attack the Pythagoreans as they were sacrificing to the Muses in a house near the temple of Apollo. Foreseeing this, the Pythagoreans fled to an inn, while Democedes with the youths retired to Plataea. The partisans of the new constitution decreed an accusation against Democedes of inciting the to capture power, putting a price of thirty talents on his head, dead or alive. A battle ensued, and the victor, Theages was given the talents promised by the city. The city's evils spread to the whole region, and the exiles were arrested even in Tarentum, Metapontum and Caulonia. The envoys from these cities that came to Crotona to get the charges were, according to the Crotonian record, bribed, with the result that the exiles were condemned as guilty, and driven out further. The Crotonians then expelled from the city all who were dissatisfied with the existing regime; banishing along with them all their families, on the two-fold pretext that impiety was unbearable, and that the children should not be separated from their parents. They then repudiated the debts, and redistributed the lands.

Many years after, when Dinarchus and his associates had been slain in another battle, and when Litagus, the chief leader of the sedition were dead, pity and repentance induced the citizens to recall from exile what remained of the Pythagoreans. They therefore sent for from messengers from Achaia who were to come to an agreement with the exiles, and file their oaths (of loyalty to the existing Crotonian regime?) at Delphi. The Pythagoreans who returned from exile were about sixty in number, not to mention the aged among whom were some physicians and dieticians on original lines. When these Pythagoreans returned, they were welcomed by the crowds, who silenced dissenters by announcing that the regime was ended. Then the Thurians invaded the country, and the Pythagoreans were sent to procure assistance but they perished in battle, mutually defending each other. So thoroughly had the city become Pythagoreanized that beside the public praise, they performed a public sacrifice in the temple of the Muses which had originally been built at the instigation of Pythagoras.

That is all of the attack on the Pythagoreans.

CHAPTER XXXVI
THE PYTHAGOREAN SUCCESSION

Pythagoras's acknowledged successor was Aristaeus, the son the Crotonian Damophon, who was Pythagoras's contemporary, and lived seven ages before Plato. Being exceedingly skillful in Pythagoric dogmas, he succeeded to the school, educated Pythagoras's children, and married his wife Theano. Pythagoras was said to have taught his school 39 years, and to have lived a century. Aristaeus growing old, he relinquished the school to Pythagoras's son Mnesarchus. He was followed by Bulagoras, in whose time Crotona was plundered. After the war, Gartydas the Crotonian, who has been absent on a journey, returned, and took up the school; but he so grieved about his country's calamity the he died prematurely. Pythagoreans who became very old were accustomed to liberate themselves from the body, as a prisoner.

Later, being saved through certain strangers, Aresas Lucanus undertook the school; and to him came Diodorus Aspendius, who was received into the school because of the small number of genuine Pythagoreans. Clinias and Philelaus were at Heraclea; Theorides and Eurytus at Metapontum, and at Tarentum, Archytas, Epicharmus was also said to have been one of the foreign Hearers, but he was not one of the school. However, having arrived at Syracuse he refrained form public philosophizing, in consideration of the tyranny of Hiero. But he wrote the Pythagoren views in metre, and published the occult Pythagorean dogmas in comedies.

It is probable that the majority of the Pythagoreans were anonymous, and remain unknown. But the following names are known and celebrated:

Of the Crotonians, Hippostratus, Dymas, Aegon, Armon, Sillus, Cleosthenes, Agelas, Episylus, Phyciades, Echpntus, Timaeus, Buthius, Eratus, Itmaeus, Rhodippus, Bryas, Evandrus, Myllias, Antimedon, Ageas, Leophron, Agylus, Onatus, Hipposthenes, Cleophron, Alcmaecsi, Damocles, Milon, Menon.

At Metapontum resided Brontinus, Parmiseus, Crestadas, Leon, Damarmenus, Aeneas, Chilas, Melisias, Aristeas, Laphion, Evandrus, Agesarchus, Thrasus, Euryphemus, Aristomenes, Agesarchus, Alceas, Xenophantes, Thraseus, Arytus, Epiphron, Eriscus, Megistisas, Leocydes, Thrasymedes, Euphemus, Proclos, Antimenes, Lacritus, Demotages, Pyrrho, Rhexbius, Alopecus, Astylus, Dacidas, Aliochus, Lacrates and Glycinus,

Of the Agrigentines was Empedocles,

Of the Eleatae, was Parmanides.

Of the Tarentines were Philolaus, Euzytus, Arcytas, Theodorus, Aristippus, Lycon, Hestiyacus, Polemarchus, Asteas, Clinias, Cleon, Eurymedon, Arceas, Clinagoras, Archippus, Zopyrus, Euthynus, Dicearchus, Philonidas, Phrontidas, LYSIS, Lysibius, Dinocrates, Echecrates, Paction, Acusalidas, Iomus, Pisicrates, and Clearatus.

Of the Leontines were Phrynichus, Smichias, Aristoclidinas, Clinias, Abroteles, Pisyrrhydus, Bryas, Evandrus, Archemachus, Mimnomachus, Achmonidas, Dicas and Cariphantidas.

Of the Sybarites were Metopus, Hippasus, Proxenus, Evanor, Deanax, Menestor, Diodes, Empedus, Timasius, Polemaeus, Evaeus, and Tyrsenus.

Of the Carthaginians was Miltiades, Anthen, Odius and Leocritus.

Of the Parians, Aetius, Phaenecles, Dexitheus, Alchimachus, Dinarchus, Meton, TIMAEUS, Timesianax, Amaerus, and Thymarides.

Of the Locrians,. Gyptius, Xenon, Philodamus, Evetes, Adicus, Athenonidas, Sosistratus, Euthynus, Zaleucus, Timares.

Of the Posidonians, Athamas, Simus, Proxenus, Cranous, Myes, Bathylaus, Phaedon.

Of the Lucani, Ocellus, and his brother Occillus, Oresandrus, Cerambus, Dardaneus, and Malion.

Of the Aegeans, Hippomedon, Timosthenes, Euelthus, Thrasydamus, Crito, and Polyctor.

Of the Hyperboreans, ABARIS.

Of the Lacones, Autocharidas, Cleanor, Eurycrates.

Of the Rheginenses, Aristides, Demosthenes, Aristocrates, Phytius, Helicaon, Mnesibulus, Hipparchides, Athosion, Euthycles, Opsimus.

Of the Selinuntians, Calais.

Of the Syracusans, Leptines, Phintias, and Damon.

Of the Samians, Melissus, Lacon, Archippus, Glorippus, Helcris, Hippon.

Of the Caulonienses, Callibrotus, Dicon, Nastas, Drymon and Xentas.

Of the Phliasians, Diocles, Echecrates,Phanton and Polymnastus.

Of the Sicyonians, Poliades, Demon, Sostratius, and Sosthenese.

Of the Cyrenians, Prorus, Melanippus, Aristangelus and Theodorus.

Of the Cyriceni Pythodorus, Hipposthenes,Butherus and Xenophilus.

Of the Catanaei, Charondas; and Lysiades.

Of the Corinthians, Chrysippus.

Of the Tyrrhenians, Nausitheus.

Of the Athenians, Neocritus.

Of the Pontians, Lyramnus.

In all, two hundred and eighteen.

The most illustrious Pythagorean women are Timycha, the wife of Myllias the Crotonian;

Phyltis, the daughter of Theophrius the Crotonian.

Byndacis, the sister of Ocellus ml Ocillus, Lucanians.

Chilonis,the daughter of Chilon the Lacedenonian.

Cratesiclea, the Lacedemonian, the wife of the Lacedemonian Cleanor.

Theane, the wife of Brontinus of Metapontum.

Mya, the wife of Milon the Crotonian.

Lasthenia the Arcadian, Abrotelia, the daughter of Abroteles the Tarentine.

Echecratia the Phliasian.

Tyrsenis the Sybarite;

Pisirrhonde, the Tarentine.

Nisleadusa, the Lacedemonian.

Byro, the Argive.

Babelyma the Argive,

and Cleaechma, the sister of Autocharidas the Lacedemonia.

In all, seventeen.

LIFE OF PYTHAGORAS
BY PORPHYRY [233-306 A.D.]

I. Many think that Pythagoras was the son of Mnesarchus, but they differ as to the latter's race; some thinking him a Samian, while Neanthes, in the fifth book of his *Fables* states he was a Syrian, from the city of Tyre. As a famine had arisen in Samos, Mnesarchus went thither to trade, and was naturalized there. There also was born his son Pythagoras, who early manifested studiousness, but was later taken to Tyre, and there entrusted to the Chaldeans, whose doctrines he imbibed. Thence he returned to Ionia, where he first studied under the Syrian Pherecydes, then also under Hermodamas the Creophylian who at that time was an old man residing in Samos.

2. Neanthes says that others hold that his father was a Tyrrhenian, of those who inhabit Lemnos, and that while on a trading trip to Samos was there naturalized. On sailing to Italy, Mnesarchus took the youth Pythagoras with him. Just at this time this country was greatly flourishing. Neanthes adds that Pythagoras had two older brothers, Eunostus and Tyrrhenus. But Apollonius, in his book about Pythagoras, affirms that his mother was Pythais, a descendant, of Ancaeus, the founder of Samos. Apollonius adds that he was said to be the off-spring of Apollo and Pythais, on the authority of Mnesarchus; and a Samian poet sings:

"Pythais, of all Samians the most fair;
Jove-loved Pythagoras to Phoebus bare!"

This poet says that Pythagoras studied not only under Pherecydes and Hermodamas, but also under Anaximander.

3. The Samian Duris, in the second book of his "Hours," writes that his son was named Arimnestus, that he was the teacher of Democritus, and that on returning from banishment, he suspended a brazen tablet in the temple of Hera, a tablet two feet square, bearing this inscription:

"Me, Arimnestus, who much learning traced,
Pythagoras's beloved son here placed."

This tablet was removed by Simus, a musician, who claimed the canon graven thereon, and published it as his own. Seven arts were engraved, but when Simus took away one, the others were destroyed.

4. It is said that by Theano, a Cretan, the daughter of Pythonax, he had a son, Thelauges and a daughter, Myia; to whom some add Arignota, whose Pythagorean writings are still extant. Timaeus relates

that Pythagoras's daughter, while a maiden, took precedence among the maidens in Crotona, and when a wife, among married men. The Crotonians made her house a temple of Demeter, and the neighboring street they called a museum.

5. Lycus, in the fourth book of his *Histories*, noting different opinions about his country, says, "Unless you happen to know the country and the city which Pythagoras was a citizen, will remain a mere matter of conjecture. Some say he was a Samian, others, a Phliasian, others a Metapontine.

6. As to his knowledge, it is said that he learned the mathematical sciences from the Egyptians, Chaldeans and Phoenicians; for of' old the Egyptians excelled, in geometry, the Phoenicians in numbers and proportions, and the Chaldeans of astronomical theorems, divine rites, and worship of the Gods; other secrets concerning the course of life he received and learned from the Magi.

7. These accomplishments are the more generally known, but the rest are less celebrated. Moreover Eudoxus, in the second book of his *Description of the Earth*, writes that Pythagoras used the greatest purity, and was shocked at all bloodshed and killing; that he not only abstained from animal food, but never in any way approached butchers or hunters. Antiphon, in his book on illustrious *Virtuous Men* praises his perseverance while he was in Egypt, saying, "Pythagoras, desiring to become acquainted with the institutions of Egyptian priests, and diligently endeavoring to participate therein, requested the Tyrant Polycrates to write to Amasis, the King of Egypt, his friend and former host, to procure him initiation. Coming to Amasis, he was given letters to the priests; of Heliopolis, who sent him on to those of Memphis, on the pretense that the were the more ancient. On the same pretense, he was sent on from Memphis to Diospolis.

8. From fear of the King the latter priests dared not make excuses; but thinking that he would desist from his purpose as result of great difficulties, enjoined on him very hard precepts, entirely different from the institutions of the Greeks. These he performed so readily that he won their admiration, and they permitted him to sacrifice to the Gods, and to acquaint himself with all their sciences, a favor theretofore never granted to a foreigner.

9. Returning to Ionia, he opened in his own country, a school, which is even now called Pythagoras's Semicircles, in which the Samians meet to deliberate about matters of common interest. Outside the city he made a cave adapted to the study of his philosophy, in which he

abode day and night, discoursing with a few of his associates. He was now forty years old, says Aristoxenus. Seeing that Polycrates's government was becoming so violent that soon a free man would become a victim of his tyranny, he journeyed towards Italy.

10. Diogenes, in his treatise about the *Incredible Things Beyond Thule*, has treated Pythagoras's affairs so carefully, that I think his account should not be omitted. He says that the Tyrrhenian Mnesarchus was of the race of the inhabitants of Lemnos, Imbros and Scyros and that he departed thence to visit many cities and various lands. During his journeys he found an infant lying under a large, tall poplar tree. On approaching, he observed it lay on its back, looking steadily without winking at the sun. In its mouth was a little slender reed, like a pipe; through which the child was being nourished by the dew-drops that distilled from the tree. This great wonder prevailed upon him to take the child, believing it to be of a divine origin. The child was fostered by a native of that country, named Androcles, who later on adopted him, and entrusted to him the management of affairs. On becoming wealthy, Mnesarchus educated the boy, naming him Astrasus, and rearing him with his own three sons, Eunestus, Tyrrhenus, and Pythagoras; which boy, as I have said, Androcles adopted.

11. He sent the boy to a lute-player, a wrestler and a painter. Later he sent him to Anaximander at Miletus, to learn geometry and astronomy. Then Pythagoras visited the Egyptians, the Arabians, the Chaldeans and the Hebrews, from whom he acquired expertery in the interpretation of dreams, and he was the first to use frankincense in the worship of divinities.

12. In Egypt he lived with the priests, and learned the language and wisdom of the Egyptians, and three kinds of letters, the epistolic, the hieroglyphic, and symbolic, whereof one imitates the common way of speaking, while the others express the sense by allegory and parable. In Arabia he conferred with the King. In Babylon he associated with the other Chaldeans, especially attaching himself to Zabratus, by whom he was purified from the pollutions of this past life, and taught the things which a virtuous man ought to be free. Likewise he heard lectures about Nature, and the principles of wholes. It was from his stay among these foreigners that Pythagoras acquired the greater part of his wisdom.

13. Astraeus was by Mnesarchus entrusted to Pythagoras, who received him, and after studying his physiognomy and the emotions of his body, instructed him. First he accurately investigated the science about the nature of man, discerning the disposition of everyone he met.

None was allowed to become his friend or associate without being examined in facial expression and disposition.

14. Pythagoras had another youthful disciple from Thrace. Zamolxis was he named because he was born wrapped in a bear's skin, in Thracian called Zalmus. Pythagoras loved him, and instructed him in sublime speculations concerning sacred rites, and the nature of the Gods. Some say this youth was named Thales, and that the barbarians worshipped him as Hercules.

15. Dionysiphanes says that he was a servant of Pythagoras, who fell into the hands of thieves and by them was branded. Then when Pythagoras was persecuted and banished, (he followed him) binding up his forehead on account of the scars. Others say that, the name Zamolxis signifies a stranger or foreigner. Pherecydes, in Delos fell sick; and Pythagoras attended him until he died, and performed his funeral rites. Pythagoras then, longing to be with Hermodamas the Creophylian, returned to Samos. After enjoying his society, Pythagoras trained the Samian athlete Eurymenes, who though he was of small stature, conquered at Olympia through his surpassing knowledge of PythagorasÔs wisdom. While according to ancient custom the other athletes fed on cheese and figs, Eurymenes, by the advice of Pythagoras, fed daily on flesh, which endued his body with great strength. Pythagoras imbued him with his wisdom, exhorting him to go into the struggle, not for the sake of victory, but the exercise; that he should gain by the training, avoiding the envy resulting from victory. For the victors, are not always pure, though decked with leafy crowns.

16. Later, when the Samians were oppressed with the tyranny of Polycrates, Pythagoras saw that life in such a state was unsuitable for a philosopher, and so planned to travel to Italy. At Delphi he inscribed an elegy on the tomb of Apollo, declaring that Apollo was the son of Silenus, but was slain by Pytho, and buried in the place called Triops, so named from the local mourning for Apollo by the three daughters of Triopas.

17. Going to Crete, Pythagoras besought initiation from the priests of Morgos, one of the Idaean Dactyli, by whom he was purified with the meteoritic thunder-stone. In the morning he lay stretched upon his face by the seaside; at night, he lay beside a river, crowned with a black lamb's woolen wreath. Descending into the Idaean cave, wrapped in black wool, he stayed there twenty-seven days, according to custom; he sacrificed to Zeus, and saw the throne which there is yearly made for

him. On Zeus's tomb, Pythagoras inscribed an epigram, "Pythagoras to Zeus," which begins: "Zeus deceased here lies, whom men call Jove."

18. When he reached Italy he stopped at Crotona. His presence was that of a free man, tall, graceful in speech and gesture, and in all things else. Dicaearchus relates that the arrival of this great traveler, endowed with all the advantages of nature, and prosperously guided by fortune, produced on the Crotonians so great an impression, that he won the esteem of the elder magistrates, by his many and excellent discourses. They ordered him to exhort the young men, and then to the boys who flocked out of the school to hear him; and lastly to the women, who came together on purpose.

19. Through this he achieved great reputation, he drew great audiences from the city, not only of men, but also of women, among whom was a specially illustrious person named Theano. He also drew audiences from among the neighboring barbarians, among whom were magnates and kings. What he told his audiences cannot be said with certainty, for he enjoined silence upon his hearers. But the following is a matter of general information. He taught that the soul was immortal and that after death it transmigrated into other animated bodies. After certain specified periods, the same events occur again; that nothing was entirely new; that all animated beings were kin, and should be considered as belonging to one great family. Pythagoras was the first one to introduce these teachings into Greece.

20. His speech was so persuasive that, according to Nicomachus, in one address made on first landing in Italy he made more than two thousand adherents. Out of desire to live with him, [.........] , to which both women and built a large auditorium, to which both women and boys were admitted. (Foreign visitors were so many that) they built whole cities, settling that whole region of Italy now known as Magna Grecia. His ordinances and laws were by them received as divine precepts, and without them would do nothing. Indeed they ranked him among the divinities. They held all property in common. They ranked him among the divinities, and whenever they communicated to each other some choice bit of his philosophy, from which physical truths could always be deduced, they would swear by the *Tetractys*, adjuring Pythagoras as a divine witness, in the words.

"I call to witness him who to our souls expressed The *Tetractys*, eternal Nature's fountain-spring."

21. During his travels in Italy and Sicily he founded various cities subjected one to another, both of long standing, and recently. By his

disciples, some of whom were found in every city, he infused into them an aspiration for liberty; thus restoring to freedom Crotona, Sybaris, Catana, Rhegium, Himera, Agrigentum, Tauromenium, and others, on whom he imposed laws through Charondas the Catanean, and Zaleucus the Locrian, which resulted in a long era of good government, emulated by all their neighbors. Simichus the tyrant of the Centorupini, on hearing Pythagoras's discourse, abdicated his rule and divided his property between his sister and the citizens.

22. According to Aristoxenus, some Lucanians, Messapians, Picentinians and Romans came to him. He rooted out all dissensions, not only among his disciples and their successors, for many ages, but among all the cities of Italy and Sicily, both internally and externally. He was continuously harping on the maxim, "We ought, to the best of our ability avoid, and even with fire and sword extirpate from the body, sickness; from the soul, ignorance; from the belly, luxury; from a city, sedition; from a family, discord; and from all things excess."

23. If we may credit what ancient and trustworthy writers have related of him, he exerted an influence even over irrational animals. The Daunian bear, who had committed extensive depredations in the neighborhood, he seized; and after having patted her for awhile, and given her barley and fruits, he made her swear never again to touch a living creature, and then released her. She immediately hid herself in the woods and the hills, and from that time on never attacked any irrational animal.

24. At Tarentum, in a pasture, seeing an ox [reaping] beans, he went to the herdsman, and advised him to tell the ox to abstain from beans. The countryman mocked him, proclaiming his ignorance of the ox-language. So Pythagoras himself went and whispered in the ox's ear. Not only did the bovine at once desist from his diet of beans, but would never touch any thenceforward, though he survived many years near Hera's temple at Tarentum, until very old; being called the sacred ox, and eating any food given him.

25. While at the Olympic games, he was discoursing with his friends about auguries, omens, and divine signs, and how men of true piety do receive messages from the Gods. Flying over his head was an eagle, who stopped, and came down to Pythagoras. After stroking her awhile, he released her. Meeting with some fishermen who were drawing in their nets heavily laden with fishes from the deep, he predicted the exact number of fish they had caught. The fishermen said that if his estimate was accurate they would do whatever he commanded. They

counted them accurately, and found the number correct. He then bade them return the fish alive into the sea; and, what is more wonderful, not one of them died, although they had been out of the water a considerable time. He paid them and left.

26. Many of his associates he reminded of the lives lived by their souls before it was bound to the body, and by irrefutable arguments demonstrated that he had bean Euphorbus, the son of Panthus. He specially praised the following verses about himself, and sang them to the lyre most elegantly:
"The shining circlets of his golden hair;
Which even the Graces might be proud to wear,
Instarred with gems and gold, bestrew the shore,
With dust dishonored, and deformed with gore.
As the young olive, in some sylvan scene,
Crowned by fresh fountains with celestial green,
Lifts the gay head, in snowy flowerets fair,
And plays and dances to the gentle air,
When lo, a whirlwind from high heaven invades,
The tender plant, and withers all its shades;
It lies uprooted from its genial head,
A lovely ruin now defaced and dead.
Thus young, thus beautiful, Euphorbus lay,
While the fierce Spartan tore his arms away."
(Pope, Homer's Iliad, Book 17).

27. The stories about the shield of this Phrygian Euphorbus being at Mycenae dedicated to Argive Hera, along with other Trojan spoils, shall here be omitted as being of too popular a nature. It is said that the river Caicasus, while he with many of his associates was passing over it, spoke to him very clearly, "Hail, Pythagoras!" Almost unanimous is the report that on one and the same day he was present at Metapontum in Italy, and at Tauromenium in Sicily, in each place conversing with his friends, though the places are separated by many miles, both at sea and land, demanding many days' journey.

28. It is well known that he showed his golden thigh to Abaris the Hyperborean, to confirm him in the opinion that he was the Hyperborean Apollo, whose priest Abaris was. A ship was coming into the harbor, and his friends expressed the wish to own the goods it contained. "Then," said Pythagoras, "you would own a corpse!" On the ship's arrival, this was found to be the true state of affairs. Of Pythagoras many other more wonderful and divine things are

persistently and unanimously related, so that we have no hesitation in saying never was more attributed to any man, nor was any more eminent.

29. Verified predictions of earthquakes are handed down, also that he immediately chased a pestilence, suppressed violent winds and hail, calmed storms both on rivers and on seas, for the comfort and safe passage of his friends. As their poems attest, the like was often performed by Empedocles, Epimenides and Abaris, who had learned the art of doing these things from him. Empedocles, indeed, was surnamed Alexanemos, as the chaser of winds; Epimenides, Cathartes, the lustrator. Abaris was called Aethrobates, the walker in air; for he was carried in the air on an arrow of the Hyperborean Apollo, over rivers, seas and inaccessible places. It is believed that this was the method employed by Pythagoras when on the same day he discoursed with his friends at Metapontum and Tauromenium.

30. He soothed the passions of the soul and body by rhythms, songs and incantations. These he adapted and applied to his friends. He himself could hear the harmony of the Universe, and understood the universal music of the spheres, and of the stars which move in concert with them, and which we cannot hear because of the limitations of our weak nature. This is testified to by these characteristic verses of Empedocles:
"Amongst these was one in things sublimest skilled,
His mind with all the wealth of learning filled,
Whatever sages did invent, he sought;
And whilst his thoughts were on this work intent,
All things existent, easily he viewed,
Through ten or twenty ages making search."

31. Indicating by *sublimest things*, and, he *surveyed all existent things*, and *the wealth of the mind*, and the like, Pythagoras 's constitution of body, mind, seeing, hearing and understanding, which was exquisite, and surpassingly accurate, Pythagoras affirmed that the nine Muses were constituted by the sounds made by the seven planets, the sphere of the fixed stars, and that which is opposed to our earth, called "anti-earth." He called *Mnemosyne*, or Memory, the composition, symphony and connexion of then all, which is eternal and unbegotten as being composed of all of them.

32. Diogenes, setting forth his daily routine of living, relates that he advised all men to avoid ambition and vain-glory, which chiefly excite envy, and to shun the presences of crowds. He himself held morning

conferences at his residence, composing his soul with the music of the lute, and singing certain old paeans of Thales. He also sang verses of Homer and Hesiod, which seemed to soothe the mind. He danced certain dances which he conceived conferred on the body agility and health. Walks he took not promiscuously, but only in company of one or two companions, in temples or sacred groves, selecting the quietest and pleasantest places.

33. His friends he loved exceedingly, being the first to declare that the goods of friends are common, and that a friend was another self. While they were in good health he always conversed with them; if they were sick, he nursed them; if they were afflicted in mind, he solaced them, some by incantations and magic charms, others by music. He had prepared songs for the diseases of the body, by the singing of which he cured the sick. He had also some that caused oblivion of sorrow, mitigation of anger and destruction of lust.

34. As to food, his breakfast was chiefly of honey; at dinner he used bread made of millet, barley or herbs, raw and boiled. Only rarely did he eat the flesh of victims; nor did he take this from every part of the anatomy. When he intended to sojourn in the sanctuaries of the divinities, he would eat no more than was necessary to still hunger and thirst. To quiet hunger, he made a mixture of poppy seed and sesame, the skin of a sea-onion, well washed, till entirely drained of the outward juice; of the flower of the daffodil, and the leaves of mallows, of paste of barley and pea; taking an equal weight of which, and chopping it small, with Hymettian honey he made it into mass. Against thirst he took the seed of cucumbers, and the best dried raisins, extracting the seeds, and the flower of coriander, and the seeds of mallows, purselain, scraped cheese, meal and cream; these he made up with wild honey.

35. He claimed that this diet had, by Demeter, been taught to Hercules, when he was sent into the Libyan deserts. This preserved his body in an unchanging condition; not at one time well, and at another time sick, nor at one time fat, and at another lean. Pythagoras's countenance showed the same constancy was in his soul also. For he was neither more elated by pleasure, nor dejected by grief, and no one ever saw him either rejoicing or mourning.

36. When Pythagoras sacrificed to the Gods, he did not use offensive profusion, but offered no more than barley bread, cakes and myrrh; least of all, animals, unless perhaps cocks and pigs. When he discovered the proposition that the square on the hypotenuse of a right angled triangle was equal to the squares on the sides containing the

right angle, he is said to have sacrificed an ox, although the more accurate say that this ox was made of flour.

37. His utterances were of two kinds, plain or symbolical. His teaching was twofold: of his disciples some were called Students, and others Hearers. The Students learned the fuller and more exactly elaborate reasons of science, while the Hearers heard only the chief heads of learning, without more detailed explanations.

38. He ordained that his disciples should speak well and think reverently of the Gods, muses and heroes, and likewise of parents and benefactors; that they should obey the laws; that they should not relegate the worship of the Gods to a secondary position, performing it eagerly, even at home; that to the celestial divinities they should sacrifice uncommon offerings; and ordinary ones to the inferior deities. (The world he Divided into) opposite powers; the "one" was a better *monad*, light, right, equal, stable and straight; while the "other" was an inferior *duad*, darkness, left, unequal, unstable and movable.

39. Moreover, he enjoined the following. A cultivated and fruit-bearing plant, harmless to man and beast, should be neither injured nor destroyed. A deposit of money or of teachings should be faithfully preserved by the trustee. There are three kinds of things that deserve to be pursued and acquired; honorable and virtuous things, those that conduce to the use of life, and those that bring pleasures of the blameless, solid and grave kind, of course not the vulgar intoxicating kinds. Of pleasures there were two kinds; one that indulges the bellies and lusts by a profusion of wealth, which he compared to the murderous songs of the Sirens; the other kind consists of things honest, just, and necessary to life, which are just as sweet as the first, without being followed by repentance; and these pleasures he compared to the harmony of the Muses.

40. He advised special regard to two times; that when we go to sleep, and that when we awake. At each of these we should consider our past actions, and those that are to come. We ought to require of ourselves an account of our past deeds, while of the future we should have a providential care. Therefore he advised everybody to repeat to himself the following verses before he fell asleep:
"Nor suffer sleep to close thine eyes
Till thrice thy acts that day thou hast run o'er;
How slipt? What deeds? What duty left undone?"
On rising:

"As soon as ere thou wakest, in order lay
The actions to be done that following day"

41. Such things taught he, though advising above all things to speak
the truth, for this alone deifies men. For as he had learned from the
Magi, who call God Oremasdes, God's body is light, and his soul is
truth. He taught much else, which he claimed to have learned from
Aristoclea at Delphi. Certain things he declared mystically, symbolically,
most of which were collected by Aristotle, as when he called the sea a
tear of Saturn; the two bear (constellations) *the hand of Rhea*; the
Pleiades, *the lyre of the Muses*; the Planets, *the dogs of Persephone*; and
he called be sound caused by striking on brass the voice of a genius
enclosed in the brass.

42. He had also another kind of symbol, such as, pass not over a
balance; that is, Shun avarice. Poke not the fire with a sword, that is, we
ought not to excite a man full of fire and anger with sharp language.
Pluck not a crown, meant not to violate the laws, which are the crowns
of cities. Eat not the heart, signified not to afflict ourselves with
sorrows. Do not sit upon a [pack]-measure, meant, do not live ignobly.
On starting a journey, do not turn back, meant, that this life should not
be regretted, when near the bourne of death. Do not walk in the public
way, meant, to avoid the opinions of the multitude, adopting those of
the learned and the few. Receive not swallows into your house, meant,
not to admit under the same roof garrulous and intemperate men. Help
a man to take up a burden, but not to lay it down, meant, to encourage
no one to be indolent, but to apply oneself to labor and virtue. Do not
carry the images of the Gods in rings, signified that one should not at
once to the vulgar reveal one's opinions about the Gods, or discourse
about them. Offer libations to the Gods, just to the ears of the cup,
meant, that we ought to worship and celebrate the Gods with music, for
that penetrates through the ears. Do not eat those things that are
unlawful, sexual or increase, beginning nor end, nor the first basis of all
things.

43. He taught abstention from the loins, testicle, pudenda, marrow,
feet and heads of victims. The loins he called *basis*, because on them as
foundations living beings are settled. Testicles and pudenda he called
generation, for no one is engendered without the help of these. Marrow
he called *increase* as it is the cause of growth in living beings. The
beginning was the feet, and the head the end; which have the most
power in the government of the body. He likewise advised abstention
from beans, as from human flesh.

44. Beans were interdicted, it is said, because the particular plants grow and individualize only after (the earth) which is the principle and origin of things, is mixed together, so that many things underground are confused, and coalesce; after which everything rots together. Then living creatures were produced together with plants, so that both men and beans arose out of putrefaction whereof he alleged many manifest arguments. For if anyone should chew a bean, and having ground it to a pulp with his teeth, and should expose that pulp to the warm sun, for a short while, and then return to it, he will perceive the scent of human blood. Moreover, if at the time when beans bloom, one should take a little of the flower, which then is black, and should put it into an earthen vessel, and cover it closely, and bury in the ground for ninety days, and at the end thereof take it up, and uncover it, instead of the bean he will find either the head of an infant, or the pudenda of a woman.

45. He also wished men to abstain from other things, such as a swine's paunch, a mullet, and a sea-fish called a "nettle," and from nearly all other marine animals. He referred his origin to those of past ages, affirming that he was first Euphorbus, then Aethalides, then Hermotimus, then Pyrrhus, and last, Pythagoras. He showed to his disciples that the soul is immortal, and to those who were rightly purified he brought back the memory of the acts of their former lives.

46. He cultivated philosophy, the scope of which is to free the mind implanted within us from the impediments and fetters within which it is confined; without whose freedom none can learn anything sound or true, or perceive the unsoundedness in the operation of sense. Pythagoras thought that mind alone sees and hears, while all the rest are blind and deaf. The purified mind should be applied to the discovery of beneficial things, which can be effected by, certain artificial ways, which by degrees induce it to the contemplation of eternal and incorporeal things, which never vary. This orderliness of perception should begin from consideration of the most minute things, lest by any change the mind should be jarred and withdraw itself, through the failure of continuousness in its subject-matter.

47. That is the reason he made so much use of the mathematical disciplines and speculations, which are intermediate between the physical and the incorporeal realm, for the reason that like bodies they have a threefold dimension, and yet share the impassibility of incorporeals; as degrees of preparation to the contemplation of the really existent things; by an artificial reason diverting the eyes of the

mind from corporeal things, whose manner and state never remain in the same condition, to a desire for true (spiritual) food. By means of these mathematical sciences therefore, Pythagoras rendered men truly happy, by this artistic introduction of truly [consistent] things.

48. Among others, Moderatus of Gades, who [learnedly] treated of the qualities of numbers in seven books, states that the Pythagoreans specialized in the study of numbers to explain their teachings symbolically, as do geometricians, inasmuch as the primary forms and principles are hard to understand and express, otherwise, in plain discourse. A similar case is the representation of sounds by letters, which are known by marks, which are called the first elements of learning; later, they inform us these are not the true elements, which they only signify.

49. As the geometricians cannot express incorporeal forms in words, and have recourse to the descriptions of figures, as that is a triangle, and yet do not mean that the actually seen lines are the triangle, but only what they represent, the knowledge in the mind, so the Pythagoreans used the same objective method in respect to first reasons and forms. As these incorporeal forms and first principles could not be expressed in words, they had recourse to demonstration by numbers. Number one denoted to them the reason of Unity, Identity, Equality, the purpose of friendship, sympathy, and conservation of the Universe, which results from persistence in Sameness. For unity in the details harmonizes all the parts of a whole, as by the participation of the First Cause. .

50. Number two, or *Duad*, signifies the two-fold reason of diversity and inequality, of everything that is divisible, or mutable, existing at one time in one way, and at another time in another way. After all these methods were not confined to the Pythagoreans, being used by other philosophers to denote unitive powers, which contain all things in the universe, among which are certain reasons of equality, dissimilitude and diversity. These reasons are what they meant by the terms *Monad* and *Duad*, or by the words uniform, biform, or diversiform.

51. The same reasons apply to their use of other numbers, which were ranked according to certain powers. Things that had a beginning, middle and end, they denoted by the number Three, saying that anything that has a middle is triform, which was applied to every perfect thing. They said that if anything was perfect it would make use of this principle and be adorned, according to it; and as they had no other name for it, they invented the form *Triad*; and whenever they tried to bring us to the knowledge of what is perfect they led us to that

by the form of this *Triad.* So also with the other numbers, which were ranked according to the same reasons.

52. All other things were comprehended under a single form and power which they called *Decad,* explaining it by a pun as decad, meaning comprehension. That is why they called Ten a perfect number, the most perfect of all as comprehending all difference of numbers, reasons, species and proportions. For if the nature of the universe be defined according to the reasons and proportions of members, and if that which is produced, increased and perfected, proceed according to the reason of numbers; and since the *Decad* comprehends every reason of numbers, every proportion, and every species, Ñ why should Nature herself not be denoted by the most perfect number, Ten? Such was the use of numbers among the Pythagoreans.

53. This primary philosophy of the Pythagoreans finally died out first, because it was enigmatical, and then because their commentaries were written in Doric, which dialect itself is somewhat obscure, so that Doric teachings were not fully understood, and they became misapprehended, and finally spurious, and later, they who published them no longer were Pythagoreans. The Pythagoreans affirm that Plato, Aristotle, Speusippus, Aristoxenus and Xenocrates; appropriated the best of them, making but minor changes (to distract attention from this their theft), they later collected and delivered as characteristic Pythagorean doctrines whatever therein was most trivial, and vulgar, and whatever had been invented by envious and calumnious persons, to cast contempt on Pythagoreanism.

54. Pythagoras and his associates were long held in such admiration in Italy, that many cities invited them to undertake their administration. At last, however, they incurred envy, and a conspiracy was formed against them as follows. Cylon, a Crotonian, who in race, nobility and wealth was the most preeminent, was of a severe, violent and tyrannical disposition, and did not scruple to use the multitude of his followers to compass his ends. As he esteemed himself worthy of whatever was best, he considered it his right to be admitted to Pythagorean fellowship. He therefore went to Pythagoras extolled himself, and desired his conversation. Pythagoras, however, who was accustomed to read in human bodies' nature and manners the disposition of the man, bade him depart, and go about his business. Cylon, being of a rough and violent disposition, took it as a great affront, and became furious.

55. He therefore assembled his friends, began to accuse Pythagoras, and conspired against him and his disciples. Pythagoras then went to

Delos, to visit the Syrian Pherecydes, formerly his teacher, who was dangerously sick, to nurse him. Pythagoras's friends then gathered together in the house of Milo the wrestler; and were all stoned and burned when Cylo's followers set the house on fire. Only two escaped, Archippus and Lysis, according to the account of Neanthes. Lysis took refuge in Greece, with Epaminondas, whose teacher he had formerly been.

56. But Dicaearchus and other more accurate historians relate that Pythagoras himself was present when this conspiracy bore fruit, for Pherecydes had died before he left Samos. Of his friends, forty who were gathered together in a house were attacked and slain; while others were gradually slain as they came to the city. As his friends were taken, Pythagoras himself first escaped to the Caulonian haven, and thence visited the Locrians. Hearing of his coming, the Locrians sent some old men to their frontiers to intercept him. They said," Pythagoras, you are wise and of great worth; but as our laws retain nothing reprehensible, we will preserve them intact. Go to some other place, and we will furnish you with any needed necessaries of travel." Pythagoras turned back, and sailed to Tarentum, where, receiving the same treatment as at Crotona, he went to Metapontum. Everywhere arose great mobs against him, of which even now the inhabitants make mention, calling them the Pythagorean riots, as his followers were called Pythagoreans.

57. Pythagoras fled to the temple of the Muses, in Metapontum. There he abode forty days, and starving, died. Others however state that his death was due to grief at the loss of all his friends who, when the house in which they were gathered was burned, in order to make a way for their master, they threw themselves into the flames, to make a bridge of safety for him, whereby indeed he escaped. When died the Pythagoreans, with them also died their knowledge, which till then than they had kept secret, except for a few obscure things which were commonly repeated by those who did not understand them. Pythagoras himself left no book; but some little sparks of his philosophy, obscure and difficult, were preserved by the few who were preserved by being scattered, as were Lysis and Archippus.

58. The Pythagoreans now avoided human society, being lonely, saddened and dispersed. Fearing nevertheless that among men the name of philosophy would be entirely extinguished, and that therefore the Gods would be angry with them, they made abstracts and commentaries. Each man made his own collection of written authorities and his own memories, leaving them wherever he happened to die,

charging their wives, sons and daughters to preserve them within their families. This mandate of transmission within each family was obeyed for a long time.

59. Nichomacus says that this was the reason why the Pythagoreans studiously avoided friendship with strangers, preserving a constant friendship among each other. Aristoxenus, in his book on the *Life of Pythagoras*, says he heard many things from Dionysius, the tyrant of Sicily, who, after his abdication, taught letters at Corinth. Among these were that they abstained from lamentations and grieving and tears; also from adulation, entreaty, supplication and the like.

60. It is said that Dionysius at one time wanted to test their mutual fidelity under imprisonment. He contrived this plan. Phintias was arrested, and taken before the tyrant, and charged with plotting against the tyrant, convicted, and condemned to death. Phintias, accepting the situation, asked to be given the rest of the day to arrange his own affairs, and those of Damon, his friend and associate, who now would have to assume the management. He therefore asked for a temporary release, leaving Damon as security for his appearance. Dionysius granted the request, and they sent for Damon, who agreed to remain until Phintias should return.

61. The novelty of this deed astonished Dionysius; but those who had first suggested the experiment, scoffed at Damon, saying he was in danger of losing his life. But to the general surprise, near sunset Phintias came to die. Dionysius then expressed his admiration, embraced them both, and asked to be received as a third in their friendship. Though he earnestly besought this, they refused this, though assigning no reason therefore. Aristoxenus states he heard this from Dionysius himself. [Hippobotus] and Neanthes relate about Myllia and Timycha.

ANONYMOUS BIOGRAPHY OP PYTHAGORAS
Preserved by PHOTIUS

I. Plato was the pupil of Archytas, and thus the ninth in succession from Pythagoras; the tenth was Aristotle. Those of Pythagoras's disciples that were devoted to contemplation were called *sebastici*, the reverend, while those who were engaged in business were called *politicians*. Those who cultivated the disciplines of geometry and astronomy, were called *students*. Those who associated personally with Pythagoras were called *Pythagoreans*, while those who merely imitated his teachings were called *Pythagoristians*. All these generally abstained from the flesh of animals; at a certain time they tasted the flesh of victims only.

2. Pythagoras is said to have lived 104 years; and Mnesarchus, one of his sons, died a young man. Telauges was another son, and Sara and Myia were his daughters. Theano, it is said, was not only his disciple, but practically his daughter.

3. The Pythagoreans preach a difference between the *Monad*, and the One; the *Monad* dwells in the intelligible realm, while the One dwells among numbers. Likewise, the Two exists among numerable things, while the *Duad* is indeterminate.

4. The *Monad* expresses equality and measure, the *Duad* expresses excess and defect. Mean and Measure cannot admit of more or less, while excess and defect, which proceed to infinity, admit it; that is why the *Duad* is called indeterminate. Since, because of the all-inclusion of the *Monad* and *Duad*, all things refer to number, they call all things numbers; and number is perfected in the Ten. Ten is reached by adding in order the first four figures; that is why Ten is called the Quaternary (or, *Tetrachtys*).

5. They affirm that man may improve in three ways; first, by conversation with Gods, for to them none can approach unless he abstain from all evil, imitating the divinity, even unto assimilation; second, by well doing, which is a characteristic of the divinity; third by dying; for if the slight soul-separation from the body resulting from discipline improves the soul so that she begins to divine, in dreams; and if the disease-ecstasies produce visions, then the soul must surely improve far more when entirely separated from the body by death.

6. The Pythagoreans abstained from eating animals, on their foolish belief in transmigration; also because this flesh-food engages digestion

too much, and is too fattening. Beans also they avoided, because they produced flatulency, produced over-satiety, and other reasons.

7. The Pythagoreans considered the *Monad* as the beginning of all things, just as a point is the beginning of a line, a line of a surface, and a surface of a solid, which constitutes a body. A point implies a preceding *Monad*, so that it is really the principle of bodies, and all of them arise from the *Monad*.

8. The Pythagoreans are said to have predicted many things, and Pythagoras's predictions always came true.

9. Plato is said to have learned his speculative and physical doctrines from the Italic Pythagoreans; and his ethics from Socrates; and his logic from Zeno, Parmenides and the Eleatics. But all of these teachings descended from Pythagoras.

10. According to Pythagoras, Plato and Aristotle, sight is the judge of the ten colors; white and black being the extremes of all others, between: yellow, tawny, pale, red, blue, green, light blue, and grey. Hearing is the judge of the voice, sharp and flat. Smell judges of odors, good and bad, and putridity, humidity, liquidness and evaporation. Taste judges of tastes, sweet and bitter, and between them five: sharp, acid, fresh, salt and hot. Touch judges of many things between the extremes of heavy and lightness, such as heat and cold; and those between them, hardness and softness; and those between them, dryness and moistness, and those between them. While the main four senses are confined to their special senses in the head, touch is diffused throughout the head and the whole body, and is common to all the senses; but is specialised in the hands.

11. Pythagoras taught that in heaven there were twelve orders: the first and outermost being the fixed sphere, where, according to Aristotle, dwelt the highest God, and the intelligible deities; and where Plato located his ideas. Next are the seven planets: Saturn, Jupiter, Mars, Venus, Mercury, Sun and Moon. Then comes the sphere of Fire, that of Air, Water, and last, Earth. In the fixed sphere dwells the First Cause, and whatever is nearest thereto is the best organized, and most excellent, while that which is furthest therefrom is this worst. Constant order is preserved as low as the Moon; while all things sublunary are disorderly. Evil, therefore, must necessarily exist in the neighborhood of the Earth; which has been arranged as the lowest, as a basis for the world, and as a receptacle for the lowest things. All superlunary things are governed in firm order, and Providentially; and the decree of God, which they follow; while beneath the moon operate four causes: God,

Fate, our election, and Fortune. For instance, to go aboard a ship, or not, is in our power; but the storms and tempests that may arise out of a calm, are the result of Fortune; and the preservation the ship, sailing through the waters, is in the hands of providence, of God. There are many different modes of Fate. There is a distinction to be made between Fate, which is determined, orderly and consequent, while Fortune is spontaneous and casual. For example, it is one mode of Fate that guides the growth of a boy; through all the sequent ages to manhood.

12. Aristotle, who was a diligent investigator, agreed with the Pythagoreans that the Zodiac runs obliquely, on account of the generations of those [worthy] things which become complements to the Universe. For if these moved evenly, there would be no change of seasons, of any kind. Now the passage of the sun and the other planets from one [moon] to another effect the four seasons of the year, which determine the growth of plants, and generation of animals.

13. Others thought that the sun's size exceeded that of the earth by no more than thirty times; but Pythagoras, as I think correctly, taught it was more than a hundred times as great.

14. Pythagoras called the revolution of Saturn the great year, inasmuch as the other planets run their course in a shorter time: Saturn, thirty years; Jupiter, in twelve; Mars in tow; the Sun in one; Mercury and Venus the same as the Sun. The moon, being nearest to the Earth, has the smallest cycle, that of a month. It was Pythagoras who first called heaven *Cosmos* because it is perfect, and "adornedÓ with infinite beauty and living beings. With Pythagoras agreed Plato and Aristotle, that soul is immortal; although some who did not understand Aristotle claimed he taught the soul was mortal.

15. Pythagoras said that man was a microcosm; which means, a compendium of the universe not because, like other animals, even the least, he is constituted by the four elements, but because he contains all the powers of the world. For the world contains Gods, the four elements, animals and plants. All of these powers are contained in man. He has reason, which is a divine power; he has the nature of the elements, the powers of moving, growing, and reproduction. However, in each of these he is inferior to the others. For example, an athlete who practices five kinds of sports, and diverting his powers into five channels, is inferior to the athlete who practises a single sport, so man having all of the powers, is inferior in each. Than the gods, we have less reasoning powers; and less of each of the elements than the elements

themselves. Our anger and desire are inferior to these passions in the irrational animals; while our powers of nutrition and growth are inferior to that in plants. Constituted therefore of different powers, we have a difficult life to lead.

16. While all other things are ruled by one nature only, we are drawn by different powers; as for instance, when by God we are drawn to better things, or when we are drawn to evil courses by the prevailing of the lower powers. He who, like a vigilant and expert charioteer, within himself cultivates the divine element, will be able to utilize the other powers by a mingling of the elements, by anger, desire and habit, just as far as may be necessary. Though it seems easy to know yourself, this is the most difficult of all things. This is said to derive from the Pythian Apollo, though it is also attributed to Chilo, one of the seven sages. Its message is, in any event, to discover our own power, which amounts to learning the nature of the whole extant world, which, as God advises us, is impossible without philosophy.

17. There are eight organs of knowledge: sense, imagination, art, opinion, prudence, science, wisdom and mind. Art, prudence, science and mind we share with the Gods; sense and imagination, with the irrational animals; while opinion alone is our characteristic. Sense is a fallacious knowledge derived through the body; imagination is a notion in the soul; art is a habit of cooperating with reason. The words "with reason," are here added, for even a spider operates, but it lacks reason. Prudence is a habit selective of the rightness of planned deeds; science is a habit of those things which remain ever the same, with Sameness; wisdom is a knowledge of the first causes; while mind is the principle and fountain of all good things.

18. Docility is divided into three: shrewdness, memory and acuteness. Memory guards the things which have been learned; acuteness is quickness of understanding, and shrewdness is the ability of deducing the unlearned from what one has learned to investigate.

19. Heaven may be divided into three: the first sphere; second, the space from the fixed sphere to the moon; third, the whole world, heaven and earth.

20. The extreme elements, the best and the worst, operate unintermittently. There is no intermission with God, and things near him in mind and reason; and plants are continuously nourished by day and night. But man is not always active, nor irrational animals, which rest and sleep most of the time.

21. The Greeks always surpassed the Barbarians on manners and habits, on account of the mild climate in which they live. The Scythians are troubled by cold, and the Aethiopians by heat; which determines a violent interior heat and moisture, resulting in violence and audacity. Analogously, those who live near the middle zone and the mountains participate in the mildness of the country they inhabit. That is why, as Plato says, Greeks, and especially the Athenians improved disciplines that they derived from the barbarians.

22. (From them had come) strategym, painting, mechanics, polemics, oratory, and physical culture. But the sciences of these were developed by the Athenians, owing to the favorable natural conditions of light, and purity of air, which had the double effect of drying out the earth, as it is in Attica, but making subtle the minds of men. So a rarefied atmosphere is unfavorable to the fertility of the earth, but is favorable to mental development.

(In Photius's work, this is followed by a paragraph on the Etesian winds, which has nothing whatever to do with the subject, and which, therefore, is omitted.)

LIFE OF PYTHAGORAS
by DIOGENES LAERTIUS [circa 180 A.D.]
I
EARLY LIFE

Since we have now gone through the Ionian philosophy, which was derived from Thales, and the lives of the several illustrious, men who were the chief ornaments of that school, we will now proceed to treat of the Italian School, which was founded by Pythagoras, the son of Mnesarchus, a seal engraver, as he is recorded to have been by Hermippus; a native of Samos, or, as Aristoxenus, asserts a Tyrrhenian, and a native of one of the islands which the Athenians, after they had driven out the Tyrrhenians, had occupied. But some authors say that he was the son of Marmacus, the son of Hippasus, the son of Euthyphron, the son of Cleonymus, who was an exile from Phlias; and that Marmacus settled in Samos, and that from this circumstance Pythagoras was called a Samian. After that, he migrated to Lesbos; having come to Pherecydes, with letters from his uncle Zoilus. Then he made three silver goblets, and carried them to Egypt as a present for each of the three priests. He had brothers, the eldest of whom was named Eunomus, the middle one Tyrrhenius, and a slave named Zamolxis, to whom the Getae sacrifice, believing him to be the same as Saturn, according to the account of Herodotus (4:93).

II
STUDIES

He was a pupil, as I have already mentioned, of Pherecydes the Syrian; and after his death he came to Samos, and became a pupil of Hermadamas, the descendant of Creophylus, who was already an old man now.

III
INITIATIONS

As he was a youth devoted to learning, he quitted his country, and got initiated in all the Grecian and barbarian sacred mysteries. Accordingly he went to Egypt, on which occasion Polycrates gave him a letter of introduction to Amasis; and he learned the Egyptian language as Antiphon tells us, in his treatise on those men who have become conspicuous for virtue; and he associated with the Chaldeans and Magi.

Afterwards he went to Crete, and in company with Epimenides, he descended into the Idaean cave---and in Egypt too he had entered into the holiest parts of their temples, --and learned all the most secret mysteries that relate to their Gods. Then he returned again to Samos, and finding his country reduced under the absolute dominion of Polycrates, he set sail, and fled to Crotona in Italy. Having given laws to the Italians, he there gained a very high reputation, together with his scholars, who were about three hundred in numbers, and governed the republic in a most excellent manner; so that the constitution was very nearly an aristocracy.

IV
TRANSMIGRATION

Herclides Ponticus says that he was accustomed to speak of himself in this manner: that he had formerly been Aethalides, and had been accounted the son of Mercury; and that Mercury had desired him to select any gift he pleased except immortality. Accordingly he had requested that, whether living or dead, he might preserve the memory of what had happened to him. While, therefore, he was alive, he recollected everything; and when he was dead, he retained the same memory. At a subsequent period he passed into Euphorbus, and was wounded by Menelaus. While he was Euphorbus, he used to say that he had formerly been Aethalides, and that he had received as a gift from Mercury, the perpetual transmigration of his soul; so that it was constantly transmigrating and passing into whatever plants or animals it pleased; and he had also received the gift of knowing and recollecting all that his soul had suffered in hell, and what sufferings too are endured by the rest of the souls.

But after Euphorbus died, he said that his soul had passed into Hermotimus; and when he wished to convince people of this, he went into the territory of the Branchidas, and going into the temple of Apollo, he showed his shield which Menelaus had dedicated there as an offering. For he said that he, when he sailed from Troy, had offered up his shield which was already getting worn-out, to Apollo, and that nothing remained but the ivory face which was on it. He said that when Hermotimus died he had become Pyrrhus, a fisherman of Delos; and that he still recollected everything, how he had formerly been Aethalides, then Euphorbus, then Hermotimus, and then Pyrrhus. When Pyrrhus died, he became Pythagoras, and still recollected all the circumstances I have been mentioning.

V
WORKS OF PYTHAGORAS

Now they say that Pythagoras did not leave behind him a single book; but they talk foolishly; for Heraclitus, the natural philosopher, speaks plainly enough of him, saying, "Pythagoras, the son of Mnesarchus, was the most learned of all men in history and having, selected from these writings, he thus formed his own wisdom and extensive learning, and mischievous art." Thus he speaks, because Pythagoras, in the beginning of his treatise on natural philosophy, writes in the following manner: "By the air which I breathe, and by the water which I drink, I will not endure to be blamed on account of this discourse."

There are three volumes extant written by Pythagoras: one on education, one on politics, and one Natural Philosophy. The treatise which is now extant under the name of Pythagoras is the work of [Lysis], of Tarentum, a philosopher of the Pythagorean school, who fled to Thebes, and became the teacher of Epaminondas. Heraclides, the son of Sarapion, in his *Abridgment of [N]otion* says that he wrote a poem in epic verse upon the Universe; and besides that a sacred poem which begins thus:

"Dear youths, I warn you cherish peace divine,
And in your hearts lay deep these words of mine."

A third about the Soul; a fourth on Piety; a fifth entitled Helothales, which was the name of the father of Epicharmus of Cos; a sixth, called Crotona; and other poems too. But the mystic discourse which is extant under his name, they say is really the work of Hippasus, having been composed with a view to bring Pythagoras into disrepute. There were also many other books composed by Aston of Crotona, and attributed to Pythagoras. Aristoxenus asserts that Pythagoras derived the greater part of his ethical doctrines from Themistoclea, the priestess at Delphi. Ion of Chios, in his *Victories*, says that he wrote some poems and attributed them to Orpheus. His also, it is said, is the poem called *Scopadaea*, which begins thus; ÒBehave not shamelessly to any one."

VI
GENERAL VIEWS ON LIFE

Sosicrates, in his Successions, relates that, having been asked by Leon, the tyrant of the Phliasians, who he was, replied, "A philosopher." He adds that Pythagoras used to compare life to a festival. "And as some people come to the festival to contend for the prizes, and others for the purpose of traffic, and the best as spectators, so also in life the men of slavish dispositions are born hunters after glory and covetousness; but philosophers are seekers after the truth." Thus he spoke on this subject. But in the three treatises above mentioned the following principles are laid down by Pythagoras.

He forbids men to pray for anything in particular for themselves, because they do not know what is good for them. He calls drunkenness an expression identical with ruin, and rejects all superfluity, saying, "That no one ought to exceed the proper quantity of meat and drink." On the subject of venereal pleasures, he writes thus: "One ought to sacrifice to Venus in the winter, not in the summer; and in autumn and spring in a lesser degree. But the practice is pernicious at every season and is never good for the health." And once, when he was asked when a man might indulge in the pleasures of love, he replied, "Whenever you wish to be weaker than yourself."

VII
AGES OF LIFE

Thus does he divide the ages of life. A boy for twenty years; a young man -- *neaniskos,* -- for twenty years; a middle aged man -- *neanias,* -- for twenty years, and an old man for twenty. These different ages correspond proportionately to the seasons; boyhood answers to the spring; youth to summer; middle age to autumn; and old age to winter. He uses *neaniskos* here as equivalent to *meirakion*; and *neanias* as equivalent to *aner.*

VIII
SOCIAL CUSTOMS

Timaeus says that he was the first person to assert that the property of friends is common, and that friendship is equality. His disciples used to put all their possessions together into one store, and use them in common. For five years they kept silence, doing nothing but listening to discourses, and never once seeing Pythagoras, until they were approved; after that time they were admitted into his house, and allowed to see him. They also abstained from the use of cypress coffins, because the sceptre of Jupiter was made of that wood, as Hermippus tells us in the second book of his account of Pythagoras.

IX
DISTINGUISHED APPEARANCE

He is said to have been a man of the most dignified appearance; and respecting him his disciples adopted an opinion that he was Apollo who had come from the Hyperboreans; and it is said that once when he was stripped naked he was seen to have a golden thigh. Many people affirmed that when he was crossing the river Nessus, it addressed him by his name.

X
WOMEN DEIFIED BY MARRIAGE

Timaeus, in the tenth book of his *Histories* tells us that he used to say that women who were married to men had the names of Gods, being successively sively called virgins, nymphs, and then mothers.

XI
SCIENTIFIC CULTURE

Also it was Pythagoras who carried geometry to perfection, after Moeris had first found out the principles of the elements of that science, as Aristiclides tells us in the second book of *History of Alexander*; and the part of the science to which Pythagoras applied himself above all others, was arithmetic. He also discovered the numerical relation of sounds on a single string; he also studied medicine. Apollodorus the logician recounts of him that he sacrificed a hecatomb, when he had discovered that the square of the hypothenuse of a right-angled triangle was equal to the squares of the sides containing the right angle. There is an epigram which is couched in the following terms:

"When the great Samian sage his noble problem found,
A hundred oxen with their life-blood dyed the ground."

XII
DIET AND SACRIFICES

He is also said to have been the first man who trained athletes on meat; and Eurymenes was the first man, according to the statement of Phavorinus, in the third book of his Commentaries, who ever did submit to this diet as before that men used to train themselves on dry figs, and moist cheese, and wheaten bread; as the same Phavorinus informs us in the eighth book of his *Universal History*. But some authors state that a trainer of the name of Pythagoras certainly did train his athletes on this system, but that it was not our philosopher; for that he even forbade men to kill animals at all, much less would he have allowed his disciples to eat them, as having a right to live in common with mankind. And this was his pretext; but in reality he prohibited the eating of animals because he wished to train and accustom men to simplicity of life; so that all their food should be easily procurable, as it would be, if they ate only such things as required no fire to cook them, and if they drank plain water; for from this diet they would derive health of body and acuteness of intellect. The only altar at which he worshipped was that of Apollo, the Father, at Delos, which is at the back of the altar of Caratinus, because wheat and barley, and cheesecakes are the only offerings laid upon it, as it is not dressed by fire; and no victim is ever slain there, as Aristotle tells us, in his Constitution of the Delians. It is also said that he was the first person who asserted that the soul went a necessary circle, being transformed and confined at different times in different bodies.

XIII
MEASURES AND WEIGHTS

He was also the first person who introduced measures and weights among the Greeks, as Aristoxenus the musician informs us.

XIV
HESPERUS AND LUCIFER

Parmenides assures us too that he was the first person who asserted the identity of Hesperus and Lucifer.

XV
STUDENTS AND REPUTATION

He was so greatly admired that it used to be said that his disciples looked on all his sayings as the Oracles of God. In his writings he himself said that he had come among men after having spent two hundred and seventy years in the shades below. Therefore the Lucanians, Peucetians, Messapians and Romans flocked around him, coming with eagerness to hear his discourses; but until the time of Philolaus no doctrines of Pythagoras were ever divulged; and he was the first person who published the three celebrated books which Plato wrote to have purchased for him for a hundred minae. The scholars who used to come to him by night were [no] less than six hundred. Whenever any one of them [was] permitted to see him, he wrote of it to his friends, as if they had achieved something wonderful. The people of Metapontum used to call his house the temple of Ceres; and the street leading to it was called that of the Muses, as we are informed in the universal history of Phavorinus.

According to the account given by Aristoxenus, in his tenth book of his Laws on Education, the rest of the Pythagoreans used to say that his precepts ought not to be divulged to all the world; and Xenophilus the Pythagorean, when he was asked what was the best way for a man to educate his son, said, "That he must first of all take care that he was born in a city which enjoyed good laws." Pythagoras formed many excellent men in Italy, by his precepts, and among them Zaleucus and Charondas, the lawgivers.

XVI
FRIENDSHIP FOUNDED ON SYMBOLS

Pythagoras was famous for his power of attracting friendships; and among other things, if he ever heard that anyone had any community of symbols with him, he at once made him a companion and a friend.

XVII
SYMBOLS OR MAXIMS

Now what he called his symbols were such as these:
"Do not poke the fire with a word."
"Do not sit down on a bushel."
"Do not devour your heart."
"Do not aid men in discarding a burden, but in increasing one."
"Always have your bed packed up."
"Do not bear the image of God on a ring."
"Efface the traces of a pot in the ashes."
"Do not wipe a seat with a lamp."
"Do not make water in the sunshine."
"Do not walk in the main street."
"Do not offer your hand lightly."
"Do not cherish swallows under your roof."
"Do not cherish birds with crooked talons."
"Do not defile; do not stand upon the parings of your nails, or the cuttings of your hair."
"Avoid a sharp sword."
"When traveling abroad, do not look back at your own borders."

Now the precept not to poke the fire with a sword meant, not to provoke the anger or swelling pride of powerful men; not to violate the beam of the balance meant, not to transgress fairness and justice; not to sit on a bushel is to have an equal care for the present and the future; for by the bushel is meant one's daily food. By devouring ones heart, he intended to show that we ought not to waste away our soul with grief and sorrow. In the precept that a man when traveling abroad should not turn his eyes back, he recommended those who were departing this life not to be desirous to live, and not to be too much attracted by the pleasures here on earth. And the other symbols may be explained in a similar manner, that we may not be too prolix here.

XVIII
PERSONAL HABITS

Above all things, he used to prohibit the eating of the *erythinus* and the *mepanurus*; also the hearts of animals, and beans. Aristotle informs us that to these prohibitions he sometimes added tripe and mullet. Some authors assert that he himself used to be contented with honey, honey-comb and bread; and that he never drank wine in the daytime. He usually ate vegetables, either boiled or raw; and he very rarely ate fish. His dress was white, very clean; his bed-clothes also were white and woolen, for linen had not yet been introduced in that country. He was never known to have eaten too much, or to have drunk too much; or to indulge in the pleasures of love. He abstained wholly from laughter, and from all such indulgences as jests and idle stories. He never chastised any one, whether slave or free man, while he was angry. Admonishing he used to call feeding storks.

He used to practise divination, as far as auguries and auspices; but not by means of burnt offerings, except only the burning of frankincense. All the sacrifices which he offered consisted of inanimate things. But some, however, assert that he did sacrifice animals, limiting himself to cocks, and sucking kids, which are called [-palioi], but that he very rarely offered lambs. Aristoxenus, however, affirms that he permitted the eating of all other animals, and abstained only from oxen used in agriculture, and from rams.

XIX
VARIOUS TEACHINGS

The same author tells us, as I have already mentioned, that he received his doctrines from Themiclea at Delphi. Hieronymus says, that when he descended into the shades below, he saw the soul of Hesiod bound to a brazen pillar, and gnashing it's teeth; and that of Homer suspended from a tree, snakes around it, as a punishment for the things that they had said of the Gods. Those who refrain from commerce with their wives also were punished and that on account of this he was greatly honored at Crotona. Aristippus of Cyrene, in his Account of Natural Philosophers, says that Pythagoras derived his name from the fact of his speaking (agoreuein), truth no less than the God at Delphi (touputhieu).

He used to admonish his disciples to repeat these lines to themselves whenever they returned home to their houses:

"In what have I transgressed? What Have I done? What that I should have done have I omitted?"

He used to forbid them to offer victims to the Gods, ordering them to worship only at those altars which were unstained with blood. He also forbad to swear by the Gods, saying, "That every man ought so to exercise himself as to be worthy of belief without an oath. He also taught men that it behoved them to honor their elders, thinking most honorable that which was precedent inpoint of time; just as in the world, the rising of the sun was more so than the setting; in life, the beginning more so than the end; and in animals, production more than destruction.

Another of his rules was that men should honor the Gods above the geniuses, and heroes above men and of all men, parents were those entitled to more honor. Another, that people should associate with each other in such a way as not to make their friends enemies, but to render their enemies friends. Another was that they should not think anything exclusively their own. Another was to assist the law, and to make war upon lawlessness. Not to destroy or injure a cultivated tree, nor any animal which does not injure man. Modesty and decorum consisted in never yielding to laughter, without looking stern. Men should avoid eating too much flesh, and in travelling should let rest and exertion alternate; that they should exercise memory, nor ever say or do anything in anger, not pay respect to every kind of divination, should sing songs accompanied by the lyre, and should display a reasonable gratitude to the Gods and eminent men by hymns.

His disciples were forbidden to eat beans, because, as they were flatulent, they greatly partook of animal properties; (that their stomachs would be kept in much better order by avoiding them), and that such abstinence would make the visions that appear in one's sleep gentle and free from agitation.

Alexander, in his Successions of Philosophers, reports the following doctrines as contained in Pythagoras's Commentaries: the Monad is the beginning of everything. From this proceeds an indefinite duad, which is subordinate to the monad, as to its cause. From the monad and the indefinite duad proceed numbers. From numbers proceed signs. From these, lines, of which plane figures consist. From these plane figures are derived solid bodies. From solid bodies are derived sensible bodies, of which last there are four elements, fire, water, earth and air. The world, which is endued with life and intellect, and which is of a spherical figure, in its centre containing the earth, which is also spherical, and inhabited all over, results from a combination of these elements, and from them derives its motion. There are antipodes, and what to us is below, is to them above, He also taught that light and darkness, cold and heat, dryness and moisture, were equally divided in the world; and that, while heat was predominant in summer, so when cold prevailed, it was winter; when dryness prevailed, it was spring; and when moisture preponderated, autumn. The loveliest season of the year was when all these qualities were equally balanced; of which the flourishing spring was the most wholesome, and the autumn, the most pernicious. Of day, the most flourishing period was the morn while the evening was the fading one, and the least healthy.

Another of his theories was that the air around the earth was immovable, and pregnant disease, and that in it everything was mortal while the upper air was in perpetual motion, and salubrious; and that in it everything was immortal, and on that account divine. The sun, moon and the stars were all Gods; for in them dominates the principle which is the cause of. The moon derives its light from the sun. There a relationship between men and the Gods, because men partake of the divine principle; on which count, therefore, God exercises his providence for our advantage. Fate is the cause of the arrangement of the world, both in general and in particular. From the sun a ray penetrates both the cold aether, which is the air, *aer* and the dense aether, *pachun aithera*, which is the sea and moisture. This ray descends into the depths and in this way vivifies everything. Everything which partakes of the principle of heat lives, which account, also, plants are animated beings but that not all living beings necessarily have souls. The soul is something torn off from the aether, both warm and cold, from its partaking of the cold aether. The soul is something different from life. It is immortal, because of the immortality of that from which it was torn off.

Animals are born from one another by seeds and that it is impossible for there to be any spontaneous production by the earth. Seed is a drop from the brain which in itself contains a warm vapor; and that when this is applied to the womb, it transmits moisture, virtue, and blood from the brain, from which flesh, sinews, bones and hair, and the whole body are produced. From the vapor is produced the soul and also sensation. The infant first becomes a solid body at the end of forty days; but, according to the principles of harmony, it is not perfect till seven, or perhaps nine; or at most ten months, and then it is brought forth. In itself it contains all the principles of life which are all connected together, and by their union and combination form a hormonious whole, each of them developing itself at the appointed time.

In general the senses, and especially sights, are a vapor of intense heat, on which account a man is said to see through air, or through water. For the hot principle is opposed by the cold one; since, if the vapor in the eyes were cold, it would have the same temperature as the air, and so would be dissipated. As it is, in some passages he calls the eyes the gates of the sun. In a similar manner he speaks of hearing, and of the other senses. He also says that the soul of man is divided into three parts; into intuition (nous), reason (phren), and mind (thumos); and that the first and last divisions are found also in other animals, but that the middle one, reason, is found in man only. The chief abode of the soul is in those parts of the body which are between the heart and the brain. The mind abides in the heart, while the intuition (or deliberation) and reason reside in the brain.

The senses are drops from them; and the reasoning sense is immortal, while the others are mortal. The soul is nourished by the blood, and reasons are the winds of the soul. The soul is invisible, and so are its reasons, inasmuch as the aether itself is invisible. The links of the soul are the arteries, veins and nerves. When the soul is vigorous, and is by itself in a quiescent state, then its links are words and actions. When it is cast forth upon the earth, it wanders about, resembling the body. Mercury is the steward of the souls, and that is the reason of his name Conductor, Commercial, and Infernal, since it is he who conducts the souls from their bodies, and from earth, and sea; and that he conducts the pure souls to the highest region, and that he does not allow the impure ones to approach them nor to come near one another; committing them to be. bound in indissoluble fetters by the Furies. The Pythagoreans also assert that the whole air is full of souls, and that these are those that Page I69 DIOGENES LAERTES BIOGRAPHY XIX are accounted geniuses or heroes. They are the ones that send down among men dreams, and tokens of disease and health; the latter not being reserved to human beings, but being sent also to sheep and other cattle. They are concerned with purifications, expiations, and all kinds of divinations, oracular predictions, and the l(ike).

Man's most important privilege is to be able to persuade his soul to be either good or bad. (Men) are happy when they have a good soul; yet they never quiet, never long retaining the same mind. An oath is justice; and on that account Jupiter is called Jupiter of Oaths. Virtue is harmony, health, universal good and God; on which account everything owes its existence and preservation to harmony. Friendship is a harmonious quality. Honors to Gods and heroes should not be equal. The Gods should be honored at all times, extolling them with praises, clothed in white garments, and keeping one's body chaste; but that to the heroes such honors should not be payed till after noon.

A state of purity is brought about by purifications, washings and sprinklings; by a man's purifying himself from all funerals, concubinage, or any kind of pollution; by abstaining from all flesh that has either been killed or died of itself, from mullets, from melanuri, from eggs, from such animals as lay eggs, from beans, and from other things that are prohibited by those who have chared of the mysteries in the temples.

In his treatise on Beans, Aristotle says that Pythagoras's reason for demanding abstention from them on the part of his disciples, was that either they resemble parts of the human body, or because they are like the gates of hell Ñ they are the only plants without parts; -- or because they dry up other plants, or because they are representatives of universal nature, or because they are used in elections in oligarchical governments. He also forbade his disciples to pick up what fell from the table, for the sake of accustoming them to eat moderately, or else because such things belong to the dead. Aristophanes, indeed said that what fell belonged to the heroes, in his heroes singing, "Never taste the things which fall, From the table on the floor."

He also forbade his disciples to eat white poultry, because a cock of that color was sacred to the god Month, and was also a suppliant. He was also accounted a good animal (?) and he was sacred to the god Month, for he indicates the time.

The Pythagoreans were also forbidden to eat of all fish that was sacred, on the ground that the same animals should not be served up before both gods and men, just as the same things do not belong to both freemen and slaves. Now white is an indication of a good nature, and black of a bad one.

Another of the precepts of Pythagoras was never to break bread; because in ancient, times friends used to gather around the same loaf, as they even now do among the barbarians. Nor would he allow men to divide bread which unties them. Some think that he laid down this rule in reference to the judgment which takes place in hell; some because this practice engenders timidity in war. According to others, the refence is to the Union, which presides over the government of the Universe.

Another one of his doctrines was that of all solid figures the sphere was the most beautiful; and of all plane figures, the circle. That old age, and all diminution was similar, and also; all increase and youth. That health was the permanence of form, and disease, its destruction. He thought salt should be set before people as a reminder of justice; for salt preserves everything which it touches, and is composed of the purest particles of water and the sea.

These are the doctrines which Alexander asserts that he discovered in the Pythagorean treatises; and Aristotle gives us a similar account of them.

POETIC TESTIMONIES

Timon, in his Silli, has not left unnoticed the dignified appearance of Pythagoras, though he he attacks him on other points. Thus he speaks:

"Pythagoras who often teaches
precepts of magic, and with speeches
Of long high-sounding diction draws,
From gaping crowds, a vain applause."

In his *Alcmaeon*, Innesimachus says:

"As we do sacrifice to the Phoebus whom
Pythagoras worships, never eating aught
Which has the breath of life."

Austophon says in his *Pythagorean*:

A. "He said that when he did descend below
Among the shades in Hell, he there beheld
All men who e'er had died; and there he saw
That the Pythagoreans differed much
From all the rest; for that with them alone
Did Pluto deign to eat, much honoring
Their pious habits."

B. "He's a civil God,
If he likes eating with such dirty fellows."

And again in the same play he says,

"They eat nothing but herbs and vegetables, and drink
Pure water only; but their lice are such
Their cloaks so dirty, and their unwash'd scent
So rank, that none of our younger men
Will for a moment bear them."

Referring to his having been different people at different times, Xenophanes says in an elegiac poem, that begins thus:

"Now will I upon another subject touch,
And lead the way.....
They say that once, as passing by he saw
A dog severely beaten, he did pity him;
And spoke as follows to the man who beat him:
"Stop now and beat him not; since in his body
Abides the soul of a dear friend of mine,
Whose voice I recognized as he was crying."

Cratinus also ridiculed him in his *Pythagorean Woman*, but in his *Tarentines* he speaks thus:

"They are accustomed, if by chance they see
A private individual abroad,
To try what powers of argument he has.
How he can speak and reason; and they bother him
With strange antithesis, and forced conclusions,
Errors, comparisons, and magnitudes,
Till they have filled, and quite perplexed his mind."

XXI
DEATH OF PYTHAGORAS

Pythagoras died in this manner. When he was sitting with some of his companions in Milo's house, some of those whom he did not think worthy of admission into it, was by envy excited to set fire to it. But some say that the people of Crotona themselves did this, being afraid lest he might aspire to the tyranny. Pythagoras was caught as he was trying to escape; and coming to a place full of beans, he stopped there, saying that it was better to be caught than to trample on the beans, and better to be slain than to speak; and so he was murdered by those who were pursuing him. In this way also, most of his companions were slain; being about forty in number; but that a very few did escape, among whom were Archippus of Tarentum, and Lysis, whom I have mentioned before.

But Dicaearchus states that Pythagoras died later, having escaped as far as the temple of the Muses at Metapontum, where he died of starvation, after forty days. Heraclides, in his abridgment of the *Life of Satyrus*, says that after he had buried Pherecydes at Delos, he returned to Italy, and there finding a superb banquet prepared at the house of Milo, of Crotona, he left that city or Metapontum, where, not wishing any longer to live, he put an end to his life by starvation. But Hermippus says that when there was war between the Agrigentines and the Syracusans, Pythagoras, with his usual companions, joined the Agrigentine army, which was put to flight. Coming up against a field of beans, instead of crossing it, he ran around it, and so was slain by the Syracusans; and that the rest, about thirty-five in number, were burned at Tarentum, where they were trying to excite a sedition in the state against the principal magistrates.

Hermippus also relates another story about Pythagoras. When in Italy, he made a subterranean apartment, and charged his mother to write an account of everything that took place, marking the time of each on a tablet, then sending them down to him until he came up again. His mother did so. Then after a certain time Pythagoras came up again, lean, and reduced to a skeleton; he came into the public assembly, and said that he had arrived from the shades below, and then he recited to them all that had happened to them in the meanwhile. Being charmed with what he told them, they believed that Pythagoras was a divine being, so they wept and lamented, and even entrusted to him their wives, as likely to learn some good from him; and they took upon themselves the name of Pythagoreans. Thus far Hermippus.

XXII
PYTHAGORAS' FAMILY

Pythagoras had a wife, whose name was Theano, the daughter of
Brontinus of Crotona. Some say that she was the wife of Brontinus, and
only Pythagoras's pupil. As Lysis mentions in his letter to Hipparchus,
he had a daughter named Damo. Lysis's letter speaks of Pythagoras
thus:

"And many say that you philosophize in public, as Pythagoras also
used to do; who, when he had entrusted his commentaries to his
daughter Damo, charged her not to divulge them to any one outside of
the house. Though she might have sold his discourses for much money,
she did not abandon them; for she thought that obedience to her
father's injunction; even though this entailed poverty, better than gold;
and that too, though she was a woman."

He had also a son, named Telauges, who was his father's successor
in his school, and who, according to some authors, was the teacher of
Empedocles. At least Hippobotus relates that Empedocles said,

"Telauges, noble youth, whom in due time
Theano bore, to wise Pythagoras."

But there is no book extant, which is the work of Telauges, though
there are some extant that are attributed to his mother Theano. Of her
is told a story, that once, when asked how long a woman should be
absent from her husband, and remain an pure, she said: The moment
she leaves her own husband, she is pure; but she is never pure at all after
she leaves anyone else. A woman who was going to her husband was by
her told to put off her modesty with, her clothes, and when she left
him, to resume it with her clothes; when she was asked what clothes, she
said: "Those which cause you to be called a woman."

XXIII
RIDICULING EPIGRAMS

Now Pythagoras, according to Heraclides, the son of Serapion, died
when he was eighty years of age, according to his own account; by that
of others, he was over ninety. On him we have written a sportive
epigram, as follows:
"You are not the only man who has abstained
From living food; for so have we;
And who, I'd like to know, did ever taste
Food while alive, most sage Pythagoras?
When meat is boiled, or roasted well and salted,
I do not think it well can be called living.
Which, without scruple therefore then we eat it
And call it no more living flesh, but meat."
Another, which runs thus:
"Pythagoras was, so wise a man, that he
Never ate meat himself, and called it sin.
Yet gave the good joints of beef to others;
So that I marvel at his principles;
Who others wronged, by teaching them to do
What he believed unholy for himself."
Another, which follows:
"Should you Pythagoras's doctrine wish to know,
Look on the centre of Euphorbus's shield
For he asserts there lived a man of old,
And when he had no longer an existence,
He still could say that he had been alive,
Or else he would not still be living now."
Another one follows:
"Alas! Alas! Why did Pythagoras hold
Beans in such wondrous honor? Why, besides
Did he thus die among his choice companions?
There was a field of beans; and so the sage,
Died in the common road of Agrigentum,
Rather than trample down his favorite beans."

XXIV
THE LAST PYTHAGOREANS

He flourished about the sixtieth Olympiad; and his system lasted for about nine or ten generations.

The last Pythagoreans known to Aristoxenus were Xenophilus the Chalcidean, from Thrace; Phanton the Phliasian with his countrymen Echutes, [Diode] and Polynmestus, disciples of Philolaus and Eurytus of Tarentum.

XXV
VARIOUS PYTHAGORASES

Pythagoras was the name of four men, almost contemporaneous, and living close to each other. One was a native of Crotona, a man who attained to tyrant's power; the second was Phliasian, and as some say, a trainer of wrestlers. The third was a native of Zacynthus; the fourth was this our philosopher, to whom the mysteries of philosophy are said to belong, and in whose time the proverbial phrase, *ipse dixit*, arose generally. Some also claim the existence of a fifth Pythagoras, a sculptor of Rhodes, who is believed to have been the first discoverer of rhythm and proportion. Another was a Samian sculptor. Another, an orator of small reputation. Another was a physician, who wrote a treatise on squills, and some essays on Homer. Dionysius tells us there was another who wrote a history of the affairs of the Dorians.

Eratosthenes, quoted by Phavorinus, in the eighth book of his *Universal History*, tells us that this philosopher, of whom we are speaking, was the first man who ever practised boxing in a scientific manner, in the forty-eighth Olympiad, having his hair long, and being robed in purple. From competition with boys he was rejected; but being ridicules for his application for this, he immediately entered among the men, and was victorious. Among other things, this statement is confirmed by an epigram of Theaetetus:

"Stranger, if e'er you knew Pythagoras,
Pythagoras, the man with flowing hair,
The celebrated boxer, erst from Samos,
I am Pythagoras. And if you ask
A citizen of Elis of my deeds,
You will surely think he is relating fables."

Phavorinus says that he employed definitions on account of the mathematical subjects to which he applied himself. Socrates and his pupils did still more; and in this they were later followed by Aristotle and the Stoics.

He too was the first man who applied to the universe the name *kosmos*, and who first called the earth round; though Theophrastus attributes this to Parmenides, and Zeno to Hesiod. It is also said that he had a constant adversary, named Cylon, as Socrates' was Antidicus. This epigram was formerly repeated concerning Pythagoras the athlete:

"Pythagoras of Samos, son of Crates,
Came while a child to the Olympic games;
Eager to battle for the prize in boxing."

XXVI
PYTHAGORAS' LETTER

Extant is a letter of our philosopher's, which follows:
PYTHAGORAS TO ANAXIMENES
"You ---, most excellent friend, if you were not superior to
Pythagoras in birth and reputation, would have migrated from Miletus,
and gone elsewhere. But now the reputation of your father keeps you
back, which perhaps would have restrained me too, if I had been like
Anaximenes. But if you, who are the most eminent man, abandon the
cities, all their ernaments will disappear, and the Median power will be
the more dangerous to them. Nor is it always seasonable to be studying
astronomy, but it is more honorable to exhibit a regard for one's
country. I myself am not always occupied about speculations of my own
fancy, but I am busied also with the wars which the Italians are waging
one with another."

But since we have now finished our account of Pythagoras, we must
also speak of the most eminent of the Pythagoreans. After whom, we
must mention those who are spoken of more promiscuously in
connection with no particular school; and then will connect the whole
series of philosophers worth speaking of, till we arrive at Epicurus.
Now [Jelanges] and Theano we have mentioned; and we must speak of
Empedocles, in the first place, for according to some accounts, he was a
pupil of Pythagoras.

XXVII
EMPEDOCLES AS PYTHAGOREAN

Timaeus in his ninth book, relates that he was a pupil of
Pythagoras, saying that he was afterwards convicted of having divulged
his doctrines, in the same way as Plato was, and that he was therefore
henceforth forbidden for attending his school. It is said Pythagoras has
him in mind when he said:
  "And in that band there was a learned man
Of wondrous wisdom; on who of all men
Had the profoundest wealth of intellect."
  But some say the philosopher was here referring to [Pytherides]
Neanthes relates that until the time of Philolaus and Empedocles, the
Pythagoreans used to admit into their school all persons
indiscriminately; but when Empedocles, by means of his poems, then
they made a law to admit no epic poet. They said that the same thing
happened to Plato; for that he too was excluded from the school. Who
was Empedocles's Pythagorean teacher in not mentioned; for, as the
letter of Jelanges in which he is stated to have been a pupil of Hippasus
and Brontinus, that is not worthy of belief. But Theophrastus says that
he was an imitator and rival of Parmenides in his poems, for that he too
has delivered his opinions on natural philosophy in Epic verse.
  Hermippus however says that he was an imitator not of Parmenides,
but of Xenophanes with whom he lived; and that he imitated his epic
style, and that it was at a later period that he fell in with the
Pythagoreans. But Alcimadas, in his Natural Philosophy, says that Zeno
and Erapedodes were pupils of Parmenides, about the same time; and
that they subsequently seceded from him. Zeno was said to have
adapted a philosophical system peculiar to himself; but that
Empedocles became a pupil of Anaxagoras and Pythagoras, and that he
imitated the pompous demeanor and way of life and gestures of the
one, and the system of Natural Philosophy of the other.

VOLUME TWO
Pythagorean Fragments

INTRODUCTION TO PYTHAGOREAN FRAGMENTS

The reason that Pythagoreanism has been neglected, and often treated mythically, is that until this edition, the Pythagorean fragments have never been collected, in text, or any translation. This book therefore marks an era in the study of philosophy, and is needed by every university and general library in the world, not to mention those of the students of philosophy. But there is yet a wider group of people who will welcome it, the lovers of truth in general, who will be charmed by Hierocles' modern views about the family, inspired by Iamblichus's beautiful life of Pythagoras, which has been inaccessible for over a century, and strengthened by the maxims of Sextus, which represent the religious facts of the religion of the future more perfectly than can easily be found elsewhere.

The universal culture of Pythagoras is faithfully portrayed by the manifold aspects of the teachings of Archytas, and Philolaus, and of many other Pythagoreans, among whose fragments we find dissertations on every possible subject: metaphysics, psychology, ethics, sociology, science, and art. Men of general culture, therefore, will feel the need of this encyclopedic information and study; and conversely, there is neither scientist, metaphysician, clergyman, litterateur or sociologist who will fail to discover therein something to his taste.

The Fragments have been gathered from various sources. On Philolaus, the authority is Boeckh. The Archytas fragments have been taken from Chaignet; the minor works from Gale and Taylor, and the Maxims and Golden verses from Dacier. *The Timaeus* was taken from Plato's works, among which it has been preserved. Hierocles's Commentary on the Golden verses has been temporarily omitted as late, wordy, and containing nothing new.

INTRODUCTION TO PYTHAGOREAN LIBRARY

As it is the Editor's purpose to live up to the title of this book, "A Complete Pythagorean Library," he will be grateful to any purchaser of the book who may point out to him further fragments that might be added, as the Editor has no idea that he has, in spite of his good intentions, and Herculean labors, done more than to make the first attempt in a most important direction. Moreover, as the work had to be done at off times, by night, or on holidays, it was inevitably hurried, and therefore inevitably imperfect; for all of which oversights and errors he begs consideration, forgiveness, and constructive criticism.

This work was done, however, because of its great significance in the history of philosophy, which has been elsewhere more definitely been pointed out, and for the sake of which, no doubt, the book will be procured by all students, philosophers and general lovers of truth. It was undertaken for no purpose other than the benefit of humanity, that had for so long been deprived of this its precious heritage, and the Editor will be satisfied if he succeeds in restoring these treasures of thought and inspiration to his day and generation.

SIGNIFICANCE OF THIS PYTHAGOREAN LIBRARY
IMPORTANCE OF THIS COLLECTION OF
PYTHAGOREAN FRAGMENTS

It is a general notion among the uneducated that the great geniuses of thought and poetry arose by divine decree in ready-made originality. Goethe did his best to disabuse the world of this, acknowledging that most of the merit of his work was due to the literature he had studied better than anybody else of his circle. Virgil was so ashamed of his borrowings from Ennius and others, later demonstrated by Macrobius, that on his deathbed he wished to destroy his Aeneid, not understanding that it was all the more precious to us for the fidelity with which it represented the then immediately preceding age. The uncoverers of the sources of Shakespeare, Homer, Milton (Vondel), Dante (Bruno Latini), and many ethnic scriptures have done; their victims no harm, but rather honor; enriching their significance, and making them all the more precious to the world which in the last analysis cares nothing for a British poacher and pawnbroker who wrote his name in 6 different ways, or about a blind traveler, compelled to make the most of his foreign findings, or a Florentine Bolshevik, exile and sycophant, to whom it was heaven to be guided by a stout mother of a great family, who had repulsed him; but the world is very much concerned in having, in modern, accessible and cheap form a summary of the best that has been done up to that time.

In restoring the background of philosophy and thought behind Plato and Aristotle, we are not doing them an injury, but rather making their utterances all the more precious by showing the mental associations that inspired them as they penned their immortal words. This can, of course, be done only very partially, for we have only fragments to deal with; but the inference is reasonable that if we can suggest so much from mere fragments, we could do much more from the now lost complete works of the Pythagoreans. To begin with, Plato showed his good taste by making great efforts to procure the inaccessible writings of Ocellus, and through Archytas secured several. So we have a definite historical connection on which to base our further suppositions.

Then we hear that he paid a large sum of money for a Pythagorean writing, which indeed may have been the treatise of the Locrian Timaeus, which is generally printed with his works, and whose close relations with his own "Timaeus" are unblinkable. To begin with, we do know that the titles of many of his dialogues were not taken on chance, but represented famous thinkers in that field, such as the Protagoras, and others.

The correspondences between his *Timaeus* and the Locrian work are so marked, that inevitably some connection has been assumed, and in view of Plato's fame and the Locrian's rusticity, has generally led to calling the Locrian work an abstract of Plato's.

But even they who stated and assumed this had qualms of conscience. Both De Gelder and Teneann had pointed out that the Locrian "origin of the human soul is more clearly explained" than the Platonic; and Burges adds, that in view of this it is "hard to understand how the former could have been an abridgment of the latter." De Gelder had already pointed out important discrepancies, so that the abstract theory is unsatisfactory. The Locrian calculation from 384 (instead of Plato's 192) [through] the numbers of the scale to a total of 114,695 is no easy matter, and impossible for the student abstracter; this implied great mathematical and musical skill, and could not have been made without very clear purposes, which indeed here are unmistakably Pythagorean.

In comparing the Locrian and Platonic essays we find the Locrian much shorter, logical, and without any padding. It is therefore, antecedently, much more likely to have been the source of inspiration. Thomas Taylor had already done much in this field, which deserves, and no doubt in the future will attract serious attention. We can here mention only a few of the better known correspondences.

The second chapter of Ocellus Lucanus's treatise, is practically reproduced by Aristotle in his essay on Generation and Corruption, especially the three things necessary to generation; also the four powers, and details about matter. Several paragraphs about the mixture of the elements are taken entire. Also the expression, *"as is proper, from such things as are proper, and when it is proper."*

Hippodamus's mingling of democracy, aristocracy and monarchy is found in Plato's laws, and his Statesman. Ecphantus said that any man who has a divine conception of things is in reality a king. Plato in his Statesman said that *"we must call royal he who possesses the royal science, whether or not he governs."* Callicratidas defined God as an intellectual, and incorruptible animal, while in the 12th book of his Metaphysics, Aristotle says that *ÒGod is an animal eternal and most excellent."*

Strange to say, Plato's mother was named Pericthyone, whose namesake was one of the Pythagoreans' female philosophers. She said that those who are unfaithful to their parents must expect punishment in hell, while Olimpiodorus, on the Phaedo of Plato states that the soul is by the divinity not punished through anger, but medicinally, as was implied by Pericthyone. Aristoxenus's second paragraph is quoted in extenso in Plato's Laws, (viii, p187, 188, Bipon). Pempelus's fragment on parents is also quoted by Plato in the same work. Archytas's treatment of happiness is reproduced in part in Aristotle's Nicomachean Ethics. This most interesting topic, should furnish the subject of a most valuable treatise, which will be necessary to the proper appreciation of all Greek philosophy. Who will have time for it?

PYTHAGOREAN SYMBOLS, or MAXIMS
(From Hierocles.)

I. Go not beyond the balance. (Transgress not Justice).

2. Sit not down on the bushel. (Do not loaf on your job).

3. Tear not to pieces the crown. (Do not be a joy-killer).

4. Eat not the heart. (Do not grieve over-much).

5. Do not poke the fire with a sword. (Do not further inflame the quarrelsome).

6. Having arrived at the frontiers, turn not back. (Do not wish to live over your life).

7. Go not by the public way. (Go not the broad popular way, which leads to destruction).

8. Suffer not swallows around your house. (Receive no swallows in your family).

9. Wear not the image of God on your ring. (Profane not the name of God).

10. Do not unload people, but load them up. (Encourage not idleness, but virtue).

11. Not easily shake hands with a man. (Make no ill-considered friendships).

12. Leave no the least mark of the pot on the ashes. (After reconciliation, forget the disagreement).

13. Sow mallows, but never eat them. (Use mildness to others, but not to yourself).

14. Wipe not out the place of the torch. (Let not all the lights of reason be extinguished).

15. Wear not a narrow ring. (Seek freedom, avoid slavery).

16. Feed not the animals that have crooked claws. (To your family admit no thief or traitor).

17. Abstain from beans. (Avoid farcineous food causing flatulence, avoid democratic voting).

18. Eat not fish whose tails are black. (Frequent not the company of men without reputation).

19. Never eat the gurnet. (Avoid revenge).

20. Eat not the womb of animals. (Avoid what leads to generation, to lowest affections).

21. Abstain from flesh of animals that die of themselves. (Avoid decayed food).

22. Abstain from eating animals. (Have no conversation with unreasonable men).

23. Always put salt on the table. (Always use the principle of Justice to settle problems).

24. Never break the bread. (When giving charity, do not pare too close).

25. Do not spill oil upon the seat. (Do not flatter princes, praise God only).

26. Put not meat in a foul vessel. (Do not give good precepts to a vicious soul).

27. Feed the cock, but sacrifice him not; for he is sacred to the sun and the moon. (Cherish people who warm you, sacrifice them not to resentment).

28. Break not the teeth. Do not revile bitterly. (Do not be sarcastic).

29. Keep far from you the vinegar-cruet. (Avoid malice and sarcasm).

30. Spit upon the parings of your nails, and on the clippings of your hair. (Abhor desires).

31. Do not urinate against the sun. (Be modest).

32. Speak not in the face of the sun. (Make not public the thoughts of your heart).

33 Do not sleep at noon. (Do not continue in darkness).

34. Stir up the bed as soon as you are risen, do not leave in it any print of the body. (When working, hanker not for luxurious ease).

35. Never sing without harp-accompaniment. (Make of life a whole).

36. Always keep your things packed up. (Always be prepared for all emergencies).

37. Quit not your post without your general's order. (Do. not suicide).

38. Cut not wood on the public road. (Never turn to private use what belongs to the public).

39. Roast not what is boiled. (Never take in ill part what is done in simplicity and ignorance).

40. Avoid the two-edged sword. (Have no conversation with slanderers).

41. Pick not up what is fallen from the table.(Always leave something for charity).

42. Abstain even from a cypress chest. (Avoid going to funerals).

43. To the celestial gods sacrifice an odd number, but to the infernal, an even. (To God consecrate the indivisible soul, the body to hell).

44. Offer not to the gods the wine of an unpruned vine. (Agriculture is a great piece of piety).

45. Never sacrifice without meal. (Encourage agriculture, offer bloodless offerings).

46. Adore the gods, and sacrifice bare-foot. (Pray and sacrifice in humility of heart).

47. Turn round when you worship. (Adore the immensity of God, who fills the universe).

48. Sit down when you worship. (Never worship in a hurry).

49. Pare not your nails during the sacrifices. (In the temple behave respectfully).

50. When it thunders, touch the ground. (Appease God by humility).

51. Do not primp by torch-light. (Look at things in the light of God).

52. One, Two. (God and Nature; all things are known to God).

53. Honor marks of dignity, the Throne, and the Ternary. (Worship magistrates, Kings, Heroes, Geniuses and God).

54. When the winds blow, adore echo. (During revolts, flee to deserts).

55. Eat not in the chariot. (Eat not in the midst of hurried, important business).

56. Put on your right shoe first, and wash your left foot first.(Prefer an active life, to one of ease and pleasure).

57. Eat not the brain. (Wear not out the brain, refresh yourself).

58. Plant not the palm-tee. (Do nothing but what is good and useful).

59. Make thy libations to the gods by the ear. (Beautify thy worship by music).

60. Never catch the cuttle-fish. (Undertake no dark affairs, intricate affairs, that will wound you).

61.Stop not at the threshold. (Be not wavering but choose your side).

62. Give way to a flock that goes by. (Oppose not the multitude).

63. Avoid the weasel. (Avoid tale-tellers).

64. Refuse the weapons a woman offers you. (Reject all suggestions revenge inspires).

65. Kill not the serpent that chances to fall within your walls. (Harm no enemy who becomes your guest or suppliant).

66. It is a crime to throw stones into fountains. (It is a crime to persecute good men)

67. Feed not yourself with your left hand. (Support yourself with honest toil, not robbery).

68. It is a horrible crime to wipe off the sweat with iron. (It is a criminal to deprive a man by force of what he earned by labor).

69. Stick not iron in the footsteps of a man. (Mangle not the memory of a man).

70. Sleep not on a grave. (Live not in idleness on the parents' inherited estates).

71. Lay not the whole faggot on the fire. (Live thriftily, spend not all at once).

72. Leap not from the chariot with your feet close together. (Do nothing inconsiderately).

73. Threaten not the stars. (Be not angry with your superiors).

74. Place not the candle against the wall. (Persist not in enlightening the stupid).

75. Write not in the snow. (Trust not your precepts to persons of an inconstant character).

PYTHAGORAS'S GOLDEN VERSES

1. First honor the immortal Gods, as the law demands;
2. Then reverence thy oath, and than the illustrious heroes;
3. Then venerate the divinities under the earth, due rites performing,
4. Then honor your parents, and all of your kindred;
5. Among others make the most virtuous thy friend;
6. Love to make use of soft speeches, but deeds that are useful;
7. Alienate not the beloved comrade for trifling offences,
8. Bear all you can, what you can, and you should [are near to each other]
9. Take this wall to heart: you must gain control of your habits;
10. First over stomach, then sleep, and then luxury,
11. And anger; what brings you shame, do not unto others.
12. Nor by yourself; highest of duties is honor of self,
13. Let Justice be practiced in words as in deeds;
14. Then make the habit, never inconsiderately to act;
15. Neither forget that death is appointed to all;
16. That possessions here gladly gathered, there must be left;
17. Whatever sorrow the fate of the gods may here send us,
18. Bear, whatever may strike you, with patience unmurmuring.
19. To relieve it, so far as you can, is permitted; but reflect:
20. Not much good has Fate given to the good.
21 The speech of the people is various, now good, and now evil;
22. So let them not frighten you, nor keep you from your purpose.
23. If false calumnies come to your ear, support it in patience;
24. Yet that which I now am declaring, fulfill it full faithfully:
25. Let no one with speech or with deeds e'er deceive you;
26. To do or to say what is not the best,
27. Think, ere you act, that nothing stupid result;
28. To act inconsiderately is part of a fool;
29. Yet whatever later will not bring you repentance, that you should carry through,
30. Do nothing beyond what you know; yet learn
31. What you may need; thus shall your life grow happy.
32. Neither grow anxious about the health of the body;
33. Keep measure in eating and drinking, and every exercise of the body;
34. By measure, I mean what later will not induce pain;
35. Follow clean habits of life, but not the luxurious;

36. Avoid what envy arouses,

37. At the wrong time, never be prodigal, as if you did not know what was proper;

38. Nor show yourself stingy; that which is medium is ever the best.

39. Never let slumber approach thy wearied eye-lids,

40. Ere thrice you reviewed what this day you did;

41 (Missing)

42. Wherein have I sinned? What did I? What duty is neglected?

43. All from the first to the last, review; and if you have erred,

44. Grieve in your spirit, rejoicing for all that was good.

45. With zeal and with industry, this, then repeat; and learn to repeat it with joy.

46. Thus wilt thou tread on the paths of heavenly virtue,

47. Surely, I swear it by him who into our souls' placed the Four (elements), [yes, by him who imparted to our soul the *tetraktys*,]

48. Him who is spring of Nature eternal-- Now start on your task!

49. After you have implored the blessing of the Gods. -- If this you hold fast,

50. Soon will you recognize of Gods and mortal men

51. The peculiar existence, how everything passes and returns.

52. Then will you see what is true, how Nature in all is most equal,

53. So that you hope not for what has no hope, nor that aught should escape you.

54. Men shall you find whose sorrows themselves have created,

55. Wretches who see not the God, that is to near, near,

56. Nothing they hear; few know how to help themselves in misfortune.

57. That is the Fate, that blinds humanity, in circl[ing] circles,

58. Hither and yon, they run, in endless sorrows;

59. For they are followed by a grim companion, disunion within themselves,

60. Unnoticed; ne'er rouse him, and fly from before him!

61. Father Zeus, O free them all from sufferings so great,

62. Or show unto each the Genius, who is their guide!

63. Yet, do not fear, for the mortals are divine by [-----]

64. To whom holy Nature everything will reveal and demonstrate;

65. Whereof if you have received, so keep what I teach you;

66. For I will heal you, and you shall remain insured from manifold evil.

67. Avoid foods forbidden, reflect, that this contributes to cleanliness

68. And redemption of your soul; This all, Oh, consider;

69. Let reason, the gift divine, be thy highest guide;

70. Then should you be separated from the body, and soar in the spiritual aether,

71. Then will you be imperishable, a divinity, no longer a human!

BIOGRAPHY OF PHILOLAUS
BY DIOGENES LAERTES

Philolaus of Crotona, a Pythagorean, was he from whom Plato, in some of his Letters, begged Dio to purchase Pythagorean books. He died under the accusation of having had designs on the tyranny. I have made about him the following epigram:

"I advise everybody to take, good care to avoid suspicion; even if you are not guilty, but seem so, you are ruined. That is why Crotona, the homeland of Philolaus, destroyed him, because he was suspected of wishing to establish autocracy."

He teaches that all things are produced by necessity and harmony, and he is the first who said that the earth has a circular movement; others however insist this was due to Hicetas of Syracuse.

He had written a single book which the philosopher Plato, visiting Dionysius in Sicily, bought according to Hermippus, from Philolaus's parents, for the sum of 40 Alexandrian minae, whence he drew his Timaeus. Others state that he received it as a present for having obtained the liberty of one of Philolaus's disciples, whom Dionysius had imprisoned. In his *Homonyms* Demetrius claims that he is the first of the Pythagorean philosophers who made a work on nature public property. This book begins as follows:

"The world's being is the harmonious compound of infinite and finite principles; such is the totality of the world and all it contains."

FRAGMENTS OF PHILOLAUS
From Boeckh

1. (Stob.21.7; Diog..#.8.85) The world's nature is a harmonious compound of infinite and finite elements; similar is the totality of the world in itself, and of all it contains. b. All beings are necessarily finite or infinite, or simultaneously finite and infinite; but they could not all be infinite only.

2. How, since it is clear that the beings can not be formed neither of elements that are all infinite, it is evident that the world in its totality, and its included beings are a harmonious compound of finite and infinite elements. That can be seen in works of art. Those that are composed of finite elements, are finite themselves, those that are composed of both finite and infinite elements, are both finite and infinite; and those composed of infinite elements, are infinite.

2. All things, at least those we know contain number; for it is evident that nothing whatever can either be thought or known, without number. Number has two distinct kinds: the odd and the even, and a third, derived from a mingling of the other two kinds, the even-odd. Each of its subspecies is susceptible of many very numerous varieties; which each manifests individually.

3. The harmony is generally the result of contraries; for it is the unity of multiplicity, and the agreement of discordances. (Nicom.Arith.2:509)

4. This is the state of affairs about nature and harmony. The essence of things is eternal; it is a unique and divine nature, the knowledge of which does not belong to man. Still it would not be possible that any of the things that are, and are known by us, should arrive to our knowledge, if this essence was not the internal foundation of the principles of which the world was founded, that is, of the finite and infinite elements. How since these principles are not mutually similar, neither of similar nature, it would be impossible that the order of the world should have been formed by them, unless the harmony intervened, in any manner whatever. Of course, the things that were similar and of similar nature, did not need the harmony; but the dissimilar things, which have neither a similar nature, nor an equivalent function, must be organized by the harmony, if they are to take their place in the connected totality of the world.

5. The extent of the harmony is a fourth, plus a fifth. The fifth is greater than the fourth by nine eighths; for from the lowest string to the

second lowest, there is a fourth; and from this to the next, a fifth; but from this to the next, or "third," a fourth; and from this "third" to the lowest, a fifth. The interval between the second lowest and the "third" (from the top) is nine eighths; the interval of the fourth, is four thirds; that of the fifth, three halves; that of the octave, the double relation. Thus the harmony contains five nine-eighths plus two sharps; the fifth, three nine eighths, plus one sharp; the fourth two nine-eighths, plus one.

6. (Boethius, Music, 3:5). Nevertheless the Pythagorean Philolaus has tried to divide the tone otherwise; his tone's starting-point is the first uneven number which forms a cube, and you know that the first uneven number was an object of veneration among these Pythagoreans. Now the first odd number is three; thrice three are nine, and nine times three is 27, which differs from the number 24 by the interval of one tone, and differs from it by this very number 3. Indeed, 3 is one eighth of 24, and this eighth part of 24 added to 24 itself, produces 27, the cube of 3. Philolaus divides this number 27 in two parts, the one greater than half, which he calls apotome; the other one smaller than half he calls sharp; but which latterly has become known as minor half-tone. He supposes that this [sharp] contains thirteen unities, because 13 is the difference between 256 and 243, and that this [same] number is the sum of 9, 3, and unity, in which the unity plays the part of the period, 3 of the first odd line, and 9 of the first odd square. After having, for these reasons, expressed by 13 the sharp, which is called a semi-tone, out of 14 unities he forms, the other part of the number 27 which he calls apotome, and as the difference between 13 and 14 is the unity, he insists that the unity forms the coma, and that 27 unities form an entire tone, because 27 is the difference between 215 and 243, which are distant by one tone.

7. (Boethius, Music, 3:8). These are the definitions that Philolaus has given of these intervals, and of still smaller intervals. The coma, says he, is the interval whose eighth-ninths relation exceeds the sum of two sharps, namely, the sum of two minor semi-tones. The *schisma* is half the comma, the *diaschisma* is half the sharp, namely, of the minor semi-tone.

8. (Claudius Namert.de Stat. anim.2:3) Before treating of the substance of the soul, Philolaus, according to geometrical principles, treats of music, arithmetic, measures, weights, numbers, insisting that these are the principles which support the existence of the Universe.

9. (Nicom.. Arith.2:p.72) Some, in this following Philolaus, think that this kind of a proportion is called harmonic, because it has the greatest analogy with what is called geometrical harmony; which is the cube, because all its dimensions are mutually equal, and consequently in perfect harmony. Indeed this proportion is revealed in all kinds of cubes; which has always 12 sides, 8 angles, and 6 surfaces.
b.(Cassiodorus, Exp.in Ps.9,p.36) The number 8, which the arithmeticians call the first actual square, has been named, by the Pythagorean Philolaus the name of geometrical harmony, because he thinks he recognizes in it all the hamonic relations.

10. (Stob. Eclogl.I:5:7:p.360) The world is single; it began to form from the centre outwards. Starting from this centre, the top is entirely identical to the base; still you might say that what is above the centre is opposed to what is below it; for, for the base, lowest point would be the centre, as for the top, the highest point would still be the centre; and likewise for the other parts; in fact, in respect to the centre, each one of the opposite points is identical, unless the whole be moved.
b.(Stob.Ecl.l:2l:3:p.468) The prime composite, the One placed in the centre of the sphere is called Hestia.

11. a. (Stob.Ecl.l:22:1:p.488) Philolaus has located the fire in the middle, the centre; he calls it Hestia, of the All, the house [policeipest] of Jupiter, and the mother of the Gods, the altar, the link, the measure of nature. Besides, he locates a second fire, quite at the top, surrounding the world. The centre, says he, is by its nature the first; around it, the ten different bodies carry out their choric dance; these are, the heaven, the planets, lower the sun, and below it the moon ; lower the earth, and beneath this, the anti-earth (a body invented by the Pythagoreans, says Aristotle, Met i: 5) then beneath these bodies the fire of Hestia, in the centre, where it maintains order. The highest part of the Covering, in which he asserts that the elements exist in a perfectly pure condition, is called Olympus, the space beneath the revolutionary circle of Olympus, and where in order are disposed the five planets, the sun and moon, forms the Cosmos world; finally, beneath the latter is the sublunar region, which surrounds the earth, where are the generative things susceptible to change; that is the heaven. The order which manifests in the celestial phenomena is the object of science; the disorder which manifests in the things of becoming, is the object of virtue; the former is perfect, the latter is imperfect. b. (Plut. Plac.Phil.3:ll). The Pythagorean Philolaus located the fire in the centre, it is the Hestia of the All, then the Anti-earth, then the earth we inhabit, placed opposite

the other, and moving circularly; which is the cause that its inhabitants are not visible to ours. c. (Stob.Ecl.l:21:6:p.452). The directing fire, [of] Philolaus, is in the entirely central fire; which the demiurge has placed as a sort of keel [to] serve as foundation to the sphere of the All.

12. (Plut.Plac.Phil.2:5). Philolaus explains destruction by two causes; one is the fire which descends from heaven, the other is the water of the noon, which is driven away therefrom by the circulation of air; the loss of these two stars nourish the world.

13. (Diog.Laert.8:85). Philolaus was the first who said the world moves in a circle; others attribute it to Hivatas of Syracuse. b. (Plut.Plac.Philos.3:7). Some insist that the earth is immovable but the Pythagorean Philolaus says that it moves circularly around the central fire, in an oblique circle like the sun and moon.

14. (Stob.Ecl.l:25:3:p.530) The Pythagorean Philolaus says that the sun is a vitrescent body which receives the light reflected by the fire of the Cosmos, and sends it back to us, after having filtered them, light and heat; so that you might say that there are two suns, the body of the fire which is in the heaven, and the igneous light which emanates therefrom, and reflects itself in a kind of a mirror. Perhaps we might consider as a third light that which, from the mirror in which it reflects, and falls back on us in dispersed rays.

15. (Stob.Eclog.I:26: l:p. 562) Some Pythagoreans, among whom is Philolaus, pretend that the moon's resemblance to the earth consists in its surface being inhabited, like our earth; but by animals and vegetation larger and more beautiful; for the lunar animals are fifteen times larger than ours, and do not evacuate excreta. The day is also fifteen times as long. Others pretend that the apparent form of the noon is only the reflection of the sea, which we inhabit, which passes beyond the circle of fire.

16. (Censorinus, de Die Natal.18). According to the Pythagorean Philolaus there is a year composed of 59 years and 21 intercalary months; he considers that the natural year has 364 and a half days.

17. (Iambl.ad Nicon.Arith.11). Philolaus says that number is the sovereign and autogenic force which maintains the eternal permanence of cosmic things.

18. (Stob.I:3:8). The power, efficacy and essence of number is seen in the decad; it is great, it realizes all its purposes, it is the cause of all effects; the power of the *decad* is the principle and guide of all life, divine, celestial or human into which it is insinuated; without it everything is infinite, obscure, and furtive. Indeed it is the nature of

number which teaches us comprehension, which serves us as guide, which teaches us all things, which would remain impenetrable and unknown for every man, for there is nobody who could get so clear a notion about it, things in themselves, neither in their relations, if there was no number or number-essence. By means of sensation, number instills a certain proportion, and thereby establishes among all things harmonic relations, analogous to the nature of the geometric figure called the *gnomon*; it incorporates intelligible reasons of things, separates them, inidividualises them, both in finite and infinite things. And it is not only in matters pertaining to genii or gods that you may see the force manifested by the nature and power of number, but it is in all its works, in all human thoughts, everywhere indeed, and even in the production of arts and music. The nature of number and harmony are numberless, for what is false has no part in their [-------]; for the principle of error and envy is thoughtless, irrational, infinite nature. Never could error slip into number; for its nature is hostile thereto. Truth is the proper, innate character of number.

b. (Theologoumena, 61). The decad is also named Faith because according to Philolaus, it is by the *decad* and its elements, if utilized energetically and without negligence, that we arrive at a solidly grounded faith about beings. It is also the source of memory, and that is why the *Monad* has been called (Mnemosyne?).

c. (Theon of Smyrna, Platon.Nemn.p.49) The [*Tetractys*] determines every number, including the nature of everything, of the even and the odd, of the mobile and immobile, of good and evil. It has been the subject of long discussions by Archytas, and of Philolaus, in his work on nature.

d. (Lucien, Pro. Laps. Inter. Salut. 5.) Some called the *Tetractys* the great oath of the Pythagoreans, because they considered it the perfect number, or even because it is the principle of health; among them is Philolaus.

19. (Theon of Smyrna, Plat. Math. 4.). Archytas and Philolaus use the terms *monad* and unity interchangeably.

b. (Syrianus, sub init, Comment. in Arist. Net. I.xiv?). You must not suppose that the philosophers begin by principles supposed to be opposite; they know the principle above these two elements, as Philolaus acknowledges when saying that it is God who hypostasizes the finite and the infinite. He shows that it is by the limit, that every coordinate series of things further approaches Unity, and that it is by infinity that the lower series is produced. Thus even above these two principles they posited the unique and separate cause distinguished by all of its excellence. This is the clause which Archinetus called the cause before the cause and which Philolaus vehemently insists is the principle of all, and of which Brontinus says that in power and dignity it surpasses all reason and essence.

c. (Iambl. ad Nicom. Arith. p109). In the formation of square numbers by addition, unity is as it were the starting-post from which one starts, and also the end whither one returns; for if one places the numbers in the form of a double procession, and you see them grow from unity to the root of the square, and the root is like the turning-point where the horses turn to go back through similar numbers to unity, as in the square of 5.

For example:

```
1-----2-----3-----4
          -----5 = added, 25
1-----2-----3-----4
```

It is not the same with rectangular numbers; if, just as if in the *gnomon*, one adds to any number the sum of the even, then the number two will alone seem to receive and stand addition and without the number two it will not be possible to produce rectangular numbers. If you set out the naturally increasing series of numbers in the order of the double race-track, then unity, being the principle of everything according to Philolaus (for it is he who said, "unity the principle of everything"), will indeed present itself as the barrier, the starting point which produces the rectangular numbers, but it will not be the goal or limit where the series returns, and comes back; it is not unity, but the number 2 which will fulfill this function. Thus:

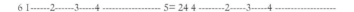

6 1------2------3-----4 ----------------- 5= 24 4 --------2-----3-----4 ------------------

d. (Ohilo, Mundi Opif .24). Philolaus confirms what I have just said by the following words; "He who commands and governs everything is a God who is single, eternally existing, immutable, self-identical, different from other things.

e. (Athenag.Legat.pro Christo). Philolaus says that all things are by God kept as if in captivity, and thereby implies, that He is single and superior to matter.

20. (Proclus, ad Euclid. Elem.I.33). Even among the Pythagoreans we find different angles consecrated to the different divinities, as did Philolaus, who devoted to some the angle of the triangle, to others the angle of the rectangle, to others other angles, and sometimes the same

to several. The Pythagoreans say that the triangle is the absolute principle of generation of begotten things, and of their form; that is why Timaeus says that the reasons of physical being, and of the regular formation of the elements are triangular; indeed, they have the three dimensions, in unity they gather the elements which in themselves are absolutely divided and changing; they are filled with the infinity characteristic of matter, and above the material beings they form bonds that indeed are frail. That is why triangles are bounded by straight lines and are [have] angles which unite the lines, and are their [ends]. Philolaus was therefore right in devoting the angle of the triangle to four divinities, [Cronos], Hades, Mars and Bacchus, under these names combining the fourfold disposition of the elements, which refers to the superior part of the Universe, starting from the sky, or sections of the zodiac. Indeed, Cronos presides over everything humid and cold essence; Mars, over everything fiery; Hades contains everything terrestrial, and Dionysius directs the generation of wet and warm things, symboled by wine, which is liquid and warm. These four divinities divide their secondary operations, but they remain united; that is why Philolaus, by attributing to them one angle only, wished to express this power of unification.

The Pythagoreans also claim that, in preference to the quadrilateral, the tetragone bears the divine impress; and by it they express perfect order....For the property of being straight imitates the power of immutability; and equality represents that of permanence; for motion is the result of inequality; and rest, that of equality. Those are the causes of the organisation of the being that is solid in its totality, and of its pure and immovable essence. They were therefore right to express it symbolically by the figure the tetragon. Besides, Philolaus, with another stroke of genius, calls the angle of the tetragon. that of Rhea, of Dimeter, and of Hestia...For considering the earth as a tetragon, and noting that this element possesses the property of continuousness, as we learned it from Timaeus, and the earth receives all that drips from the divinities and also the generative powers that they contain, he was right in consecrating the angle of the tetragon to these divinities which procreate life. Indeed, some of them call the earth Hestia and Demeter, and claim that it partakes of Rhea, in its entirety, and that Rhea contains all the begotten causes. That is why, in obscure language, he says, that the angle of the tetragon contains the single power which produces the unity of these divine creations.

And we must not forget that Philolaus assigns the angle of the triangle to four divinities, and the angle of the tetragon to three, thereby indicating their penetrative faculty, whereby they influence each other mutually; showing how all things participate in all things, the odd things in the even and the even in the odd. The *triad* and the *tetrad*, participating in the generative and creative beings, contain the whole regular organization of begotten beings. Their product is the *dodecad*, which ends in the single monad, the sovereign principle of Jupiter; for Philolaus says that the angle of the *dodecagon* belongs to Jupiter, because in unity Jupiter contains the entire of the *dodecad*.

21. (Theolog.Arithm. p.56). After the mathematical magnitude which by its three dimensions or intervals realizes the number four, Philolaus shows us the being manifesting in number five quality and color, in the number six the soul and life; in the number seven, reason, health, and what he calls light; then he adds that love, friendship, prudence, and reflexion are communicated to beings by the number eight.

b. (Theolog.Arithm. p.22). There are four principles of the reasonable animal, as Philolaus in his work on Nature, the skull, the heart, the navel, and the sexual organs. The head is the seat of reason, the heart, that of the soul or life, and sensation; the navel, the principle of the facility of striking roots and reproducing the first being; the sexual organs, of the faculty of projecting the sperm, and procreating. The skull contains the principle of man, the heart of the animal, the navel that of the plant, the sexual organs that of all living beings, for these grow and produce offspring.

c. (Stob.Edog.Physic.l:2:3: p.10). There are bodies five in the sphere; fire, water, earth, air; and the circle of the sphere, which makes the fifth.

22. (Stob.Ecog.l:2:2: p.418). From the Pythagorean Philolaus, drawn from his book *On the [Soul]*. He insists that the world is indestructible. Here is what he says in his book *On the Soul*. That is why the world remains eternally, because it cannot be destroyed by any other, nor spontaneously destroy itself. Neither within it, nor without it can be found a force greater than itself; able to destroy it. The world has existed from all eternity, and will remain eternally, because it is single, governed by a principle whose nature is similar to its own, and whose force is omnipotent and sovereign. Besides, the single world is continuous, and endowed with a natural respiration, moving eternally in a circle, having the principle of motion and change; one of its parts is immovable, the other is changing; the immovable part extends from the

soul to the moon, that embraces everything, to the moon; and the changing part from the moon to the earth; or, since the mover has been acting since eternity, and continues his action eternally, and since the changeable part receives its manner of being from the Mover who acts thereon, it necessarily results thence that one of the parts of the World ever impresses motion, and that the other ever receives it passively; the one is entirely the domain of reason and the soul, the other of generation and change; the one is anterior in power, and superior, the other is posterior and subordinate. The composite of these two things, the divine eternally in motion and of generation ever changing; is the World. That is why one is right in saying that the World is the eternal energy of God, and of becoming which obeys the laws of changing nature. The one remains eternally in the same state, self-identical, the remainder constitutes the domain of plurality, which is born and perishes. But nevertheless the things that perish save their essence and form, thanks to generation, which reproduces the identical form of the father who has begotten and fashioned them.

23. (Claudian Mamort. De Statu. Anim.2: p.7). The soul is introduced and associated with the body by number and by a harmony simultaneously immortal and incorporeal....The soul cherishes its body, because without it the soul cannot feel; but when death has separated the soul therefrom, the soul lives an incorporeal existence in the cosmos.

b. (Macrob. Dream of Scipio, I:04). Plato says that the soul is a self-moving essence; Xenocrates defines the soul as a self-moving number; Aristotle calls it an *entelechy*; and Pythagoras and Philolaus, a harmony.

c. (Olympiod. ad Plat. Phaed. p 150). Philolaus opposed suicide, because it was a Pythagorean precept not to lay down the burden but to help others carry theirs; namely, that you must assist, and not hinder it.

d. (Clem.Strom. 3: p.433). It will help us to remember the Pythagorean Philolaus's utterance that the ancient theologians and divines claimed that the soul is bound to the body as a punishment, and is buried in it as in a tomb.

24. (Arist.Eth.Eud. 2:8). As Philolaus has said, there are some reasons stronger than us. b. (Iambl. ad Nicom. Arithm. I:25). I shall later have a better opportunity to consider how, in raising a number to its square, by the position of the simple component unities, we arrive at [very] evident propositions, naturally, and not by any law, as says Philolaus.

25. (Sext. Empir, Adv.Math. 7:92: p. 388). Anaxagoras has said how reason in general is the faculty discerning and judging; the

Pythagoreans also agree that it is Reason, not reason in general, but the Reason that develops in men by the study of mathematics, as Philolaus used to say and insist that if this Reason is capable of undestanding All, it is only that its essence is kindred with this nature, for it is in the nature of things that the similar be understood by the similar.

26. (Laurent.Lydus,de Mens.p 16; Cedrenus --; 169b). Philolaus was therefore right in calling it a *decad*, because it receives (pun) the Infinite, and Prpheus was right in calling it the branch, because it is the branch from which issue all the numbers, as do many branches.

b. (Cedrenus, l.p72). Philolaus was therefore right to say that the number seven was motherless.

c. (Cedrenus, l.p.23). Philolaus was therefore right to call the spouse of Kronos, the *Dyad*.

Biography of ARCHYTAS [375 B.C.]
by DIOGENES LAERTES [180 A.D.]
(From Chaignet)

Archytas of Tarentum, son of Mnesagoras, or of Hestius, according to Aristoxenus, also was a Pythagorean. It was he who, by a letter, saved Plato from death threatened by Dionysius. He possessed all the virtues, so that, being the admiration of the crowd, he was seven times named general, in spite of the law which forbad re-election after one year. Plato wrote him two letters, in response to this one of Archytas:

"Greetings. It is fortunate for you that you have recovered from your illness; for I have heard of it not only from you, but also from [Lamiscus]. I have busied myself about those notes, and took a trip into Lucania, where I met descendants of Ocellus. I have in my possession the treatises *on Law and Royalty*, *on Holiness*, and *on the Origin of All Things*; and I am sending them to you. The others could not be discovered. Should they be found, they will be sent to you."

Plato answered:

"Greetings. I am delighted to have received the works which you have sent me, and I acknowledge a great admiration for him who wrote them. He seems to be worthy of his ancient and glorious ancestors, who are said to be [Tyreans] and among the number of those Trojans who emigrated under the leadership of Laomedon, [all] worthy people, as the legend proves. Those works of mine about which you wrote me are not in a sufficient state of perfection, but I send them such as they are. Both of us are in perfect agreement on the subject of protecting them. No use to renew the request. May your health improve!"

Such are these two letters. There were four Archytases. The first, of whom we have just spoken. The second, from Mytilene, was a musician; the third wrote about agriculture; fourth is an author of epigrams. Some mention a fifth; an architect, who left a treatise on mechanics, beginning as follows: This book contains what I have been taught by the Carthaginian Teucer.

The musician is said to have made this joke. Being reproached for not advertising himself more, he said: It is my instrument, which speaks for me. Aristoxenus claims that the philosopher Archytas was never vanquished when he commanded. Once, overcome by envy, he had been obliged to resign his command; and his fellow-citizens were immediately conquered. He was the first who methodically applied the principles of mathematics to mechanics; who imparted an organic motion to a geometric figure, by the section of the semi-cylinder seeking two means that would be proportional, to double the cube. He also first, by geometry discovered the properties the cube, as Plato records in the Republic.

SECTION I
METAPHYSICAL FRAGMENTS
(Stob.Ec.Phys. I:-?13)

I. There are necessarily two principles of beings; the one containing the series of beings organized, and finished, the other, of unordered and unfinished beings. That one which is susceptible of being expressed, by speech, and which can be explained, both embraces beings, and determines and organises the non-being.

For every time that it approaches the things of becoming, it orders them, and measures them, and makes them participate in the essence and form of the universal. On the contrary, the series of beings which escape speech and reason, injures ordered things and destroys those which aspire to essence and becoming; whenever it approaches them, it assimilates them to its own nature.

But since there are two principles of things of an opposite character, the one the principle of good, and the other the principle of evil, there are therefore also two reasons, the one of beneficent nature, the other of maleficent nature.

That is why the things that owe their existence to art, and also those which owe it to nature, must above all participate in these two principles; form and substance.

The form is the cause of essence; substance is the substrate which [it] receives the form. Neither can substance alone participate in form, by itself; nor can form by itself apply itself to substance; there must therefore exist another cause which moves the substance of things; and forms them. This cause is primary, as regards substance, and the most excellent of all. Its most suitable name is God.

There are therefore three principles: God, the substance of things, and form. God is the artist, the mover; the substance is the matter, the moved ; the essence is what you might call the art, and that to which the substance is brought by the mover. But since the mover contains forces which are self-contrary, those of simple bodies, and as the contraries are in need of a principle harmonizing and unifying them, it must necessarily receive its efficacious virtues and proportions from the numbers, and all that is manifested in numbers and geometric forms; virtues and proportions capable of binding and uniting into form the contraries that exist in the substance of things. For, by itself, substance is formless; only after having been moved towards form does it become

186

form, and receives the rational relations of order. Likewise, if movement exists, besides the thing moved, there must exist a prime mover; there must therefore be three principles; the substance of things, the form, and the principle that moves itself, and which by its power is the first; not only must this principle be an intelligence, it must be above intelligence, and we call it God.

Evidently the relation of equality applies to the being which can be defined to language, and reason. The relation of inequality applies to the irrational being; and cannot be fixed by language; it is substance; that is why all begetting and destruction take place in substance, and do not occur without it.

2. In short, the philosophers began only by so to speak contrary principles; but above these elements they knew another superior one, as is testified to by Philolaus, who says that God has produced, and realized the finite and infinite, and shown that at the limit is attached the whole series which has a greater affinity with the One, and to Infinity, the one that is below. Thus, above these two principles they have posited a unifying cause, superior to everything which, according to Archenetus, is the cause before the cause, and, according to Philolaus, the universal principle.

3a. Which unity are you referring to? Of supreme unity, or of the infinitely small unity that you can find in the parts? The Pythagoreans distinguished between the Unity and the *Monad*, as says Archytas ; Unity and the *Monad* have a natural affinity but yet they differ.

3b. Archytas and Philolaus indiscriminately call the unity a *monad*, and *monad* a unity. The majority however add to the same *monad*, the distinction of first *monad*, for there is a *monad* which is not the first, and which is posterior to the *monad* in itself, and to unity.

3c. Pythagoras said that the human soul was a tetragon with right angles. Archytas, on the contrary, instead of defining the soul by the tetragon, did so by a circle, because the soul is a self-mover, and consequently, the prime mover; but this [is] a circle or a sphere.

3d. Plato and Archytas and the other Pythagoreans claim that there are three parts in the soul; reason, courage and desire.

4. The beginning of the knowledge of beings is in the things that produce themselves. Of these some are intelligible, and others sensible; the former are immovable, the latter are moved. The criterion of intelligible things is the World; that of sensible things is sensation.

Of the things that do not manifest in things themselves, some are science, the others, opinion; science is immovable; opinion is movable.

We must, besides, admit these three things; the subject that judges, the object that is judged, and the rule by which that object is judged. What judges, is the mind, or sensation; that is judged, is the *logos* or rational essence; the rule of judgment is the act itself which occurs in the being; whether intelligible or sensible. The mind is the judge of essence, whether it tends towards an intelligible being, or a sensible one. When reason seeks intelligible things, it tends towards an intelligible element; when it seeks things of sense, it tends towards their element. Hence come, those false graphic representation in figures and numbers seen in geometry, those researches in causes and probable ends, whose object are beings subject to becoming, and moral acts, ... physiology or politics. It is while tending towards the intelligible element that reason recognizes that harmony is in the double relation; but sensation alone attests that this double relation is concordant. In mechanics, the object of science is figures, numbers, proportions; -- namely rational proportions; the effects are perceived by sensation; for you can neither study nor know them outside of the matter or movement. In short it s impossible to know the reason of an individual thing, unless you have preliminarily by the mind grasped the essence of the individual thing. The knowledge of the existence, and of quality, belongs to reason and sensations; to reason, whenever we effect a thing's demonstration by a *syllogism* whose conclusion is inevitable; to sensation, when the latter is the criterion of a thing's essence.

5. Sensation occurs in the body, reason in the soul. The former is the principle of sensible things, the latter, of intelligible ones. Popular measures are number, length, the foot, weight and equilibrium; the scales; while the rule and the measure of straightness in both vertical and longitudinal directions is the right angle.

Thus sensation is the principle and measure of the bodies; reason is the principle and measure of intelligible things. The former is the principle of beings that are intelligible and naturally primary; the latter, of sense-objects, and naturally secondary. Reason is the principle of our soul; sensation, the principle of our body. The mind is the judge of the noblest things; sensation, of the most useful. Sensation was created in view of our bodies, and to serve them; reason in view of the soul, and to initiate wisdom therein. Reason is the principle of science; sensation, of opinion. The latter derives its activity from sensible things; the former from the intelligible. Sensible objects participate in movement and change; intelligible objects participate in immutability and eternity. There is no analogy between sensation and reason; for sensation's object is the sensible, which moves, changes, and never remains self-identical; therefore as you can see it, it improves or deteriorate. Reason's object is the intelligible; whose essence is immobility, wherefore in the intelligible we cannot conceive of either more nor less, better or worse; and just as reason sees the primary being, and the (cosmic) model, so sensation sees the image, and the copied. Reason sees man in himself; sensation sees in them the circle of the sun, and the forms of artificial objects. Reason is perfectly simple and indivisible, as unity, and the point; it is the same with intelligible beings.

The idea is neither the limit nor the frontier of the body; it is only the figure of being, that by which the being exists, while sensation has parts, and is divisible.

Some beings are perceived by sensation, others by opinion, others by science, and others by reason.

The bodies that offer resistance are sensible; opinion knows those that participate in the ideas, and are its images, so to speak. Thus some particular man participates in the idea of man, and this triangle, in the triangle-idea. The object of science are the necessary accidents of ideas; thus the object of geometry is the properties of the figures; reason knows the ideas themselves, and the principles of the sciences and of their objects; for example, the circle, the triangle, ,and the pure sphere in itself. Likewise, in us, in our souls, there are four kinds of knowledge, pure thought, science, opinion and sensation; two are principles of knowledge (thought and sensation); two are its purpose, science and opinion. It is always the similar which is capable of knowing the similar; reason knows the intelligible things; science, the knowable things; opinion, conjecturable things; sensation, sensible things.

That is why thought must rise from things that are sensible, to the conjecturable ones and from these to the knowable, and on to the intelligible and he who wishes to know the truth about these objects, must in a harmonious grouping combine all these means and objects of knowledge. This being established, you might represent them under the image of a line divided into two equal parts, each of which would be similarly divided; if we separate the sensible, dividing it into two parts, in the same proportion, the one will be clearer, the other obscurer. One of the sections of the of the sensible contains images of things, such as you see reflected in water, or mirrors; the second represents the plants and animals of which the former are images. Similarly dividing the intelligible, the different kinds of sciences will represent the images; for the students of geometry begin by establishing by hypothesis, the odd and the even, figures, three kinds of angles, and from these hypotheses deduce their science; as to the things themselves, they leave them aside, as if they knew them, though they not cannot account for them to themselves or to others; they employ sensible things as images, but these things are neither the object nor the end proposed in their researches and reasonings; which pursue only things in themselves, such as the diameter or square. The second section is that of the intelligible; object of dialectics. It really makes no hypotheses, positing principles whence it rises to arrive to the unconditioned, to the universal principle; then, by an inverse movement, grasping that principle, it descends to the end of the reasoning, without employing any sensible object, exclusively using pure ideas. By these four divisions, you can also analyse the soul-states, and give the highest the name of thought, reasoning to the second, faith to the third, and imagination to the fourth.

6. Archytas, at the beginning of his book *on Wisdom* gives this advice; in all human things wisdom is as superior as sight is to all the other senses of the body, as mind is superior to soul, as the sun is superior to the stars. Of all the senses, sight is the one that extends furthest in its sphere of action, and gives us the most ideas. Mind, being supreme, accomplishes its legitimate operation by reason and reasoning; it is like sight, and the power of the noblest objects; the sun is the eye and soul of natural things, for it is through it that they are all seen, begotten, and thought; through it the beings produced by root or seed, are fed, developed, and endowed with sensation. Of all beings, man is the wisest; by far; for he is able to contemplate beings, and to acquire knowledge and understanding of all. That is why divinity has engraved in him, and has revealed to him the system of speech, which extends to everything, a system in which are classified all the beings, kinds of being, and the meanings of nouns and verbs. For the specialised seats of the voice are the pharynx, the mouth and the nose. As man is naturally organized to produce sounds, through which nouns and verbs are expressed and formed, likewise he is naturally destined to contemplate the notions contained in the visible objects; such, in my view, is the purpose for which man has been created, and was born; and for which he received from God his organs and faculties.

Man is born and is created to know the essence of universal nature; and precisely the function of wisdom is to possess and contemplate the intelligence manifested in the beings.

The object of wisdom is no particular being, but all the beings, absolutely; and it should not begin to seek the principles of an individual being, but the principles common to all. The object of wisdom is all the beings, as the object of sight is all visible things. The function of wisdom is to see all the beings in their totality, and to know their universal attributes; and that is how wisdom discovers the principles of all beings.

He who is capable of analysing all the species, and to trace and group them, by an inverse operation, into one single principle, he seems to me the wisest, and the closest to the truth; he seems to have found that sublime observatory from the peak of which he may observe God, and all the things that belong to the series and order of divine things; being master of this royal road, his mind will be able to rush forwards, and arrive at the end of the career, uniting principles to the purposes of things, and knowing that God is the principle, the middle and the end of all things made according to the rules of justice and right reason.

SECTION II
PHYSICAL AND MATHEMATICAL FRAGMENTS

7. As Eudemus reports, Archytas used to ask this question: If I was situated at the extreme and immovable limit of the world, could I, or not, extend a wand outside of it? To say I could not, is absurd; but if I can, there must be something, outside of the world, be it body or space; and in whatever manner we reason, by the same reasoning we will ever return to this limit. I will still place myself there, and ask, is there anything else on which I may place my wand. Therefore, the infinite exists; if it is a body, our proposition is demonstrated; if it its space, place is that in which a body could be; and if it exists potentially, we will have to place it among, classify it among the eternal things, and the infinite will then be a body and a place.

8. The essence of place is that all other things are in it, while itself is not in anything. For if it was in a place, there would be a place in a place, and that would continue to infinity. All other beings must therefore be in place, and place in nothing. Its relation to things is the same as limit to limited things; for the place of the entire world is the limit of all things.

9a. Some say that time is the sphere of the world; such was the sentiment of the Pythagoreans, according to those who had no doubt heard Archytas give this general definition of time: "Time is the interval of the nature of all."

9b. The divine Iamblichus, in the first book of his commentaries on the Categories, said that Archytas thus defined time: "It is the number of movement, or in general the interval of the nature of all."

9c. We must combine these two definitions, and recognise time as both continuous and discrete, though it is properly continuous. Iamblichus claims that Archytas taught the distinction of time physical, and time psychic; so at least Iamblichus interpreted Archytas; but we must recognise that there, and often elsewhere, he adds to his commentaries to explain matters.

10. The general proper essence of "When-ness" and time is to be indivisible and insubstantial. For, being indivisible, the present time has passed, while expressing it, and thinking of it; naught remains of it, becoming continuously the same, it never subsists numerically, but only specifically. In fact, the actually present time and the future are not identical with former time. For the one has past, and is no more; the other passes while being produced and thought. Thus the present is

never but a bond; it perpetually becomes, changes, and perishes; but nevertheless it remains identical in its own kind.

In fact, every present is without parts, and indivisible; it is the term of past time, the beginning to come; just as in a broken line, the point where the break occurs becomes the beginning of a line, and the end of the other. Time is continuous, and not discrete as are number, speech and harmony. In speech, the syllables are parts, and distinct parts; in the harmony, they are the sounds; in number; the unities. The line, place and space are continuous; if they are divided, their parts form common sections. For the line divides into points, the surface into lines, the solid into surfaces. Therefore time is continuous. In fact, there was no nature, when time was not; and there was no movement, when the present was not. But the present has always been, it will always be, and will never fail; it changes perpetually, and becomes an other according to the number, but remains the same according to kind. The line differs from the other continua, in that if you divide the line, place, and space, its parts will subsist; but in time, the past has perished, and the future will. That is why either time does absolutely not exist, or it hardly exists, and has but an insensible existence. For of its parts one, the past, is no more; the future is not yet, how then could the present, without parts and indivisible, possess true reality?

11. Plato says that the movement is the great and the small, the non-being. the unequal and all that reduces to these; like Archytas we had better say that it is a cause.

12. Why do all natural bodies take the spherical form? Is it, as said Archytas, because the natural movement is the proportion of equality? For everything moves in proportion; and this proportion of equality is the only one which, when it occurs, produces circles and spheres because it returns on itself.

13. He who knows must have learned from another, or have found his knowledge by himself. The science that you learn from another, is as you might say, exterior; what you find by yourself belongs to ourselves individually. To find without seeking is something difficult and rare; to find what one is seeking is commodious and easy; to ignore, and seek what you ignore, is impossible.

14. The Pythagorean opinion about sciences to me seems correct, and they seen to show an exact judgment about each of then. Having known how to form a just idea of the nature of all, they should have likewise seen the essential nature of the parts. They have left us certain evident theories about arithmetic, geometry, spherics; also about music;

for all these sciences seem to be kindred, in fact, the first two kinds of being are indistinguishable.

15a. First they have seen that it was not possible that there should be any noise, unless there was a shock of one body against another; they said. There is a shock when moving bodies meet and strike each other. The bodies moved in the air in an opposite direction and those that are moved without equal swiftness, -- in the same direction, -- the first, when overtaken, make a noise, because struck. Many of these noises are not susceptible of being perceived by our organs; some because of the slightness of the shock, the others because of their too great distance from us, some even because of the very excess of their intensity; for noises too great do not enter into our ears, as one cannot introduce anything into jars with too narrow an opening when one pours in too much at a time.

Of the sounds that fall within the range of our senses, same, -- those that come quickly from the bodies struck, seem shrill; those that arrive slowly and feebly, seem of low pitch. In fact, when one agitates some object slowly and feebly, the shock produces a low pitch; if the waving is [done] quickly and with energy, the sound is shrill. This not the only proof of the fact; which we can prove when we speak or sing; when we wish to speak loud and high, we use a great force of breath. So also something thrown; if you throw them hard, they go far; if you throw then without energy, they fall near, for they air yields more to bodies moved with much force, than to those thrown with little. This phenomenon is also reproduced in the sound of the voice; for the sounds produced by an energetic breath are shrill while those produced by a feeble breath are weak and low pitch. This same observation can be seen in the force of a signal given from any place; if you pronounce it loud, it can be heard far; if you pronounce the same signal low, we do not hear it, even from near. So also in flutes, the breath emitted by the mouth and which presents itself to the holes nearest the mouthpiece, produces a shriller sound, because the impulsive force is greater, further, they are of lower pitch. It is therefore evident that the swiftness of the movement produces shrillness and slowness, lower pitch. The same thing in seen in the magic tops which are spun in the mysteries; those that move slowly produce a low pitch, while those that move quickly with force [give] a shrill noise. Let us yet adduce the reed: if you close the lower opening, and blow into it, it will produce a certain sound; and if you stop it in the centre, or in the front, the sound will be shrill. For the same breath traversing a long space weakens, while traversing a shorter, it remains of the same power. After having developed this opinion that the movement of the voice is measured by the intervals, he resumes his discussion, saying, that the shrill sounds are the result of a swifter movement, the lower sounds, of a slower movement, this is a fact which numerous experiments demonstrate clearly.

15b. Eudoxus and Archytas believed that the reasons of the agreement of the sounds was in the numbers; they agree in thinking that these reasons consist in the movements, the shrill movement being quick, because the agitation of the air is continuous, and the vibration more rapid; the low pitch movement being slow, because it is calmer.

16. Explaining himself about the means, Archytas writes: In music there are three means; the first is the arithmetical mean, the second is the geometrical, the third is the subcontrary mean, which is called harmonic. The mean is arithmetical, when the three terms are in a relation of analogical excess, that is to say, when the difference between the first and second is the same as between second and third; in this proportion, the relation of the greater terms is smaller, and the relation of the smaller is greater. The geometric mean exists when the first term is to the second, as the second is to the third; here the relation of the greater is identical with the relation of the smaller. The subcontrary mean, which we call harmonic, exists when the first term exceeds the second by a fraction of itself, identically with the fraction by which the second exceeds the third; in this proportion, the relation of the greatest terms is greater, and that of the smaller, smaller.

SECTION III
ETHICAL FRAGMENTS

17. We must first know that the good man is not thereby
necessarily happy, but that the happy man is necessarily good; for the
happy man is he who deserves praise and congratulations; the good man
deserves only praise. We praise a man because of his virtue, we
congratulate him because of his success. The good man is such because
of the goods that proceed from virtue; the happy man is such because of
the goods that come from fortune. From the good man you cannot take
his virtue; sometimes the happy man loses his good fortune. The power
of virtue depends on nobody; that of happiness, on the contrary, is
dependent. Long diseases, the loss of our senses cause to fade the flower
of our happiness [and luck].

2. God differs from the good man in that God, not only possesses a
perfect virtue, purified from all mortal affection, but enjoys a virtue
whose power is indefectible, independent, as suits the majesty and
magnificence of his works. Man, on the contrary, not only possesses an
inferior virtue, because of the mortal constitution of his nature, but even
sometimes by the very abundance of his goods, now by the force of
habit, by the vice of nature, or from other causes, he is incapable of
attaining the perfection of the good.

3. The good man, in my opinion, is he who knows how to act
properly in serious circumstances and occasions; he will therefore know
how to support good and bad fortune; in a brilliant and glorious
condition, he will show himself worthy if it, and if fortune happens to
change, he will know how to accept properly his actual fate. In short,
the good man is he who, in every occasion, and according to the
circumstances, well plays his part, and knows how to fit to it not only
himself, but also those who have confidence on him, and are associated
with his fortunes.

4. Since amidst the goods, some are desirable for themselves, and
not for anything else, and others are desirable for something else, and
not for themselves, there must necessarily exist a third kind of goods,
which are desirable both for themselves and for other things. Which are
the goods naturally desirable for themselves, and not for anything else?
Evidently, it is happiness; for it is the end on account of which we seek
everything else, while we seek it only for itself, and not in view of
anything else.

Secondly, which are the goods chosen for something else, and not for themselves? Evidently those that are useful, and which are the means of procuring the real goods, which thus become the causes of the goods desirable for themselves; for instance, the bodily fatigues, the exercises, the tests which procure health; reading, meditation, the studies which procure virtues, and the quality of honesty. Last, which are those goods which are both desirable for themselves, and for something else? The virtues, and the habitual possession of virtues, the resolutions of the soul, the actions, and in short anything pertaining to the possession of the beautiful. Thus what is to be desired for itself, and not for anything itself, this is the only good. Now what we seek both for itself and for something else is divided into three classes; the one whose object is the soul, the body, and external goods. The first contains the virtues of the soul, the second the advantages of the body; the third, friends, glory, honor and wealth. Likewise with the goods that are desirable only for something else; one part of them procures goods for the soul, the other which regards the body, procures goods for it; the external goods furnish wealth, glory, honor and friendship.

We can prove that it is characteristic of virtue to be desirable for itself, as follows: In fact, if the naturally inferior goods, I mean those of the body, are by us sought for themselves, and if the soul is better than the body, it is evident that we like the goods of the soul for themselves, and not for the results that they might produce.

5. In human life there are three circumstances: prosperity, adversity, and intermediary comfort. Since the good man who possesses virtue and practises it, practises it in these three circumstances, either in adversity, or prosperity, or comfort, since besides in adversity he is unhappy, in prosperity he is happy and in comfort he is not happy; -- it is evident that happiness is nothing else than the use of virtue in prosperity. I speak here of human happiness. Man is not only a soul, he is also a body; the living being is a composite of both; and man also; for if the body is an instrument of the soul, it is as much a part of the man, as the soul. That is why, among the goods, some belong to the man and others belong to his component parts. The good of man is happiness; amidst its integral parts, the soul's goods are prudence, courage, justice temperance; the body's are beauty, health, good disposition of its members and the perfect condition of its senses. The wealth, glory, honor, nobility, naturally superfluous advantages of man, and naturally subordinate to the superior goods.

The inferior goods serve as satellites to the superior goods; friendship, glory, wealth are the satellites of the body and soul; health, strength and sense-perfection are satellites of the soul; prudence, courage, justice, temperance are the satellites of the reason of the soul; reason is the satellite of God; his is omnipotent, the supreme master. It is for these goods the other must exist; toe the army obeys the general, [as] sailors to the pilot, the world to God, the [soul] to reason, the happy life to prudence. For prudence is nothing that the science of the happy [---e], or the science of the goods which belong to [--an] nature.

6. To God belong happiness and the happy life;[--] cannot possess but a grouping of science, virtue and prosperity forming a single body. Call wisdom the science for the Gods and [genius]; prudence, the science of human things, the science of life; for science should be the name of virtues which rest on reasons and demonstrations, and moral virtue, the excellent habit of the irrational part of the soul, which makes you move; the name of certain qualities corresponding to our habits, namely the names of liberals, of just men, and of temperate people; and I call prosperity this affluence of goods which we re[quire] without reason, without reason being their cause. Then since virtue and science depend on us, and prosperity does not depend thereon, since happiness consists in the contemplation and practice of good things, and since contemplation and action when they meet obstacles, lend us a necessary support when they go by an easy road, they bring us distraction and happiness; since after all it is prosperity that gives us these benefits, it is evident that happiness is nothing else than the use of virtue in prosperity.

7. Man's relations with prosperity resemble a healthy and vigorous human body; he also can stand heat and cold, raise a great burden, and easily bear many other miseries.

8. Since happiness is the use of virtue in prosperity, let us speak of virtue and prosperity, the latter first. Some goods, such as virtue, are not subject to excess; for excess is impossible in virtue, for one can never be too decent a man; indeed, virtue's measure is duty, and is the habit of duty in practical life. Prosperity is subject to excess and lack, which excesses produce certain evils, disturbing man from his usual mood, so as to oppose him to virtue; this is not only the case with prosperity, but other more numerous causes also produce this effect. You need not be surprised at seeing in the hall certain impudent artists, who neglect true art, misleading the ignorant by a false picture; but do you suppose that this race does not exist as regards virtue? On the contrary, the greater

and more beautiful virtue is, the more do people feign to adorn themselves with it. There are indeed many things which dishonor the appearance of virtue; first are the deceivers who simulate it, others are the natural passions which accompany it, and sometimes twist the dispositions of the soul into a contrary direction; others are the bad habits which the body has rooted in us, or have been ingrained in us by youth, age, prosperity, adversity, or a thousand other circumstances. Wherefore we must not at all be surprised at entirely wrong judgments, because the true nature of our soul has has been falsified within us. Just as we see an artist who is excellent make errors in works we are examining; or the general, the pilot or the painter and the like may make errors without our detracting from their talent, so we must not call unworthy him who has had a moment of weakness, nor among the worthy a man who has done no more than a single action; but in respect to the evil, we must consider chance, and for the good, of error, and to make an equitable and just judgment, and not regard a single circumstance, or a single period of time, but the whole life.

Just as the body suffers from both excess and lack, but as nevertheless the excess and so-called superfluities naturally produce the greatest diseases, so the soul suffers of both prosperity and adversity when they arrive at wrong times, and yet the greatest evils come from so-called absolute prosperity that is absolute because like wine it intoxicates the reason of the worthy.

9. That is why it is not adversity but prosperity which is the hardest to stand properly. All men, when they are in adversity, at least greater part of them, seem moderate and modest; and in good fortune, ambitious, vain and proud. For adversity is apt to moderate the soul, and concentrate it; while on the contrary prosperity excites it and puffs it up; that is why the wretches are docile to advice, and prudent in conduct, while the happy are bold and venturesome.

10. There is therefore a measure and limit of prosperity; the one that the worthy man should desire to have as auxiliary in the accomplishment or his actions; just as there is a measure in the size of the ship, and in the length of the tiller; which permits the experienced pilot to traverse an immense extent of sea, and to carry through a great voyage.

The result of excess of prosperity, even among worthy people, is that the soul loses leadership, to prosperity; just as too bright, a light dazzles the eyes, so too great a prosperity dazzles the reason of the soul. Enough about prosperity.

18. I insist that virtue is sufficient to preclude unhappiness, that badness precludes happiness, if we know how properly to judge of the genuine condition of the soul in these two conditions; for the evil is necessarily always unhappy, whether in abundance, -- which he it does not know how properly to judge use, -- or in poverty; just as a blind man is always, whether he is in brilliant light or in darkness. But the worthy man is not always happy; for happiness does not consist in the possession of virtue, but its use; just as a man who sees does not see all the time; he will not see without light.

Life is as it were divided into two roads; the rougher one, followed by patient Ulysses, and the more agreeable one followed by Nestor; I mean that virtue desires the one, but can also follow the other. But nature cries aloud that happiness is life desirable in itself, whose state is assured, because one can realize one's purposes in it, so that if life is traversed by things one has not desired, one is not happy, without however being absolutely unhappy. Therefore be not so bold as to insist that the worthy man is exempt from, sickness, and suffering; dare not to say that he does not know pain; for if the body is allowed some causes of pain, the soul should also be allowed some. The griefs of the insane lack reason and measure while those of the wise are contained within the measure which reason gives to everything; but this so advertised insensibility enervates the character of generosity of virtue, when it stands trials, great sorrows, when it is exposed to death, suffering and poverty; for it is easy to support small sorrows. You must therefore practice the "metriopathy," or sorrow-standardization; so as to avoid the insensibility just as much as the over-sensibility to pain, and not in words to boast about our strength above the measure of our human nature.

19. We might define philosophy as the desire of knowing and understanding things in themselves, joined with practical virtue, inspired and realized by the love of science.

The beginning of philosophy is the science of nature; the middle, practical life; and the end, science itself. It is fortunate to have been well born, to have received a good education, to have been accustomed to obey a just rule and to have habits conformable to nature. One must also have been exercised in virtue, and have been educated by wise parents, governors and masters. It is fine to impose the role of duty on one's self, to have no need of constraint, to be docile to those who give us good advice about life, and science. For a fortunate disposition of nature, and a good education are often more powerful than lessons to bring us to the good; its only lack would be the efficacious light of reason, which science gives us. Two rival directions of life contend for mastery; practical and philosophical life. By far the most perfect life unites them both, and in each different path adapts itself to circumstances. We are born for rational activity; which we call practical. Practical reason leads us to politics; the theoretical reason, to the contemplation of the universality of things. Mind itself, which is universal, embraces the two powers necessary to happiness, which we define as the activity of virtue in prosperity; it is not exclusively either a practical life which would exclude science, nor a speculative life which would exclude the practical. Perfect reason inclines towards these two omnipotent principles, for which man is born; the principle of society and science; for if these opposite principles seem mutually to interfere in their development, the political principles turning us away from politics, and the speculative principles turning us from speculation, to persuade us to live at rest, nevertheless nature, uniting the ends of these two movements, shows them fused; for virtues are not contradictory and antipathetic mutually; than the harmony of virtues no harmony is more consonant. If, from his youth, man has subjected himself to the principles of virtues, and to the divine law of the world harmony, he will lead an easy life; and if, by his own inclination, he inclines towards evil, and has the luck of meeting better guides, he will, by rectifying his course, arrive at happiness, like passengers favored by chance, finishing a fortunate sea-passage, thanks to the pilot; and the fortunate passage of life is happiness. But if by himself he cannot know his real interests, if he does not have the luck of meeting prudent directors, what benefit would it be if he did have immense treasures ? For the fool, even if he had for himself all the other elements of luck, is eternal unhappy.

And since, in everything, you must first consider the end, -- for that is what is done by the pilots ever meditating over the harbor wither they are to land the ship, and the drivers who keep their eye on the goal of their trip, the archers and slingers who consider their objective, for it is the objective towards which all their efforts must tend, -- virtue must necessarily undertake an objective, which should become the art of living; and that is the name I give it in both directions it can take. For practical life, this objective is improvement; for the philosophical life, the perfect good; which, in their human affairs the sages call happiness. Those who are in misery are not capable of judging of happiness according to exact ideas; and those who do not see it, clearly, would not know how to choose it. Those who consider that pleasure is the sovereign good are punished therefore by foolishness, those who above all seek the absence of pain, also receive their punishment, and, to resume all, to define life-happiness as the enjoyment of the body, or in an unreflective state of soul is to expose himself to all the whirlwinds of the tempest. Those who suppress moral beauty by avoiding all discussion, all reflection about the matter, and seeking pleasure, absence of pain, simple and primitive physical enjoyments, the irreflective inclinations of body and soul, are not more fortunate; for they commit a double fault, by reducing the good of the soul and its superior functions to the level of that of the body, and in raising the good of the body to the high level due to the good of the soul. By an exact discernment of these goods, we should outline its proper part for the divine element, and for nature. They themselves do not, observe this relation of dignity from the better to the worse. But we do so, when we say that if the body is the organ of the soul, reason is the guide of the entire soul, the mistress of the body, this tent of the soul and that all the other physical advantages should serve only as instruments to the intellectual activity, if you wish it to be perfect in power, duration and wealth.

20. These are the most important conditions to become a sage: first, you must have received from fate a mind endowed with facility to understand, memory, and industry; you must then from youth up exercise your intelligence by the practice of argumentation, by mathematical studies, and the exact sciences. Then you must study healthful philosophy, after which you may undertake the knowledge of the Gods, of laws, and of human life. For there are two means of arriving at this state known as wisdom. The first is to acquire the habit of work that, is intellectual, and the taste for knowledge; the other is to seek to see many things, to undertake business frequently, and to know them either directly at first hand, or indirectly. For he who from youth up has exercised reason by dialectic reasonings, mathematical studies, and exact sciences; is not yet ready for wisdom, any more than he who has neglected these labors, and has only listened to others, and has plunged himself in business. The one has become blind; when the business is to judge particular facts; the other, when he is to judge of general deductions. Just as in calculations you obtain the total by combining the parts, so also, in business practice, reason can vaguely sketch the general formula; but experience alone can enable us to grasp the details and individual facts.

21. Age is in the same relation to youth. Youth makes men energetic, age makes them prudent; never by imprudence does it let a thought escape; it reflects on what it has done; it considers maturely what it ought to do, in order that this comparison of the future with the present, and the present with the future lead it to good conduct. To the past, it applies memory, to the present, sensation, and to the future, foresight; for our memory has always as object the past, foresight the future, and sensation the present. He therefore who wishes to lead an honest and beautiful life must not only have senses and memory, but foresight.

SECTION IV
POLITICAL FRAGMENTS

22.a. The laws of the wicked and atheists are opposed by the unwritten laws of the Gods, who inflict evils and terrible punishments on the disobedient. It is these divine laws which have developed and directed the laws and written maxims given to men.

b. The relation of law to the soul and human life is identical to that of harmony to the sense of hearing, and the voice; for the law instructs the soul, and therethrough, the life; as harmony regulates the voice through education of the ear. In my opinion, every society is composed of the commander, the commanded, and the laws. Among the latter, one is living; namely the king; the other is inanimate, the written letter. The law is therefore the essential; through it only is the king legitimate, the magistrate, regularly instituted, the commanded free, and the whole community happy. When it is violated, the king is no more than a tyrant; the magistrate illegitimate, the commanded becomes a slave, and the whole community becomes unhappy. Human acts are like a mingled tissue, formed of command, duty, obedience, and force sufficient to overcome resistance. Essentially, the command belongs to the better; being commanded to the inferior, and force belongs to both; for the reasonable part of the soul commands and the irrational part is commanded; both have the force to conquer the passions. Virtue is born from the harmonious cooperation of both; and leads the soul to rest and indifference by turning it away from pleasures and sorrows.

c. Law must conform to nature, and exercise an efficient power over things, and be useful to the political community; for if it lacks one, two, or all of these characteristics, it is no longer a law, or at least it is no longer a perfect law. It conforms to nature if it is the image of natural right; which fits itself, and distributes to each according to his deserts; it prevails, if it harmonizes with the men who are to be subject thereto; for there are may people who are not apt to receive what by nature is the first of goods; and who are fitted to practice only the good which is in relation with them, and possible for them; for that is how the sick and the suffering have to be nursed. Law is useful to the political society if it is not monarchical, if it does not constitute privileged classes, if it is made in the interest of all, and is equally imposed on all. Law must also regard the country and the lands, for not all soils can yield the same returns, neither all human souls the same virtues. That is why some establish the aristocratic constitution, while others prefer the democratic or oligarchic. The aristocratic constitution is founded on the subcontrary proportion, and is the justest, for this proportion attributes the greatest results to the greatest terms, and the smallest to the smallest. The democratic constitution is founded on the geometrical proportion, in which the results of the great and small are equal. The oligarchic and tyrannic constitutions are founded on the arithmetical proportion, which, being the opposite of the subcontrary, attributes to the smallest terms the greatest results, and vice versa.

Such are the kinds of proportions, and you can observe their image in families and political constitutions; for either the honors, punishments and virtues are equally attributed to the great and small, or they are so attributed unequally, according to superiority, in virtue, wealth or power. Equal distribution is the characteristic of democracy; and the unequal, that of aristocracy and oligarchy.

d. The best law and constitution must be a composite of all other constitutions, and contain something democratic, oligarchic, monarchic and aristocratic, as in Lacedemon; for in it the kings formed the monarchic element, the elders the aristocracy, the magistrates the oligarchy, the cavalry generals and youths the democracy. Law must therefore not only be beautiful and good, but its different parts must mutually compensate. This will give it power and durability and by this mutual opposition I mean that the same magistracy command and be commanded, as in the wise laws of Lacedemon; for the power of its kings is balanced by the magistrates, this by the elders, and between these two powers are the cavalry generals and the youths, who, as soon as they see any one party acquire the preponderance, throw themselves on the other side.

The law's first duty is to decide about the gods, the geniuses, the parents; in short, on all that is estimable and worthy; later, about utility. It is proper that the secondary regulations should follow the best, and that the laws be inscribed, not on the houses and doors, but in the depths of the souls of the citizens. Even in Lacedemon, which has excellent laws, the State is not administered by manifold written, ordinances. Law is useful to the political community, if it is not monarchical, and does not serve private interests, if it is useful to all, if it extends its obligation to all, and aims its punishments to shame the guilty, and to brand him with infamy, rather than to deprive him of his wealth. If, indeed, you are seeking to punish the guilty by ignominy, the citizens will try to lead a wiser and more honest life, so as to avoid the law's punishment; if it is only by money fines, they will rate above everything wealth, understanding that it is their best means to repair their faults. The best would be that the State should be organized in a manner such that it would need nothing from strangers, neither for virtue, power, or anything else. Just as the right constitution of a body, a house, or an army is to contain, and not to depend on outside sources for the principle of its safety; for in that way the body is more vigorous, the house better ordered, and the army will be neither mercenary nor badly drilled. Beings that are thus organized are superior to others; they are free, enfranchised from servitude, unless, for their conservation, they need many things, but have only few needs, easily satisfied. In that way the vigorous man becomes able to bear heavy burdens, and the athlete, to resist cold; for men are exercised by events and misfortunes. The temperate man, who has tested his body and soul, finds any food, drink, even a bed of leaves, delectable. He who has preferred to live like a sybarite among delights, would finally scorn and reject the magnificence of the great (Persian) king. Law must therefore deeply penetrate into the souls and habits of the citizens; it will make them satisfied with their fate, and distribute his deserts to each. Thus the sum, in traversing the zodiac, distributes to everything on the earth, growth, food, life, in the proper measure, and institutes this wise legislation which regulates the succession of the seasons. That is why we call Jupiter *nomios*, law-giver, from *Nemeios*, and we call *nomeus* he who distributes their food to the sheep; that is why we call *nomoi* the verses sung by the citharedians, for these verses impart order to the soul because they are sung according to the laws of harmony, rhythm and measure.

23. The true chief must not only possess the science and power of commanding well, but he must also love men; for it is absurd that a shepherd should hate his flock, and feel hostile disposition towards those he is educating. Besides he must be legitimate; only thus can he sustain a chief's dignity. His science will permit him to discern well, his power to punish, his kindness to be beneficent, and the law to do everything according to reason. The best chief would be he who would closest approach the law, for he would never act in his own interest, and always in that or others, since the law does not exist for itself, but for its subjects.

24. See 21a.

25. When the art of reflexion was discovered, diminished dissensions, and increased concord; those who possess it feel the pride of predominance yielding to the sentiment of equality.

It is by reflexion that we succeed in adjusting our affairs in a friendly fashion; through it the poor receive riches, and the rich give to the poor, each possessing the confidence that he possesses, the equality of rights.

26. Reflexion is like a rule which hinders and turns aside the people who know how to reflect from committing injustices, for it convinces them that they cannot remain hidden if they carry out their purposes and the punishment which has overtaken those who have not known how to abstain makes them reflect and not become back-sliders.

SECTION V
LOGICAL FRAGMENTS

27. Logic, compared with the other sciences is by far the most successful, and succeeds in demonstrating its objectives even better than geometry. Where geometric demonstration fails, the logical succeeds; and logic treats not only with general classes, but with their exceptions.

28. In my opinion it is a complete error to insist that about every subject there are two contrary opinions which are equally true. To begin with, I consider it impossible that, if both opinions are true, they should contradict each other, and that beauty should contradict beauty, and whiteness, whiteness. It cannot be so, for beauty and ugliness, whiteness and blackness are contraries. Likewise, the true is contrary to the false, and you cannot produce two contrary opinions, either true of false; the one must be true, at the expense of the falseness of the other. For instance, he who praises the soul of man and accuses his body is not speaking of the same object, unless you claim that speaking exclusive of the heaven you are speaking exclusively of the earth. Why no, they are not one, but two propositions. What am I trying to demonstrate? That he who says that the Athenians are skillful and witty and he who says they are not grateful, are not supporting contradictory propositions, for contradictories are opposed to each other on the same points, and here the two points are different.

29. ARCHYTAS'S TEN UNIVERSAL NOTIONS. First, all kinds of arts deal with five things: the matter, the instrument, the part, the definition, the end.

The first notion, the substance, is something self-existent and self-subsistent. It needs nothing else for its essence, though subject to growth, if it happens to be something that is born; for only the divine is uncreated, and veritably self-subsistent; for the other notions are considered in relation to substance when the latter by opposition to them is termed self-subsisting: but it is not such, in relation to the divine.

The nine notions appear and disappear without implying the ruin of the subject, the substrate, and that is what is called the universal accident. For the same subject does not lose its identity by being increased or diminished in quantity. Thus, excessive feeding creates excessive size and stoutness; sobriety and abstinence make men lean, but it always the same body, the same substrate. Thus also human beings passing from childhood to youth remain the same in substance, differing only in quantity. Without changing essence, the identical object may become white or black, changing only as regards quality. Again, without changing essence, the identical man may change disposition and relation, as he is friend or enemy; and being today in Thebes, and tomorrow in Athens changes nothing in his substantial nature. Without changing essence, we remain the same today that we were yesterday; the change affected only time; the man standing is the same as the man sitting; he has changed only in situation: Being aimed or unarmed is a difference only of possession; the striker and the cutter are the same man in essence, though not in action; he who is cut or struck Ñ which belongs to the category of suffering, Ñ still retains his essence. The differences of the other categories are clearer; those of quality, possession, and suffering present some difficulties in the differences; for we hesitate about the question of knowing if having fever, shivering or rejoicing belong to the category of quality, possession, or suffering. We must distinguish: if we say, it is fever, it is shivering, it is joy, it is quality; if we say, he has fever, he shivers, he rejoices, it is possession; while possession again differs from suffering, in that the latter can be conceived without the agent. Suffering is a relation to the agent, and is understood only by him who produces it; if we say, he is cut, he is beaten, we express the patient; if we say, he suffers, we express possession.

We say that (Archytas) has ten, and no more universal notions; of which we may convince ourselves by the following division: the being is in a subject, (a substance), or is not in a subject; that which is not in a subject, forms the substance; that which is in a subject or is conceived by itself, or is not conceived by itself; that which is not conceived by itself constitutes relation, for relative beings, which are not conceived by themselves, but which forcibly import the idea of an other being, are what is called scheseis, conditions. Thus the term son is associated with the term farther, that of slave, master; thus all relative beings are conceived in a necessary bond together with something else, and not by themselves. The self-conceivable being is either divisible Ñ when it is quantity, --- or indivisible, when it constitutes quality. The six other notions are produced by combination of the former. Substance mingled with quantity, if seen in place, constitutes the category of *where*, if seen in time, constitutes that of *when*. Mingled with quality, substance is either active and forms the category of *action*, or when passive, forms that of *suffering*, or, *passivity*. Combined with relation, it is either posited in another, and that is what is called *situation*, or it is attributed to somebody else, and then it is *possession*.

As to the order of the categories, quantity follows substance and precedes quality; because, by a natural law, everything that receives quality also receives mass, and that it is only of something so determinate that quality can be so affirmed and expressed. Again, quality precedes relation, because the former is self-sufficient, and the latter by a relation; we first have to conceive and express something by itself before in a relation.

After these universal categories follow the others. Action precedes passivity, because its force is greater; the category of situation precedes that of possession, because being situated is something simpler than being possessed; and you cannot conceive something attributed to another without conceiving the former as situated somewhere. That which is situated is also in a position, such as standing, seated or lying. The characteristic of substance is more or less-ness; for we say that a man is no more of an animal than a horse, by substance, and not to admit the contraries. The characteristic of quality is to admit more or less; for we say, more or less white, or black. The characteristic of; quantity is to admit equality or inequality; for a square foot is not equal to an acre, and 144 sq. inches equal a square foot; five is not equal to ten, and twice five is equal to ten. The characteristic of relation is to join contraries; for if there is a father, there is a son; and if there is a master there is a slave. The characteristic of whereness is to include; and of whenness it to remain; of situation, to be located; of possession, to be attributed. The composite of substance and quantity is anterior to the composite of quality; the composite of substance and quality in its turn precedes that of substance and relation. Whereness precedes whenness; because whereness presupposes the place that is fixed and permanent; whenness relates to time and time, ever in movement, has no fixity; and rest is anterior to movement. Action is anterior to passivity, and situation to possession.

I. CATEGORY OF SUBSTANCE. Substance is divided into corporeal and incorporeal; the corporeal into bodies animate and inanimate. Animated bodies, into those endowed with sensation, and without sensation. Senses-bodies into animals and zoophytes, which do not farther divide into opposite distinctions. The animal is divided into rational and irrational; the rational into mortal and immortal; the mortal into differences of genus, such as man, ox, horse, and the rest. The species are divided into individuals who have no abiding value.

Each of the sections that we obtained above by opposite divisions is susceptible of being in turn divided equally, until we arrive to the indivisible individuals who are of no value.

2. CATEGORY OF QUANTITY. This is divided into seven parts: the line, surface, the body, the place, the time, the number, and language. Quantity is either continuous or discrete; of continuous qualities there are five; of the discrete, number and language. In quantity, you may distinguish that which is composed of parts having position relative to each other; such as line, surface, body and place; and those whose parts have no position, such as number, language, and time; for although time is a continuous quantity, nevertheless its parts have no position; because it is not permanent, and that which has no permanence could not have any position. Quantity has produced four sciences: immovable quantity, geometry; movable continuous quantity, astronomy; immovable discrete quantity, arithmetic; and the movable, music.

3. CATEGORY OF QUALITY. This is divided into hexis or habit; and diathesis or affection; passive quality and passivity, power and impotence, figure and form. Habit is affection in a state of energetic tension; it is the permanence and fixity derived from continuity and the energy of affection; it is affection become (second) nature, a second enriched nature. Another explanation of habit is the qualities given us by nature, and which are derived neither from affection, nor from the natural progress of the being; as sight and the other senses. Both passive quality and passivity are increase, intensity, and weakening. To both of these are attributed anger, hate, intemperance, the other vicious passions, the affections of sickness, heat and cold; but these are classified at will under habit and affection, or under passive quality and passivity. You might say that so far as affection is communicable it might be called habit; so far as it cause a passion, it might be called a passive quality; which refers both to its permanence and fixity. For a modification contained in the measure is called passion. Thus from the one to whom it is communicated, heat may be called a habit; from the cause which produces the modification; we may say that it is either the passive quality, or the power of the passion; as when we say of a child that he is potentially a runner or a philosopher, and, in short, when at a given moment the being does not have the power to act, but that it is possible that after the lapse of a certain period of time, this power may belong to him. Impotence is when nature refuses itself to the possibility of accomplishing certain

actions as when the man is impotent to fly, the horse to speak, the eagle to live in water, and all the natural impossibilities.

Figure is a conformation of a determined character; form, the quality showing itself exteriorly by color, or beauty, or ugliness showing itself on the surface by color, and in short any form that is apparent, determinate and striking. Some limit figure to inanimate things; reserving form to living beings. Some say that the word figure gives the idea of the dimension of depth; and that the form is applied only to the superficial appearance; but you have been taught all of that.

4. CATEGORIES OF RELATION. Generally, the relatives are divided into four classes; nature, art, chance and will. The relation of father to son is natural; that of master to disciple, that of art; that of master to slave, that of chance; and that of friend to friend, and enemy to enemy, that of will; although you might say that these are all natural relations.

5. CATEGORY OF WHERENESS. The simplest division is into six: up, down, forwards, backwards, right and left. Each of these' subdivisions contains varieties. There are many differences in up-ness, in the air, in the stars, to the pole, beyond the pole; and such differences are repeated below; the infinitely divided places themselves are further subject to an infinity of differences, but this very ambiguous point will be explained later.

6. CATEGORY OF WHENNESS. This is divided in present, past and future; the present is indivisible, the past is divided into nine subdivisions, the future into five; we have already spoken of them.

7. CATEGORY OF ACTION. This is divided into action, discourse and thought; action in work of the hands, with tools, and with feet; and each of' these divisions is subdivided into technical divisions which also have their parts. Language is divided into Greek, barbarian, and each of these divisions have their parts, namely, its dialects. Thought is divided into and infinite world of thoughts, whose objects are the worlds, other people, and the hypercosmic. Language and thought really belong to action, for they are the acts of the reasonable nature; in fact, if we are asked: What is Mr. X doing? we answer, he is chatting, conversing, thinking, reflecting, and so on.

8. CATEGORY OF PASSIVITY. Passivity is divided in suffering of the soul, and of the body; and each of these is subdivided into passions which result from actions of somebody else, as for instance, when somebody is struck; and passions which arise without the active

212

intervention of someone else; which occur in a thousand different forms.

9. CATEGORY OF SITUATION. This is divided into three: standing, sitting, and lying; and each of these is subdivided by differences of location. We may stand on our feet, or on the tips of our fingers; with the leg unflexed, or the knee bent; further differences are equal or unequal steps; or walking on one or two feet. Being seated has the same differences; one may be straight, bent, reversed; the knees may form an acute or obtuse angle; the feet may be placed over each other, or in some other way. Likewise with lying down; prone or head forwards, or to the side, the body extended, in a circle, or angularly. Far from uniform are these divisions; they are very various. Position is also subject to other divisions, for an instance, an object may be spread out like corn, sand, oil, and all the other solids; that are susceptible of position, and all the liquids that we know. Nevertheless being extended belongs to position, as cloth and nets.

10. CATEGORY OF POSSESIONS. "Having" signifies things that we put on, as shoes, arms, coverings; things which are put on others, such as a peck, a bottle, and other vases; for we say that the peck has oats, that the bottle has wine; also of wealth and estates; we say, he has a fortune, fields, cattle and other similar things.

30. The order of the categories is the following; in the first rank is substance, because it alone serves as substrate to all the others, that we can conceive it alone, and by itself, and that the others cannot be conceived without it; for all attributes' subject reside therein, or are affirmed thereof. The second is quality; for it is impossible for a thing to have a quality without an essence.

31. Every naturally physical and sensible substance must, to be conceived by man, be either classified within the categories, or be determined by them, and cannot be conceived without them.

32. Substance has three differences; the one consists in matter, the other in form, and the third in the mixture of both.

33. These notions, these categories, have characteristics that are common and individual. I say that they are characteristics common to substance, not to receive more or lessness; for it is not possible to be more or less man, God or ant; to have no contraries for man is not the contrary of man, neither god of a god; neither is it contrary to other substances, to exist by oneself, and not to be in another, as green or blue color is the characteristic of the eye, since all substance depends on itself. All the things that belong to it intimately, or the accidents are in

it; or cannot exit without it;....quality is suited by several characteristics of substance, for example, not to be subject to more or lessness.

34. It is the property to remain self-identical, one in number, and to be susceptible of the contraries. Waking is the contrary of sleep; slowness to swiftness, sickness to health; and the same man, identically one, is susceptible of all these differences. For he awakes, sleeps, moves slowly or quickly, is well or sick, and in short is able to receive all similar contraries, so long as they be not simultaneous.

35. Quantity has three differences: one consists in weight, like bullion; the other in size, as the yard; the other in multitude, as ten.

36. Including its accidents, substance is necessarily primary; that is how they are in relation to some thing else; after the substance come the relations of accidental qualities.

37. A common property which must be added to quality, is to admit certain contraries, and privation. The relation is subject to more or lessness; for though a being remain ever the same, to be greater or smaller than anything else is moreness; but all the relations are not susceptible thereto; for you cannot be more or less father, brother, or son; whereby I do not mean to express the sentiments of both parents, nor the degree of tenderness is held mutually by beings of the same blood, and the sons of the same parents; I only mean the tenderness which is in the nature of these relations.

38. Quality has certain common characters, for example, of receiving the contraries, and privation; more and less affect the passions. That is why the passions are marked by the characteristics of indetermination, because they are in a greater or less indeterminate measure.

39. Relation is susceptible of conversion, and this conversion is founded either on resemblance, as the equal, and the brother, or on lack of resemblance, the large and the small. There are relatives which are not converted, for instance, science and sensation; for we may speak of the science of the intelligible, and of the sensation of the sensible; and the reason is that the intelligible and the sensible can exist independently of science and sensation; while science and sensation cannot exist without the intelligible and the sensible;......The characteristic of relatives is to exist simultaneously in each other; for if we grant the existence of doubleness, the half must necessarily exist; and if the half exists; necessarily must the double exist, as it is the cause of the half, as the half is the cause of thy double.

40. Since every moved thing moves in a place, since action and passivity are actualized movements, it is clear that there must be a primary place in which exist the acting and the passive objects.

41. The characteristic of the agent is to contain the cause of the motion; while the characteristic of the thing done, which is passive, is to have it in some other. For the sculptor obtains the cause of the making of the statue, the bronze possesses the cause of the modification it undergoes, both in itself and in the sculptor. So also with the passions of the soul, for it is in the nature of anger to be aroused as the result of something else; that it be excited by some other external thing, for example, by scorn, dishonor, and outrage; and he who acts thus towards another, contains the cause of his action.

42. The highest degree of the action, is the act; which contains three differences; it may be accomplished in the contemplation of the stars, or in doing, such as healing or constructing; or in action, as in commanding an army, or in administering the affairs of state. An act may occur even without reasoning, as in irrational animal. These are the most general contraries.

43. Passion differs from the passive state; [as] passion is accompanied by sensation, like anger, pleasure and fear; while one can undergo something without sensation, such as the wax that melts, or the mud that dries. Then also the [deed] done differs also from the passive state, when the deed done has undergone a certain action, [whi]le everything that has undergone a certain action is not a deed done; for a thing may be in a passive state as a result of lack of privation.

44. On the one side there is the agent, on the other, the patient; for example, in nature, God is the being who acts; matter is the being which undergoes, and the elements are neither the one nor the other.

45. The characteristic of possession is to be something adventitious, something corporeal, separated from essence. Thus a veil or shoes, are distinct from the possessor; those are not natural characteristics, nor essential accidents, like the blue color of the eyes, and rarefaction; these are two incorporeal characteristics, while possession relates to something corporeal and adventitious.

46. Since the signs and the things signified have a purpose, and since the man who uses these signs and signified things is to fulfill the perfect function of speech, let us finish what we have said by proving that the harmonious grouping of all these categories does not belong to man in general, but to a certain finite individual. Necessarily, it must be a definite man existing somewhere who possesses quality, quantity,

relation, action, passivity, location and possession, who is in a place and time. The man in himself receives only the first of these expressions; I mean essence and form; but he has no quality, no age, he is not old, he neither does, nor suffers anything, he has no location, he possesses nothing, he is neither in place nor time. All those are only accidents of the physical and corporeal being; but not of the intelligible, immovable, and indivisible being.

47. Among contraries, some are said to be mutually opposed by convention and nature, as good to evil, the sick to the well man, truth to error [and] others, as possession is opposed to privation, such as life and death, sight and blindness, science and ignorance; others as relatives as the double and the half, the commander and the commanded, the master and the slave; others, like affirmation and negation, as being man and not a man, being honest, and not.

48. The relatives arise and disappear necessarily simultaneously; the existence of the double is impossible, without implying that of the half and vice versa. If something becomes double, the half must arise, and if the double is destroyed, the half passes away with it.

49. Of the relatives, some respond to each other in two senses; as, the greater, the smaller, the brother, the relative. Others again respond, but not in the two senses, for we say equally, the science of the intelligible, and the science of the sensible, but we do not say the reciprocal, the intelligible of science, and the sensible of sensation. The reason is that the object of judgment can exist independently of him who judges, for instance, the sensible can exist without sensation, and the intelligible without science; while it is not possible that the subject which bears a judgment exists without the object which he judges; for example, there can be no sensation without sensible object, nor science without intelligible object. Relatives which respond reciprocally are of two kinds; those that respond indifferently, as the relative, the brother, the equal; for they are mutually similar, and equal. Some respond reciprocally, but not in-differently; for this one is greater than that one, and that one is smaller than this one; and this one is the father of that one, and that one the son of this one.

50. These opposites divide into kinds which hang together; for of the contraries, some are without middle term, and the others have one. There is no middle term between sickness and health, rest and movement, waking and sleep, straightness and curvedness, and such other contraries. But between the much and the little, there is a just medium; between the shrill and the low, there is the unison; between the

rapid and slow, there is the equality of movement; between the greatest and the smallest, the equality of measure. Of universal contraries there must be one that belongs to what receives them; for they do not admit any medium term. Thus there is no medium term between health and sickness; every living being is necessarily sick or well; neither between waking and sleeping, for every living being is either awake or asleep; nor between rest and movement, for every human being is either at rest or at movement. The opposites of which neither of any or both necessarily belong to the subject that may receive them; have any middle terms; between black and white, there is the [----]; and it is not necessary that an animal be black or white; between the great and the small, there is the equal; and it is not necessary that a living being be either great or small; between the rough and the soft, there is the gentle, and it is not necessary that a living being be either rough or soft. In the opposites there are three differences: some are opposed, as the good is to evil, for instance, health to sickness; the others like evil to evil, as for instance, avarice to lechery; the others, as being neither the one or the other for instance, as white is opposed to black, and the heavy to the light. Of the opposites, some occur in the genus of genera; for the good is opposed to evil, and the good is the genus of virtues, and evil that of the evils. Others occur in the genera of species, virtue is the opposite of vice and virtue is the genus of prudence and temperance, and vice is the genus of foolishness and debauch. Others occur in the species, courage is opposed to cowardliness, justice of injustice, and justice and virtue are species of virtue, injustice and debauch species of vice. The primary genera, which we call genera of genera, can be divided; the last species, which are the immediate nearest to the object, that is sensible, could no longer be genera, and are only species. For the triangle is the genus of the rectangle, of the equilateral and of the scalene...the species of good......

51. The opposites differ from each other in that for some, the contraries, it is not necessary that they arise at the same time, and disappear simultaneously. For health is the contrary of sickness, and rest that of movement; nevertheless neither of them arises or perishes at the same time as its opposite. Possession and privation of production differ in this, that it is in the nature of contraries that one passes from one to the other, for instance, from sickness to health and vice versa. It is not so with possession and privation; you do indeed pass from possession to privation, but the privation does; not return to possession; the living, die, but the dead never return to life. In short, possession is the

217

pesistance of what is according to nature, while privation is its lack, and decay. Relatives necessarily arise and disappear simultaneously; for it is impossible for the double to exist without implying the half ; or vice versa. If some double happens to arise, it, is impossibly that the half should not arise, or if some double be destroyed, that the half be not destroyed. Affirmation and negation are forms of preposition, and they eminently express the true and the false. Being a man is a true proposition, if the thing exists, and false if it does not exist. You could say as much of negation, it is true or false according to the thing expressed.

Besides, between good and evil there is medium, which is neither good nor evil; between much and little, the just measure; between the slow and the fast, the equality of speed; between possession and privation, there is no medium. For there is nothing between life and death; between sight and blindness; unless indeed you say that the living who is not. yet born, but who is being born, is between life and death, and that the puppy who does not yet see is between blindness and sight. In such an expression, we are using an accidental medium, and not according to the true and proper definition of contraries.

Relatives have middle terms; for between the master and the slave, there is the free man, and between the greatest and the smallest, there is equality; between the wide and the narrow there is the proper width; one might likewise find be between the other contraries a medium, whether or no it has a name.

Between affimation (and negation) there are no contraries, for instance, between being a man and not being a man, being a musician and not being a musician. In short, we have to affirm or deny.

Affirming is showing of something that it is a man, for instance, or a horse, or an attribute of these beings, as of the man that he is a musician, and of the horse, that he is warlike; we call denying, when we show of something that it is not something, not man, not horse, or that it lacks an attribute of these beings, for instance, that the man is not a musician and that the horse is not warlike; and between this affirmation and this negation, there is nothing.

52. Privation, and being deprived is taken in three senses; or one does not at all have at all have the thing, as that the blind man does not have sight, the mute does not have voice, and the ignorant, no science; or that one does not have it but partially, as that the man hard of hearing has hearing, and that the man with sore eyes has sight; or one can say that partially he does not have it, as one says that a man whose

legs are crooked that he has no legs, and of a man who has a bad voice, that he has no voice.

BIOGRAPHY OF OCELLUS LUCANUS

Practically nothing is known of the life of Ocellus, except that Iamblichus mentions the name of his brother Ocillus, and his sister Byndacis, all Pythagorean philosophers. In the biography of Archytas we read his writings were preserved by his family, so we may assume he returned home, after studying Pythagoreanism.

His significance, however, is great, for those letters of Plato witness how much he sought them, and that he indeed received some of them. Of the books that we have, Philo Judaeus reedited the first, in his writing *on the Incorruptibility of the World.* The second was used, almost word for word by Aristotle, in his tract *on Generation and Corruption*; and the fourth was used word for word by Iamblichus in his Life of Pythagoras. Ocellus was therefore much appreciated, and a very useful writer.

In his way, Archytas was almost as useful to Aristotle, in fragments: 6, 8, I, II, 17 (4), (5), (8); 9 (2), (4), (9), (10); 32; etc....

The truth is that Pythagoreanism was bodily adapted by Plato and Aristotle, who thereby made their fortunes. Pythagoreanism was an unselfish inspiration; and not until these fragments are united has it been possible to pass through Plato and Aristotle, to the real spring of Greek philosophy. As an instance, Plato wrote his Timaeus as an amplification of the book of the Pythagorean's [Locrian] Timaeus's tract which has been preserved along with Plato's works.

I
THE PYTHAGOREAN'S TREATISE ON THE UNIVERSE

Ocellus Lucanus has written what follows concerning the nature of the universe; having learnt some things through clear arguments from nature herself, but others from opinion, in conjunction with reason, it being his intention (he) to derive what is probable from intellectual perception. Therefore it appears to me, that the universe is indestructible and unbegotten, since it always was, and always will be; for if it had a temporal beginning, it would not always have existed: thus therefore, the universe is unbegotten and indestructible; for if someone should opine that it was once generated, he would not be able to find anything into which it can be corrupted arid dissolved, since that from which it was generated would be the first part of the universe; and again, that into which it would be dissolved would be the last part of it.

But if the universe was generated, it was generated together with all things; and if it should be corrupted, it would be corrupted together with all things. This however is impossible. This universe is therefore without a beginning, and without an end: nor is it possible that it can have any other mode of subsistence.

To which may be added, that everything which. has received a beginning of generation, and which ought also to participate of dissolution, receive two mutations; one of which, indeed proceeds from the less to the greater, and from the worse to the better; and that from which it begins change is denominated generation, but that a which its length it arrives at is called climax. The other mutation, however, proceeds from the greater to the less, and from the better to the worse; but the end of this mutation is called corruption and dissolution.

If therefore the whole and the universe were generated, and are corruptible they must, when generated have been changed from the less to the greater, and from the worse to the better; but when corrupted, they must be changed from the greater to the less, and from the better to the worse. Hence, if the world was generated, it would receive increase and would arrive at its consummation; and again, it would afterwards decrease and end. For every thing which has a progression possesses three boundaries, and two intervals; the three boundaries are generation, consummation and end; and the intervals are, progression from generation to consummation, and from consolation to end.

The whole, however, and the universe, affords as from itself, no indication of anything of this kind; for neither do we perceive it rising into existence, or becoming to be, nor changing to the better and the greater, nor changing to worse or less; but it always continues to subsist in identical manner, and perpetually remains self-identical.

Clear signs and indications of this are the orders of things, their symmetry, figurations, positions, intervals, powers, swiftness and slowness in respect to each other; and, besides these, their numbers and temporal periods, are clear signs and indications. For all such things as these change and diminish, conformably to the course of generation; for things that are greater and better tend towards consummation through power, but those that are less and worse decay through the inherent weakness of nature.

The whole world is what I call the whole universe; for this word "cosmos" was given it as a result of its being adorned with all things. From itself it is a consummate and perfect system of all things, for there is nothing external to the universe, since whatever exists is contained in the universe, and the universe subsists together with this, comprehending in itself all things, both parts and superfluous.

The things contained in the world are naturally congruous with it; but the world harmonizes with nothing else, symphonizing with itself. Other things do not possess self-sub sistence, but require adjustment with the environment. Thus animals require conjunction with air for the purpose of respiration; and with light, in order to see; and similarly the other senses with other environment, to function satisfactorily. A conjunction with earth is necessary for the germination of plants. The sun, moon, planets and fixed stars likewise integrate with the world, as parts of its general arrangement. The world, however, has no conjunction with any thing outside of itself. The above is supported by the following. Fire which imparts heat to others, is self-hot; honey which is sweet to the taste, is self-sweet. The principles of demonstrations, which conclude to things unapparent, are self-evident. Therefore the cause of the perfection of other things is itself perfect. That which preserves and renders permanent other things must itself be preserved and permanent. What harmonizes must itself be self-harmonic. Now as the world is the cause of the existence, preservation and perfection of other things, must itself be perpetual and perfect; and because its duration is everlasting, it becomes the cause of the permanence of all other things. In short, if the universe should be dissolved, it would be dissolved either into the existent, or nonexistent. As it could not be dissolved into existence, for in this case the dissolution would not be a corruption; as being is either the universe, or some part of it. Nor can it be dissolved into nonentity, since being cannot possibly arise from non-being; or be dissolved into nonentity. Therefore the universe is incorruptible, and never can be destroyed. If, however, somebody should think that it can be corrupted, it must be corrupted either from something external to, or contained in the universe, but it cannot be corrupted by anything external to it, for nothing such exists, since all other things are comprehended in the universe, and the world is the whole and the all. Nor can it be corrupted by the things it contains, which would imply their greater power. This however is impossible; for all things are led and governed by the universe, and thereby are preserved and adjusted, possessing life and soul. But if the universe can neither be corrupted by anything external to it, nor by anything contained within it, the world must therefore be incorruptible and indestructible; for we consider the world identical with the universe.

Further, the whole of nature surveyed through its own totality, will be found to derive continuity from the first and most honorable bodies, proportionally attenuating this continuity, introducing it to everything mortal, and receiving the progression of its peculiar subsistence; for the first (and most honorable) bodies in the universe revolve according to the same and similarly. The progression of the whole of nature, however, is not successive and continuous, nor yet local, but is subject to mutation. When condensed, fire generates air; air water, and water earth. A return circuit of transformation extends backward from earth to fire, whence it originated. However fruits, and most rooted plants, originate from seeds. When however they fruit and mature, that are again resolved into seed, nature producing a complete circular progression.

In a subordinate manner, men and other animals change the universal boundary of nature; for in these there is no periodical return to the first age; nor is there a transfusion, such as between fire and air, and water and earth; but the mutations of their ages being accomplished in a four-cycled circle, they are dissolved, and reformed.

These therefore are the signs and indications that the universe which comprehends (all things) which, will always endure and be preserved, but that, its parts, and its nonessential additions are corrupted and dissolved. Further, it is credible that the universe, without a beginning, and without end, from s figure, motion, time and essence; and there, may be concluded that the world is begotten and incorruptible; for its figure is circular; and as a circular figure is similar and equal on all sides, it is therefore without a beginning or an end. Circular is also the motion of the universe, but this motion is stable and without transition. Time, likewise, in which motion exists, infinite; for neither had this a beginning, nor will it have an end of its revolution. The universe's essence also does not waste elsewhere, and is immutable, because it is not naturally adapted to charge, either from worse to better, or from better to worse. From all these arguments, therefore, it is obviously credible, that the world is unbegotten and incorruptible. So much about the world and the universe.

II
CREATION

Since, however, in the universe there is a difference between generation and the generated, and since generation occurs where there is a mutation and egress from things which rank as subjects, then must the cause of generation subsist as long as the generated matter. The cause of generation must be both efficient and motive, while the recipient must be passive, and moved. The Fates themselves, distinguish and separate the impassive part of the world from that which is perpetually in motion. For the course of the moon is the meeting-line of generation and immortality. The region above the moon, as well as the lunar domain, is the residence of the divinities; while sub-lunar regions are the abode of strife and nature; here is change of the generated things, and regeneration of those that have perished.

So that part of the world, however, in which nature and generation predominate, it is necessary that the three following things be present. In the first place, the body which yields to the touch, and which is the subject of all generated natures. But this will be an universal recipient, a characteristic of generation itself, having the same relation to the things that are generated from it, as water to taste, silence to sound, darkness to light, and the matter of artificial forms to the forms themselves. For water is tasteless and devoid of quality, yet is capable of receiving the sweet and the bitter, the tart and the salt. Air also, which is formless as regards sound, is the recipient of words and melody. Darkness, which is without color, and without form, becomes the recipient of splendor, and of the yellow color, and the white; but white pertains to the statuary's art, and the wax sculptor's art. Matter's relation, however, is different from the sculptor's art, for in matter, prior to generation, all things are in capacity, but they exist in perfection when they are generated, and receive their proper nature. Hence matter (or a universal recipient) is necessary to the existence of generation.

The second necessity is the existence of contrarieties, in order to effect mutations and changes in quality, matter, for this purpose, receiving passive qualities, and an aptitude to [the] participations of forms. Contrariety is also necessary in order that powers which are naturally mutually repugnant may not finally conquer, or vanquish each other. These powers are hot and cold, dryness and moistness.

In the third place rank essences: and those and fire and water, air and earth, of which heat and cold, dryness and moistness, are powers.

But essences differ from powers, essences being locally corrupted or generated, as their reasons or forms are incorporeal.

Of those four powers, however, heat and cold subsist as causes and things of an effective nature; but the dry and the moist rank as matter and things that are passive, though matter is the first recipient of things, for it is that which is spread under all things in common. Hence the body, whose capacity is the object of sense, and ranks as a principle, is the first thing while contraries, such as heat and cold, moistness and dryness, rank as primary differences; but heaviness and lightness, density and rarity, are related as things produced from primary differences. These amount to sixteen: heat an cold, moistness and dryness, heaviness and lightness, rarity and density, smoothness and roughness, hardness and softness, thinness and thickness, acuteness and obtuseness. Knowledge of all of these is had by touch, which forms a judgment; hence also any body whatever which contains capacity for these can be apprehended by touch.

Heat and dryness, rarity and sharpness are the powers of fire; coldness and moistness, density and obtuseness are those of water; those of air are softness, smoothness, light, and the quality of being attenuated; while those of earth are hardness and roughness, heaviness and thickness.

Of these four bodies, however fire and earth are the intensities of contraries. Fire is the intensity of heat, as ice is of cold; and if ice is a concretion of moisture and farigidity, fire will be the fervor of dryness and heat. That is why neither fire nor ice generate anything.

Fire and earth, therefore, are the extremities of the elements, while water and air are the media, for they have a mixed corporeal nature. Nor is it possible that there could be only one of the extremes, a contrary thereto being necessary. Nor could there be two only, for it is necessary to have a medium, as media oppose extremes.

Fire therefore is hot and dry, but air is hot and moist; water is moist and cold, and earth cold and dry. Hence heat is common to air and fire; cold is common to water and earth; dryness to earth and fire, and moisture to water and air. But with respect to the peculiarities of each, heat is the peculiarity of fire, dryness of earth, moisture of air, and frigidity of water. These essences remain permanent, through the possession of common properties; but they change through such as are peculiar, when one contrary overcomes another.

Hence, when the moisture in air overcomes the dryness in fire, or when water's frigidity overcomes air's heat, and earth's dryness water's moistness, and vice versa, then are effected the mutual mutations and generations of the elements.

The body, however, which is the subject and recipient of mutations, is a universal receptacle, and is in capacity the first tangible substance. But the mutations of the elements are effected either from a change of earth into fire, or from fire into air, or from air into water, or from water into earth. Mutations is also effected, in the third place, when each element's contrariness is corrupted, simultaneously with the preservation of everything kindred and coeval. Generation therefore is effected when one contrary quality is corrupted. For fire, indeed, is hot and dry, but air is hot and moist, and heat is common to both; but the peculiarity of fire is dryness, and of air, moisture. Hence when the moisture in air overcomes the dryness in fire, then fire is changed into air.

Again, since water is moist and cold, but air is moist and hot, moisture is common to both. Water's peculiarity is coldness, and of air, heat. When therefore the coldness in water overcomes the heat in air, air is altered into water.

Further, earth is cold and dry, and water cold and moist; coldness being common to both. But earth's peculiarity is dryness, and water's, moisture. When therefore earth's dryness overcomes water's moisture, water is altered into earth.

Earth's mutation in the ascending alteration occurs in a contrary way. One alternate mutation is effected when one whole vanquishes another; and two contrary powers are corrupted, nothing being common to them, at the same time. For since firs is hot and dry, while water is cold and moist, when the moisture in water overcomes the dryness in fire, and water's coldness, fire's heat; then fire is altered into water.

Again, earth is cold and dry, while air is hot and moist. When therefore earth's coldness overcomes air's heat, and earth's dryness air's moisture, then air is altered into earth.

When air's moisture corrupts fire's heat, then from both of them will be generated fire; for air's heat, and fire's dryness will remain, fire being hot and dry.

When earth's coldness is corrupted, and also water's moisture, then from both of them will be generated earth. For earth's dryness and water's coldness will be left, as earth is cold and dry.

But when air's heat and fire's heat are corrupted, no element will be generated; for in both of these will remain contraries, air's moisture and fire's dryness. Moisture is however contrary to dryness.

Again, when earth's coldness, and that of water are corrupted, neither thus will any generation occur; for earth's dryness, and water's moisture will remain. But dryness is contrary to moisture.

Thus we have briefly discussed the generation of the first bodies, and how and from what subjects it is effected.

Since, however, the world is indestructible and unbegotten, and neither had a beginning or generation, nor an end, it is necessary that the nature which produces generation in another thing, and also that which generates in itself, should be simultaneously present. That which produces generation in another thing, is the whole superlunary region; though the more proximate cause is the sun, who by its comings and goings continually changes the air; from cold to heat, which again changes the earth, which alters all its contents.

The obliquity of the zodiac, also, is well placed in respect to the sun's motion, for it likewise is the cause of generation. This is universally accomplished by the universe's proper order; wherein some things are active, and others passive. Different therefore is the generator, which is superlunary, while that which generated is sublunary; and that which consists of both of these, namely, an over-running body, and an ever-mutable generated nature, is the world itself.

III
THE PERPETUITY OF THE WORLD

Man's generation, did not originate from the earth, other animals, or plants; but the world's proper order being perpetual, its contained, aptly arranged natures should share with it never-failing subsistence. As primarily the world existed always, its parts must coexist with it; and by these I mean the heavens, the earth, and what is contained between them; which is on high, and is called aerial; for the world does not exist without, but with and from these.

As the world's parts are con subsistent, their comprehended natures must coexist with them; with the heavens, indeed, the sun, moon, fixed stars and planets; with the earth, animals and plants, gold and silver; with the aerial region, spiritual substances and wind, heating and cooling; for it is the property of the heavens to subsist in conjunction with the natures which it comprehends, and of the earth to support its native plants and animals; of the aerial regions, to be consubsistent with the natures it has generated. Since the therefore in each division of the world there is arranged a certain genus of animals which surpasses its fellows, the heavens are the habitat of the gods, on the earth men, and in the space between, the geniuses. Therefore the race of men must be perpetual, since reason convinces us that not only are the world's parts consubsitent with it, but also their comprehended natures.

Sudden destructions, and mutations however take place in the parts of the earth; the sea overflows on to the land, or the earth shakes and spits, through the unobserved entrance of wind or water. But an entire destruction of the earth's whole arrangement never took place, nor ever will. Hence the story that Grecian history began with the Argive Inachus is false, if understood to be a first principle, but true, as some mutations of Greek politics; for Greece has frequently been, and will again be barbarous, not only from the irruption of foreigners, but from Nature herself, which, although she does not become greater or less; yet is always younger, and has a beginning in reference to us.

So much about the whole, and the universe; the generation and corruption of natures generated in it; how they subsist, and for ever; one part of the universe consisting of a nature which is perpetually moved, and another passive one; the former governing, the latter ever governed.

IV
GROWTH OF MEN

Law, temperance and piety conspire in explaining as follows the generation of men from each other, after what manner, from what particulars, and how effected. The first postulate is that sexual association should occur never for pleasure but only for procreation of children.

Those powers and instruments, and appetites ministering to copulation were implanted in man by divinity, not for the sake of voluptuousness, but for the perpetuation of the race. Since it was impossible that man, who is born mortal, should participate in a divine life were his race not immortal, divinity operated this immortality through individuals, and lent continuousness to mankind's generation. This is the first essential, that cohabitation should not be effected for mere pleasure.

Next, man should be considered in connection with the social organism, a house or city, and especially that each human progeny should work at the completion of the world, unless he plans to be a deserter of either the domestic, political or divine Vestal hearth.

For those who are not entirely connected with each other for the sake of begetting children, injure the most honorable system of convention. But if persons of this description procreate with libidinous insolence and intemperance, their offspring will be miserable and flagitious, and will be execrated by God and geniuses, by men, families and cities.

Those therefore who deliberately consider these things ought not, in a way similar to irrational animals, to engage in venereal connections, but should think copulation a necessary good. For it is the opinion of worthy men that it is necessary and beautiful, not only to fill houses with large families, and also the greater part of the earth (for man is the most mild and the best of all animals), but as a thing of the greatest consequence, to cause them to abound with the most excellent men.

For on this account men inhabit cities governed by the best laws, rightly manage their domestic affairs and if they are able, impart to their friends such political employments as are conformable to the polities in which they live, since they not only provide for the multitude at large, but especially for worthy men.

Hence many men err who enter into connubial state without regarding the magnitude off the power of fortune, or public utility, but direct their attention to wealth, or dignity of birth. For in consequence of this, instead of uniting with females who are young and in the flower of their age, they become connected with extremely old women; and instead of having wives with a disposition according with, and most similar to their own, they marry those who are of an illustrious family, or are extremely rich. On this account, they procure for themselves discord instead of concord; and instead of unanimity, dissension; contending with each other for the mastery. For the wife who surpasses her husband in wealth, in birth, or in friends, is desirous of ruling over him, contrary to the law of nature. But the husband justly resisting this desire of superiority in his wife, and wishing not to be the second, but the first in domestic sway, is unable, in the management of his family, to take the lead.

This being, the case, it happens that not only families, but cities become miserable. For families are parts of cities, while the composition of the whole and the universe derives its subsistence from its parts. It is therefore, reasonable to admit that such as are the parts, such likewise will be the whole and the all which consists of things of this kind. As in fabrics of a primary nature the first structures operate greatly to the good or bad completion of the whole work; as for instance the manner in which the foundation is laid in a house-building, the structure of a keel in ship-building, and the utterance and closing of voice in musical modulation, so the concordant condition of families greatly contributes to the well or ill establishment of a polity.

Those therefore who direct their attention to the propagation of the human species, ought guard against everything which is dissimilar and imperfect; for neither plants nor animals when imperfect are prolific, but their fructification demands a certain amount of time, so that when the bodies are strong and perfect, they may produce seeds and fruits.

Hence it is necessary that boys and girls while they are virgin should be trained up in exercising and proper endurance, and that they be nourished with that kind of food which is adapted to a laborious, temperate, and patient life.

Moreover, in human life there are many things of such a kind that it is better for the knowledge of them to be deferred, for a certain time. Hence a boy should be so tutored as not to seek after venereal pleasure before he is twenty years of age, and then should rarely engage in them. This however will take place if he conceives that a good habit of body and continence are beautiful and honorable.

The following laws should be taught in Grecian cities: that connection with a mother, or a daughter, or a sister, should not be permitted either in temples or in a public place; for it would be well to employ numerous impediments to this energy.

All natural connexions, should be prevented, especially those attended with wanton insolence. But such as harmonize with nature should be encouraged, such as are effected with temperance for the purpose of producing a temperate and legitimate offspring.

Again, those who intend to beget children should providentially attend to the welfare of their future offspring. A temperate and salutary diet therefore is the first and greatest thing to be considered by the would be begetter; so that he should neither be filled with unseasonable food, nor become intoxicated, nor subject himself to any other perturbation which may injure the body -habits. But above all things he should be careful that the mind in the act of copulation should remain in a tranquil state, for bad seed is produced from depraved, discordant and turbulent habits.

With all possible earnestness and attention, we should endeavor that children be born elegant and graceful, and that when born, they should be well educated. For it is foolish that those who rear horses, birds or dog should, with the utmost diligence render the breed perfect, and from proper food, and when it is proper; and likewise consider how they ought to be disposed when they copulate with each other, that the offspring be not the result of chance; while men are inattentive to their progeny, begetting them by chance; and when begotten, should neglect both their food and education. It is the disregard of these that causes all the vice and depravity, since those born thus will resemble cattle, ignoble and vile.

ON LAWS
(Fragment preserved by Stobaeus, E.Ph.8:16)

As life contains bodies, whose cause is the soul, so harmony, connectedly, comprehends the world, whose cause is God. Likewise concord unites families, whose cause is the law. Therefore there is a certain cause and nature which perpetually adapts to each other the parts of the world, hindering their being disordered and unconnected. However, cities and families continue only for a short time; as the formerÕs constituent matter, and the latterÕs progeny contain the cause of dissolution, deriving their subsistence from a mutable and perpetually passive nature. For the destruction of things which are generated is the salvation of the matter from which they are generated. That nature, however, which is perpetually moved governs; while that which is always passive is governed; the capacity of the former being prior, and of the latter posterior. The former is divine, possessing reason and intellect, the latter being generated, irrational and mutable.

ON FELICITY

Of animals, some are capable of felicity, while others are incapable. Felicity cannot subsist without virtue; and, this is impossible to any lacking reason; so that those animals are incapable of felicity who are destitute of reason. The blind cannot exercise or practise sight, nor can the irrational attain to the work and virtue dependent on reason. To that which possesses reason, felicity is a work, and virtue an art. Of rational animals, some are self-perfect, in need of nothing external, either for their existence, or artistic achievement. Such indeed is God. On the contrary those animals are not self-perfect whose perfection is not due to themselves, or who are in need of anything external. Such an animal; is man. Of not self-perfect animals some are perfect, and others not. The former derive their subsistence from both their own proper causes, and from the external. They derive it indeed from their own causes, because they obtain from thence both an excellent nature; and deliberate choice; but from external causes, because they receive from thence equitable legislation, and good rulers. The animals which are not perfect are either such as participate of neither of these, or of some one of those, or whose souls are entirely depraved. Such will be the man who is of a description different from the above.

Moreover, of perfect men there are two kinds. Some of them are naturally perfect, while others are perfect only in relation to their lives. Only the good are naturally perfect, and these possess virtue. For the virtue of the [of] anything is a consummation and perfection. Thus the virtue of the eye is the eye's nature's [--] consummation and perfection. So man's virtue is man's nature's consummation and perfection.

Those also are perfect according to life, who are not only good, but happy. For indeed felicity is the perfection of human life. But human life is a system of actions; and felicity completes actions. Virtue and fortune, also complete life; (but only partially; virtue according to use; and good fortune according to prosperity. God, therefore, is neither good through learning virtue f rom anyone, nor is he happy through being attended by good fortune. For he is good and happy by nature, and always was, is and never will cease to be; since he is incorruptible, and naturally good. But man is neither happy nor good by nature, requiring discipline and providential care. To become good, he requires virtue; but to become happy, good fortune. On this account, human felicity may be summarily said to consist of these two things: praise, and being called happy. Praise indeed, because of virtue; but being called happy, from prosperity. Therefore it possesses virtue, through divine destiny; but prosperity through a mortal allotment. But mortal concerns depend on divine ones, and terrestrial on celestial. Likewise, subordinate things depend on the more excellent. That is why the good man who follows the Gods is happy, but he who follows mortal nature is unhappy. For to him who possesses wisdom, prosperity is good and useful; being good, through his knowledge of the use of it; but it is useful through his cooperating with actions. It is beautiful, therefore when prosperity is present with intellect, and when, as it we were sailing with a prosperous wind, action are performed that tend towards virtue; just as a pilot watches the motions of the stars. Thus he who does this will not only follow God, but will also harmonize human with divine good.

This also is evident, that human life becomes different from disposition and action. But it is necessary that the disposition should be either worthy or depraved; and that action should be attended with either felicity or misery. A worthy disposition indeed participates of virtue, while a bad one of vice. With respect to actions, also, those that are prosperous are attended with felicity; (for they derive their completion by looking to reason;) but those that are unfortunate, are attended with misery; for they are disappointed of their end. Hence it is not only necessary to learn virtue, but also to possess and use it; either for security, or growth; (of property, when it is too small), or, which is the greatest thing of all, for the improvement of families and cities. For it is not only necessary to have the possession of things beautiful, but also their use. All these things, however, will take place, when a man lives in a city that enjoys equitable laws. This is what is signified by the horn of Amalthea; for all things are contained in equitable legislation. Without this, the greatest good of human nature can neither be effected, nor, when effected, can be increased and become permanent. For this contains both virtue and tendency towards it; because excellent natures are generated according to it. Likewise manners, studies and laws through this subsist in the most excellent condition; and besides these, rightly-decided reason, and piety and sanctity towards the most honorable natures.

Therefore he who is to be happy, and whose life is to be prosperous, should live and [work] in a country governed by equitable laws, relinquishing all lawlessness. All the above is necessary for man is a part of society, and according to the same reasoning will become entirely [im]perfect, if he associates with others, but not in a becoming manner.

For some things are naturally adapted to subsist in many things, and not in one thing; others in one thing and not in many; others both in many and in one, and on this account in one thing because in many. For indeed harmony, symphony and number are naturally adapted to be insinuated into many things. Nothing which makes a whole from these parts is sufficient in itself. But acuteness of seeing and hearing, and swiftness of feet, subsist in one thing alone. Felicity, however, and virtue of soul, subsist both in one thing and many, in a whole, and in the universe. On this account they subsist in one thing, because they also subsist in many; and they subsist in many because, they inhere in the whole and the universe. For the orderly distribution of the whole nature of things methodically arranges each particular. The orderly distribution of particulars gives completion to the whole of things, and to the universe. But this follows from the whole being naturally prior to the part, and not the part to the whole. For if the world was not, neither the sun nor the moon would exist, not the planets, nor the fixed stars. But the world existing, each of these also exists.

The truth of this may also be seen in the nature itself of animals. For if the animal had no existence, there would be neither eye, mouth, or ear. But the animal existing, each of these likewise exists. However, as the whole is to the part, so is the virtue of the whole to that of the part. For if harmony did not exist, nor a divine inspection of human affairs, adorned things could no longer remain in good condition. Were there no equitable legislation in a city, the citizen could be neither good nor happy. Did the animal lack health, neither foot nor hand could be in health. The world's virtue is harmony; the city's virtue is equitable legislation, and the bodyÕs virtue are health and strength. Likewise, each of the parts is adjusted to the whole and the universe. For the eye sees on account of the whole body; and the other parts and members are adjusted for the sake of the whole (body) and the universe.

ON A REPUBLIC

I say that the whole of a polity is divided into three parts; the good men who manage the public affairs, those who are powerful, and those who are employed in supplying and procuring the necessaries of life. The first group is that of the counselors, the auxiliaries, and the mechanical and sordid arts. The first two groups belong to the liberal condition of life; the third, of those who labor to procure subsistence. Of these the council is best, the laborers, the worst; and the auxiliaries, a medium between the two. The council should govern, and the laborers should be governed; and the auxiliaries should both govern and be governed. For that which consults for the general good previously deliberates what ought to be done; while that which is of an auxiliary nature, so far as it is belligerent, rules over the whole mechanical tribe; but it is itself governed in so far as it has previously received advice from others.

Of these parts, however, each again receives a triple division. For of that which consults, one part presides, another governs, and another counsels for the general good. With respect to the presiding part, is that which plans, contrives, and deliberates about what pertains to the community, prior to the other parts, and afterwards refers its counsels to the senate. But the governing part is either that which now rules (for the first time), or which has before performed that office. With respect to the third part, which consults for the general good, this receives the advice of the earlier parts, and by its suffrages and authority confirms whatever it [referred] to its decisions. In short, those who provide should refer the community's affairs to that part which consults for the general good; while the latter part should refer these affairs through the presiding officers to the convention.

Likewise, of that part which is auxiliary, powerful and efficacious, one part is of a governing nature; another part is defensive, and the remaining, and greater part, is private and military. It is the governing part, therefore, from which the leaders of the armies, the officers of the bands, the bands of soldiers, and the vanguard are derived; and universally all those who rank as leaders. The vanguard consists of the bravest, the most impetuous, and the most daring, the remaining military multitude being gregarious. Of the third part engaged in sordid occupations, and in laboring to procure the necessaries of life, one part consists of husbandmen, and those employed in the cultivation of land; another are artisans, making such instruments and machines as are required by the occasions of life, and another part travels and bargains, exporting to foreign regions such things as are superabundant in the city, and importing into it other things from foreign countries. The systems of political society are organized in many such parts.

Next we must study their adaptation and union. Since, however, the whole of political society may be well compared to a lyre, as it requires apparatus and mutual adjustment, and also because it must be touched and used musically; Ñ this is enough.

Political society is organized by disciplines, the study of customs, and laws; through these three, man is educated, and improved. Disciplines are the source of erudition, and lead the desires to tend towards virtue. The laws, both repelling men from the commissions of crimes, and alluring them by honors and gifts incite them (to virtue). Manners and studies fashion the soul like wax, and through their continued energy impress thereon propensities that become second nature. These three should however cooperate with the beautiful, the useful and the just; each of these three should if possible aim at all these three; but if not all of them, it should at least have two or one of than as its goal, so that disciplines, manners and laws may be beautiful, just and advantageous. In the first place, the beautiful in conduct should be preferred; in the second place the just, and in the third place the useful. Universally the endeavor should be that through these the city may become, in the most eminent degree, consentaneous and concordant with its parts, and may be free from sedition and hostile contention. This will happen if the passions in the youths' souls are disciplined, and in things pleasing and painful are led to mediocrity, and if the possessions of men are moderate, and they derive their subsistence from the cultivation of the earth. This will also be accomplished, if good men rule over those that are in want of virtue; skillful men over those that are wanting in skill, and rich men over those things that require a certain amount of generosity and expenditure; and if also appropriate honors are distributed to those who govern in all these in a becoming manner. But there are three causes which are incitements to virtue,Ñ fear desire and shame. Law can produce fear, but custom shame; for those that are accustomed to act well will be ashamed to do anything that is base. Desire is produced by disciplines; for they simultaneously assign the causes of things and attract the soul, and especially so when accompanied by exhortation. Hence the souls of young men should be sufficiently instructed in what pertains to senates, fellowship and associations, both military and political, but that the tribe of elderly men should be trained to things of this kind; since young men indeed require correction and instruction, but elderly men need benevolent associations, and a mode of living unattended by pain. Since therefore we have said that the worthy man is perfected through three things, customs, laws and disciplines, we must consider how customs or manners are corrupted usually, and how they grow permanent. We shall then find that customs are corrupted in two ways; through ourselves, or foreigners. Through ourselves indeed, through our flying from pain, whereby we fail to endure labor; or through pursuit of pleasure; whereby we reject the good, for labors procure good, and pleasures evil. Hence through pleasures, becoming incontent and remiss, men are rendered effeminate in their souls, and more prodigal. Customs and manners are corrupted through foreigners when their numbers swamp the natives, and best of the success of their mercantile employments; or when those who dwell in the suburbs, becoming lovers of pleasures and luxury, their manners spread to the single neighbors. Therefore the legislators, officers and mass of the people should diligently take notice whether the customs of the city are being carefully preserved, and that throughout the whole people. Moreover they should see to the preserving pure of the home race, avoiding crossing with other nations, and whether the general wealth's total remains the same, without undue increase. For the possession of superfluities is accompanied by the desire of still more of the superfluous. In such ways the customs should be preserved.

With respect to disciplines, however, the same legislators and officers, should diligently inspect and examine the sophists, whether they are teaching what is useful to the laws, to the established political principles, and to the local economy of life. For sophistic doctrines may infect men with no passing, but greatest infelicity; when they dare make innovations in anything pertaining to human or divine affairs, contrary to the popular views; than which nothing can be more pernicious either with respect to truth, security or renown. In addition to this, they introduce into the minds of the general people obscurity and confusion. Of this kind are all doctrines that teach either that there is no God, or if there is, that he is not affected towards the human race so as to regard it with providential care, but despises and deserts it. In men such doctrines produce folly and injustice, to a degree that is inexpressible. Any anarchist who has dismissed fear of disobedience to the laws, violates them with wanton boasts. Hence the necessity of political and traditionally venerable principles; adapted to the speakers' disposition, free from dissimulation. Thus what is said exhibits the speakers's manners. The laws will inevitably introduce security if the polity is organized on lines of natural laws, and not on the unnatural. From a tyranny cities derive no advantage, and very little from an oligarchy. The first need, therefore, is a kingdom, and the second is and aristocracy.

For a kingdom, indeed, is as it were an image of God, and which is with difficulty preserved and defended by the human soul. For it rapidly degenerates through luxury and insolence. Hence it is not proper to employ it universally, but only so far as i tmay be useful to the state; and an aristocracy should be liberally mingled with it, as this consists of many rulers, who emulate each other, and often govern alternately. There must however also be democratic elements; for as the citizen is part of the whole state, he, also should receive a reward from it. Yet he must be sufficiently restrained, for the common people are bold and rash.

By a necessity of nature, everything mortal is subject to changes; some improving, others growing worse. Things born, increase until they arrive at their consummation, whereafter they age and perish. Things that grow of themselves, by the same nature decay into the hidden beyond; and then return to mortality through transformation of growth; then by repeated decay, retrograde in another circle. Sometimes, when houses or cities have attained the peak of supreme happiness in exuberant wealth, they have, through an ebullition of insolent self-satisfaction, through human folly, perished together with their vaunted possessions.

Thus every human empire has shown three distinct stages: growth, fruition, and destruction. For in the beginning, being destitute of goods, empires are engrossed in acquisition; but after they become wealthy, they perish. Such things, therefore, are under the dominion of the gods, being incorruptible, are preserved through the whole of time, by incorruptible natures; but such things as are under the government of men, being mortal; from mortals receive perpetual disturbance. The end of self-satisfaction and insolence is destruction; but poverty and narrow circumstances often result in a strenuous and worthy life. Not poverty alone, but many other things, bring human life to an end.

ON SANCTITY

It is necessary that the laws should not be enclosed in houses, or by gates, but in the manners of the citizens. Which, therefore is the basic principle of any state? The education of the youth. For vines will never bear useful fruit, unless they are well cultivated; nor will horses ever excel, unless the colts are properly trained. Recently ripened fruit grows similar to its surroundings. With utmost prudence do men study how to prune and tend the vines; but to things pertaining to the education of their species the behave rashly and negligently; though neither wines nor wine govern men, but man and the soul of man. The nurture of a plant, indeed, we commit to an expert, who is supposed to deserve no less than two minae (a day); but the education of youth we commit to some Illyrian or Thracian, who is worthless. As the earliest legislators could not render the bourgeoisie stable, they prescribed (in the curriculum) dancing and rhythm, which instills motion and order; and besides these they added sports, some of which induced fellowship, but others truth and mental keenness. For those who thought that intoxication or guzzling had committed any crime, the prescribed the pipe of harmony, which by maturing and refining the manners so-shaped the mind that it became capable of culture.

It is well to invoke God at the beginning and end both of supper and dinner, not because he is in want of anything of the kind, but in order that the soul may be transfigured by the recollection of divinity. For since we proceed from him, and participate in a divine nature, we should honor him. Since also God is just, we also should act justly in all things.

In the next place, there are four causes which terminate all things; and bring them to an end; namely nature, law, art and fortune. Nature is admittedly the principle of all things. Law is the inspective guardian and creator of all things that change manners into political concord. Art is justly said to be the mother and guide of things consummated through human prudence. But of things which accidentally happen to the worthy and unworthy, the cause is ascribed to fortune, which does not produce anything orderly, moderate, or controlled.

CONCERNING A KINGDOM

A king should be one who is most just; and he will be most just who most closely attends to the laws. Without justice it is impossible to a king; and without law there can be no justice. For justice is such only through law, justice's effective cause. A king is either animated law, or a legal ruler, whence he will be just, and observant of the laws. There are however three peculiar employments of a king: leading an army, administering justice, and worshipping the Gods. He will be able to lead an army properly only if he knows how to carry on war properly. He will be skilled in administering justice and in governing all his subjects only if he has well learned the nature of justice and law. He will worship the gods in a pious and holy manner only if he has diligently considered the nurture and virtue of God..... a good king must necessarily be a good general, judge and priest; which things are inseparable from the goodness and virtue of a king. It is the pilot's business to preserve the ship; the charioteer to preserve the chariot; and the physician's to save the sick, but it is a king's or a general's business to save those who are in danger in battle. For a leader must also be a provident inspector, and preserver. While judicial affairs are in general every body's interest, this is the special work of the king; who, like a god, is a world-leader and protector. While the whole state should be generally organized in a unitary manner, under unitary leadership, individual parts should be submissive to the supreme domination. Besides though the king should oblige and benefit his subjects, this should not be in contempt of justice and law. The third characteristic of a king's dignity is the worship of the Gods. The most excellent should be worshipped by the most excellent; and the leader and ruler by that which leads and rules. Of naturally most honorable things, God is the best; but of things on the earth, and human, a king is the supreme. As God is to the world, so is a king to his kingdom; and as a city is to the world, so is a king to God. For a city, indeed, being organized from things many and various, imitates the organization of the world; and its harmony; but a king whose rule is beneficent, and who himself is animated law, to men outlines the divinity.

It is hence necessary that a king should not be overcome by pleasure, but that he should overcome it; that he should not resemble, but excel the multitude; and that he should not conceive his proper employment to consist in the pursuit of pleasure, but rather in the achievement of character. Likewise he who rules others should be able first to govern his own passions.

As to the desire of obtaining great property, it must be observed that a king ought to be wealthy so as to benefit his friends, relieve those in want, and justly punish his enemies. Most delightful is the enjoyment of wealth in conjunction with virtue. So also about the preeminence of a king; for since he always surpasses others in virtue, a judgment of his empire might be formed with reference to virtue; and not to riches, power, or military strength. Riches he possesses in common with any one of his subjects; power, in common with animals, and military strength in common with tyrants. But virtue is the prerogative of good men; hence, whatever king is temperate with respect to pleasures, liberal with respect to money, and prudent and sagacious in government, he will in reality be a king. The people, however, have the same analogy with respect to the virtues and the vices, as the parts of the human soul. For the desire to accumulate the superfluous continues with the irrational part of the soul; for desire is not rational. But ambition and ferocity cling to the irascible part; for this is the furious part of the soul. The love of pleasure clings to the passionate part, which is effeminate and yielding. Injustice, however, which is the supreme vice, is composite and clings to the whole soul. The king should organize the well-legislated city like a lyre; first with himself establishing the just boundary and order of Law; knowing that the people's proper arrangement should be organized according to this interior boundary, the divinity having given him dominion over them. The good king should also establish proper positions and habits in the delivery of public orations, behaving in a cultured manner, seriously and earnestly, lest he seem either rough or abject to the multitude; but show agreeable and easy manners. These things he will obtain if in the first place his aspect and discourse be worthy of respect, and if appears to deserve the sovereign authority which he possesses. But in the second place, if he proves himself to be benign in behavior to those he may meet, in countenance and beneficence. In the third place, if his hatred of depravity is formidable, by the punishment he inflicts thereon, from his quickness in inflicting it, and in short from his skill and exercise in the art of government. For venerable gravity being something which imitates divinity, is capable of winning for him the admiration and honor of the multitude. Benignity will render him pleasing and beloved. His formidableness will frighten his enemies, and save him from being conquered; and make him magnanimous and confident to his friends.

His gravity, however, should have no abject or vulgar element; it should be admirable, and worthy of the dignity of rule and sceptre. He should never contend with his inferiors or equals, but with those that are greater than himself; and, conformably to the magnitude of his empire, he should count those pleasures greatest which are derived from beautiful and great deeds and not those which arise from sensual gratifications; separating himself indeed from human passions and approximating the Gods, not through arrogance, but through magnanimity and the invincible preeminence of virtue. Hence he should invest his aspect and reasonings with such a gracefulness and majesty, and also in his mental conceptions and soul-manners, in his actions, and body motions and gestures, that those who observe him may perceive that he is adorned and fashioned with modesty and temperance, and a dignified disposition. A good king should be able to charm those who behold him, no less than the sound of a flute and harmony attract those that hear them. Enough about the venerable gravity of a king. I must now mention his benignity. Generally, any king who is just, equitable and beneficent will be benign. Justice is a connective and collective communion, and is that disposition of the soul which adapts itself to those near us. As rhythm is to motion, and harmony to the voice, so is justice to diplomacy; since it is the governors' and the governedsÕ common good, harmonizing political society. But justice has two fellow administrators, equity and benignity; the former softening severity of punishment, the latter extending pardon to the less guilty offenders. A good king must extend assistance to those in need of it; and be beneficent; and this assistance should be given not in one way only, but in every possible manner. Besides, this beneficence should not be (hypocritical), regarding the honor to be derived therefrom, but come from the deliberate choice of the giver. Towards all men a king should conduct himself so as to avoid being troublesome to them, especially to men of inferior rank, and of slender fortune; for these, like diseased bodies, can endure nothing of a troublesome nature. Good kings, indeed, have dispositions similar to the Gods, especially resembling Jupiter, the universal ruler, who is venerable and honorable through the magnanimous preeminence of virtue. He is benign, because he is beneficent, and the giver of good; hence by the Ionic poet (Homer) he is said to be father of men and gods. He is also eminently terrible, punishing the unjust, reigning and ruling over all things. In his hand he carries thunder, as a symbol of his formidable excellence. All these particulars remind us that a kingdom is something resembling the divine.

THEAGES
ON THE VIRTUES

The soul is divided into reasoning power, anger and desire. Reasoning power rules knowledge, anger deals with impulse, and desire bravely rules the soul's affections. When these three parts unite into one action, exhibiting a composite energy, then in the soul results concord and virtue. When sedition divides them, then appear discord and vice. Virtue therefore contains three elements; reason, power, and deliberate choice. The soul's reasoning power's virtue is prudence, which is a habit of contemplating and judging. The irascible part's virtue is fortitude; which is a habit of enduring dreadful things, and resisting them. The appetitive part's virtue is temperance; which is a moderation and detention of the pleasures which arise from the body. The whole soul's virtue is justice; for men indeed become bad either through vice, or through incontinence, or through a natural ferocity. They injure each other either through gain, pleasure or ambition. More appropriately therefore does vice belong to the soul's reasoning part. While prudence is similar to good art, vice resembles bad art, inventing contrivances to act unjustly. Incontinence pertains to the soul's appetitive part, as continence consists in subduing, and incontinence in failure to subdue pleasures. Ferocity belongs to the soul's irascible part, for when some ennactivated by evil desires is gratified not as a man should be, but as a beast would be, then this is called ferocity.

The effects of these dispositions also result from the things for the sake of which they are performed. Vice, hailing from the soul's reasoning part results in avarice; the irascible part's fault is ambition, which results in ferocity; and as the appetitive part ends in pleasure, this generates incontinence. As unjust actions are the results of so many causes, so also are just deeds; for virtue is a naturally beneficent and profitable as vice is maleficent and harmful.

Since, however, of the parts of the soul one leads while the others follow, and since the virtues and vice subsist about these and in these, it is evident that with respect to the virtues also, some are leaders and others followers, while others are compounds of these. The leaders are such as prudence; the followers being fortitude and temperance; their composites are such as justice. How the virtues subsist in and about the passions, so we may call the latter the matter of the former. Of the passions, one is voluntary, and the others involuntary; pleasure being the voluntary, and pain the involuntary. Men who have the political virtues increase and decrease these, organizing the other parts of the soul to that which possesses reason. The desirable point of this adaptation is that intellect should not be prevented from accomplishing its proper work, either by lack of excess. We adapt the less good to that which is more so; as in the world every part that is always passive subsists for the sake of that which is always moved. In the conjunction of animals, the female subsists for the sake of the male; for the latter sows, generating a soul, while the former alone imparts matter to that which is generated. In the soul, the irrational subsists for the sake of the rational part. Anger and desire are organized in dependence on the first part of the soul, the former as a satellite and guardian of the body, the latter as a dispenser and provider of necessary wants. Intellect being established in the highest summit of the body, and having a prospect in that which is on all sides splendid and transparent, investigates the wisdom of real beings. This indeed is its natural function, to investigate and obtain possession of the truth, and to follow those beings which are more excellent and honorable than itself. For the knowledge of things divine and most honorable is the principle, cause and rule of human blessedness.

The principles of all virtue are three; knowledge, power and deliberate choice. Knowledge indeed is that by which we contemplate and form a judgment of things; power is a certain strength of nature from which we derive our subsistence, and which gives stability to our actions; and deliberate choice is as it were the hands of the soul by which we are impelled to, and lay hold on the objects of our choice...When the reasoning power prevails over the irrational part of the soul, then endurance and continence are produced; endurance indeed in the retention of pains, but continence in the absence of pleasures. But when the irrational parts of the soul prevail over the reasoning part of the soul, then are produced effeminacy in flying from pain, and incontinence in being vanquished by the pleasures. When however the better part of the soul prevails, the less excellent part is governed; the former leads, and the latter follows, and both consent and agree, and then in the whole soul is generated virtue and all the goods. Again, when the appetitive part of the soul follows the reasoning, then is produced temperance, when this is the case with the irascible, appears fortitude; and when it takes place in all the parts of the soul, then the result is justice. Justice is that which separates all the vices and all the virtues of the soul from each other. Justice is an established order and organization of the parts of the soul, and the perfect and supreme virtue; in this every good is contained, while the other goods of the soul cannot subsist without it. Hence justice possesses great influence both among gods and men. It contains the bond by which the whole and the universe are held together, and also that by which the gods and men are connected. Among the celestials it is called Themis, and among the terrestrials it is called Dice; while among men it is called the Law. These are but symbols indicative that justice is the supreme virtue. Virtue, therefore, when it consists in contemplating and judging, is called prudence; when in sustaining dreadful things, is called fortitude; when in restraining pleasure, it is called temperance; and when in abstaining from injuring our neighbors, justice.

Obedience to virtue according to, and transgression thereof contrary to right reason, tend towards decorousness, and its opposite. Propriety is that which ought to be. This requires neither addition or detraction, being what it should be. The improper is of two kinds: excess and defect. The excess is over -scrupulousness, and its deficiency, laxity. Virtue however is a habit of propriety. Hence it is both a climax and a medium of which are proper things. They are media because they fall between excess and deficiency; they are climaxes, because they endure neither increase nor decrease, being just what they ought to be.

Since however the virtue of manners consists in dealing with the passions, over which pleasure and pain are supreme, virtue evidently does not consist in extirpating the passions of the soul, pleasure and pain, but in regulating them. Not any more does health, which is an adjustment of the bodily powers, consist in expelling the cold and the hot, the moist and the dry, but in adjusting them suitably and symmetrically. Likewise in music, concord does not consist in expelling the sharp and the flat, but in exterminating dissonance by concord arising from their adjustment. Therefore it is the harmonious adjustment of heat and cold, moisture and dryness which produces health, and destroys disease. Thus by the mutual adjustment of anger and desire, the vices and other passions are extirpated, while virtue and good manners are induced. How the greatest peculiarity of the virtue of manners in beauty of conduct is deliberate choice. Reason and power may be used without virtue, but deliberate choice cannot be used without it; for deliberate choice inspires dignity of manners.

When the reasoning power by force subdues anger and desire, it produces continence and endurance. Again when the reasoning force is dethroned violently by the irrational parts, then result incontinence and effeminacy. Such dispositions of the soul as these are half-perfect virtues and vices. For (according to its nature) the reasoning power of the soul induces health, while the irrational induces disease. So far as anger and desire are governed and led by the soul's rational part, continence and endurance become virtues; but in so far as this is effected by violence, involuntarily, they become vices. For virtue must carry out what is proper not with pain but pleasure. So far as anger and desire rule the reasoning power there is produced effeminacy and incontinence, which are vices; but in so far as they gratify the passions with pain, knowing that they are erroneous in consequence of the eye of the soul being healthy, so far as this is the case, they are not vices. Hence it is evident that virtue must voluntarily do what is proper, as the involuntary implies pain and fear, while the voluntary implies pleasure and delight.

This may be corroborated by division. Knowledge and the perception of things are the province of the rational part of the soul; while power pertained to the irrational part, whose peculiarity is in an ability to resist pain, or to vanquish pleasure. Both of these, the rational and the irrational, subsists deliberate choice, which consists of intention and appetite, intention pertaining to the rational part, and appetite to the irrational. Hence every virtue consists in a mutual adaptation of the souls parts while, both will and deliberate choice subsist entirely in virtue. In general, therefore, virtue is a mutual [adaptation] of the irrational part of the soul to the irrational to the irrational. Virtue, however, is produced through pleasure and pain striking the right resultance of propriety. But propriety is that which ought to be, and the improper, what ought not;....... The fit and the unfit are to each other as the equal and the unequal, as the ordered and the disordered; of, which the two former are finite, and the two latter are the infinite (limit and infinity are the two great principles of things, below the universal ineffable cause). On this account the parts of the unequal are referred to the middle, but not to each other. An angle greater than a right angle is called obtuse; the acute one being less than it. (In a circle) also, the right line is greater than the radius, drawn from the centre. Any day beyond the equinox is greater is greater than it. Overheat or undercold produce diseases. Overheatedness exceeds moderation, which over-coldness does not reach.

The same analogy holds good in connection with the soul. Boldness is an excess of propriety in the endurance of things of a dreadful nature; while, timidity is a deficiency. Prodigality is an excess of proper expenditure of money; while illiberality is its excess. Rage is an excess of the proper use of the soul's irascible part, while insensibility ii the corresponding deficiency. The same reasoning applies to the opposition of the other dispositions of the soul. Since however virtue is a habit of propriety, and a medium of the passions, it should be neither wholly passive, nor immoderately passive. Impassivity causes unimpelledness of the soul and lack of enthusiasm for the beautiful in conduct, while immoderate passivity perturbs the soul, and makes it inconsiderate. We should then, in virtue, see passions as shadow and outline in a picture; which depend on animation and delicacy, imitation of the truth and contrast of coloring. The soul's passions are animated by the natural incitation and enthusiasm of virtue, which is generated from the passions, and subsisting with them. Similarly, harmony includes the sharp and the flat, and mixtures consist of heat and cold, and equilibrium results from weight and lightness.

Therefore, neither would it be necessary nor profitable to remove the passions of the soul: but they must be mutually adjusted to the rational part; under the direction of propriety and moderation.

ZALEUCUS THE LOCRIAN
PREFACE TO HIS LAWS

All inhabitants of city or country should in the first place be firmly persuaded of the existence of divinities, as result of their observation of the heavens and the world and the orderly arrangement of their contained beings. These are not the productions of fortune or of men. We should reverence and honor them as causes of every reasonable good. We should therefore prepare our souls so they may be free from vice. For the gods are not honored by the worship of a bad man, nor through sumptuousity of offerings, nor with the tragical expense of a depraved man; but by virtue, and the deliberate choice of good and beautiful deeds. All of us, therefore, should be as good as possible, both in actions and deliberate choice; if he wishes to be dear to divinity. He should not fear the loss of money more than that of renown; such a one would be considered the better citizen. Those who do not easily feel so impelled, and whose soul is easily excited to injustice, are invited to consider the following. They, and their fellow residents of a house should remember that there are Gods who punish the unjust, and should remember that no one escapes the final liberation from life. For in the supreme moment they will repent, from remembering their unjust deeds, and wishing that their deeds had been just. Everyone, in every action should be mindful of this time, as if it were present; which is a powerful incentive to probity and justice.

Should any one feel (tempted by) the presence of an evil genius, tempting him to injustice, he should go into a temple, remain at the altar, or in sacred groves, flying from injustice as from an impious and harmful mistress, supplicating the divinities to cooperate with him in turning it away from himself. He should also seek the company of men known for their probity, in order to hear them discourse about a blessed life and the punishment of bad men, that he may be deterred from bad deeds, dreading none but the avenging geniuses.

Citizens should honor all the Gods according to the particular country's legal rites, which should be considered as the most beautiful of all others. Citizens should, besides obeying the laws, show their respect for the rulers by rising before them, and obeying their instructions. Men who are intelligent, and wish to be saved should, after the Gods, geniuses and heroes most honor parents, laws, and rulers.

Let none love his city better than his country, the indignation of whose gods he would thus be exciting; for such conduct is the beginning of treachery. For a man to leave his country and reside in a foreign land, is something most afflicting and unbearable; for nothing is more kindred to us than out natal country. Nor let anyone consider a naturalized citizen an implacable enemy; such a person could neither judge, nor govern properly, for his anger predominates over his reason. Let none speak ill either of the whole city, or of a private citizen.

Let the guardians of the laws keep a watchful eye over offenders, first by admonishing them, and if that is not sufficient, by punishment. Should any established law seem unsatisfactory, let it be changed into a better one; but whichever remain should be universally obeyed; for the breaking of established laws is neither beautiful nor beneficial; though it is both beautiful and beneficial to be restrained by a more excellent law, as if vanquished thereby.

Transgressors of established laws should however be punished, as promoting anarchy, which is the greatest evil. The magistrates should neither be arrogant, nor judge insultingly, nor in passing sentence regard friendship, or hate, being partial, thus deciding more justly, and being worthy of the magistracy. Slaves should do what is just through fear, but free men, through shame, and for the sake of beauty in conduct. Governors should be men of this kind, to arouse reverence.

Anyone who wishes to change any one of the established laws, or to introduce another law, should put a halter around his neck, and address the people. And if from the suffrages it should appear that the established law should be dissolved, or that a new law should be introduced, let him not be punished. But if it should appear that the preexisting law is better, or, that the new proposition is unjust, let him who wishes to change an old, or introduce a new law, be executed by the halter.

CHARONDAS THE CATANEAN
PREFACE TO HIS LAWS

From the Gods should begin any deliberation or performance; for according to the old proverb: "God should be the cause of all our deliberation and works." Further, we should abstain from base actions especially on account of consulting with the gods; for there is no communication between God and the unjust.

Next, everyone should help himself, inciting himself to the undertaking and performance of such things as are conformable to his abilities; for it seems sordid and illiberal for a man to extend himself similarly to small and great undertaking. You should carefully avoid rushing into things too extensive, or of too great importance. In every undertaking you should measure your own desert and power, so as to succeed and gain credit.

A man or woman condemned by the city should not be assisted by anybody; anyone who should associate with him should be disgraced, as similar to the condemned. But it is well to love men who have been voted approved and to associate with them; to imitate and acquire similar virtue and probity, thus being initiated in the greatest and most perfect of the mysteries; for no man is perfect without virtue.

Assistance should be given to an injured citizen, whether he is in his own, or in a foreign country. But let every stranger who was venerated in his own country, and conformably to the proper laws of that country, be received or dismissed with auspicious cordiality, calling to mind hospitable Jupiter, as a God who is established by all nations in common, and who is the inspective guardian of hospitality and inhospitality.

Let the older men preside over the younger, so that the latter may be deterred from, and ashamed of vice, through reverence and fear of the form.

For where the elders are shameless, so also are their children and grand children. Shamelessness and impudence result in insolice and injustice; and of this the end is death.

Let none be impudent, but rather modest and temperate; for he will thus earn the propitiousness of the Gods, and for himself, achieve salvation: no vicious men is dear to the divinities. Let every one honor probity and truth, hating what is base and false. These are the indications of virtue and vice. From their very youth children should therefore be accustomed (to worthy manners); by punishing those who love falsehood, and delighting those who love the truth, so as to implant in each what is most beautiful, and most prolific of virtue.

Each citizen should be more anxious for a reputation for temperance than for wisdom, which pretense often indicates ignorance of probity, and pusillanimity. The pretense to temperance should lead to a possession of it; for no one should feign with his tongue that he performs beautiful deeds, when destitute or worthless and good intentions.

Man should preserve kindness towards their rulers, obeying and venerating them as if they were parents; for whoever cannot see the propriety of this will suffer the punishment of bad counsels from the geniuses who are the inspective guardians of the seat of empire. Rulers are the guardians of the city, and of the safety of the citizens.

Governors must preside justly over their subjects in a manner similar to that over their own children, in passing sentences on others, propitiating hatred, and anger.

Praise and renown is due the rich who have assisted the indigent; they should be considered saviors of the children and defenders of their country. The wants of those who are poor through bad fortune should be relieved; but not the wants resulting from indolence or intemperance. While fortune is common to all men, indolence and intemperance is peculiar to bad man. Let it be considered as a worthy deed to point out anyone who has acted unjustly, in order that the state may be saved, having many guardians of its proprieties. Let the informer be considered a pious man, though his information affect his most familiar acquaintance; for nothing is more intimate or kindred to a man than his country. However let not the information regard things done through involuntary ignorance, but of such crimes as have been committed from a previous knowledge of their enormity. A criminal who shows enmity to the informer should be generally hated, that he may suffer the punishment of ingratitude, through which he deprives himself of being cured of the greatest of diseases, namely, injustice.

Further, let contempt of the Gods be considered as the greatest of iniquities, also voluntary injury to parents, neglecting of rulers and laws, and voluntary dishonoring of justice. Let him be considered as a most just and holy citizen who honors these things, and to the rulers indicates the citizens that despise them.

Let it be esteemed more honorable for a man to die for his country, than through a desire of life to desert it, along with probity; for it is better to die well than to live basely and disgracefully.

We should honor each of the dead not with tears or lamentations, but with good remembrance, and with an oblation of annual fruits. For when, we grieve immoderately for the dead, we are ungrateful to the terrestrial geniuses.

Let no one curse him by whom he has been injured; praise is more divine than defamation.

He who is superior to anger should be considered a better citizen than he who therethrough offends.

Not praiseworthy, but shameful is it to surpass temples and palaces in the sumptuousness of his expense. No thing private should be more magnificent and venerable than things of a public nature.

Let him who is a slave to wealth and money be despised, as pusillanimous and illiberal, being impressed by sumptuous possessions, yet a tragical and vile life. The magnanimous man foresees all human concerns, and is not disturbed by any accident of fortune.

Let no one speak obscenely; lest his thoughts lead him to base deeds, and defile his soul with impudence. Proper and lovely things it is well and legal to advertise; but such things are honored by being kept silent. It is base even to mention something disgraceful.

Let every one dearly love lawful wife and beget children by her. But let none shed the seed due his children into any other person, and let him not disgrace that which is honorable by both nature and law. For nature produced the seed for the sake of producing the children, and not for the sake of lust.

A wife should be chaste, and refuse impious connection with other men, as by so doing she will subject herself to the vengeance of the geniuses, whose office it is to expel those to they are hostile from their houses, and to produce hatred.

He who gives a step-mother to his children should not be praised, but disgraced, as the cause of domestic dissension. As it is proper to observe these mandates, let him who transgresses them be subjected to political execration.

The law also orders that these introductory suggestions be known by all citizens, and should be read in festivals after the hymns to Apollo called paens, by him who is appointed for this purpose by the master of the feast, so that these precepts may germinate in the minds of all who hear them.

CALLICRATIDAS
ON THE FELICITY OF FAMILIES

The universe must be considered as a system of kindred communion or association. But every system consists of certain dissimilar contraries, and is organized with reference to one particular thing, which is the most excellent, and also with a view to benefit the majority. What we call choir is a system of musical communion in view of one common thing, a concert of voices. Further, a ship's construction-plan contains many dissimilar contrary things, which are arranged with reference to one thing which is best, the pilot and the common advantage of a prosperous voyage.

Now a family is also a system of kindred communion, consisting of dissimilar proper parts; organised in view of the best thing, the father of the family, the common advantage being unanimity.

In the same manner as a zither, family requires three things: apparatus, organization, and a certain manner of practice, or musical use. An apparatus being the composition of all its parts, is that from which the whole, and the whole system of kindred communion derives its consummation. A family is divided into two divisions; man and the possessions; which latter is the thing governed, that affords utility. Thus also, an animal's first and greatest parts are soul and body; soul being that which governs and uses, the body being that which is governed, and affords utility. Possessions indeed are the adventitious instruments of human life, while the body is a tool born along with the soul, and kindred to it. Of the persons that complete a family, some are relatives, and others only attracted acquaintances.

The kindred are born from the same blood, or race. The affinities are an accidental alliance, commencing with the communion of wedlock. These are either fathers or brothers, or maternal and paternal grandfathers, or other relatives by marriage.

But if the good arising from friendship is also to be referred to a family, Ñ for thus it will become greater and more magnificent, not only through an abundance of wealth and many relations, but also through numerous friends, Ñ in this case it is evident that the family will thus become more ample, and that friendship is s social relation essential to a family.

Possessions are either necessary or desirable. The necessary subserve the wants of life; the desirable produce an elegant and well-ordered life, replacing many other [necessaries]. However, whatever exceeds what is needed for an elegant and well-ordered life are the roots of wantonness, insolence and destruction. Great possessions swell out with pride, and this leads to arrogance, and fastidiousness, conceiving that their kindred, nation and tribe do not equal them. Fastidiousness leads to insolence, whose end is destruction. Wherever then, in family or city there is a superfluity of possessions, the legislator must cut off and amputate the superfluities, as a good husbandman prunes luxurious leafage.

In the family's domestic part there are three divisions: the governor, the husband; the wife; and the auxiliary, the offspring.

With respect to practical and rational domination, one kind is despotic, another protective, and another political. The despotic is that which governs with a view to the advantage of the governor, and not of the governed, as a master rules his slaves, or a tyrant his subjects. But the guardian's domination subsists for the sake of the governed, and not the governor: as the masseurs rule the athletes, physicians over the sick, and preceptors over their pupils. Their labors are not directed to their own advantage, but to the benefit of those they govern; those of the physician being undertaken for the sake of the sick, that of the masseurs for the sake of exercising somebody else's body, and those of the erudite for the ignorant. Political domination, however, aims at the common benefit of both governors and governed. For in human affairs, according to this domination are organized both a family and a city; just as the world and divine affairs are in correspondence. A family and a city stand in a relation, analogous to the government of the world. Divinity indeed is the principle of nature, and his attention is directed neither to his own advantage, nor to private good, but to that of the public. That is why the world is called *cosmos*, from the orderly disposition of all things, which are mutually organized of the most excellent, which is God, who, according to our notions of him, is a celestial living being, incorruptible, and the principle and cause of the orderly disposition of the wholes.

Since therefore the husband rules over the wife, he rules with a power either despotic, protective or political. Despotic is out of the question, as he diligently attends to her welfare; nor is it protective entirely, for he has to consider himself also. It remains therefore that he rules over her with a political power, according to which both the governor and governed seek the common advantage. Hence wedlock is established with a view to the communion of life. Those husbands that govern their wives despotically are by them hated; those that govern them protectively are despised; being as it mere appendages and flatterers of their wives. But those that govern them politically are both admired and beloved. Both these will be effective if he who governs exercises his power so that it may be mingled with pleasure and veneration; pleasure at his fondness, but veneration at his doing nothing vile or abject.

He who wishes to marry ought to take for a wife one whose fortune is conformable to his own, neither above nor beneath, but of equal property. Those who marry a woman above their condition have to contend for the mastership; for the wife, surpassing her husband in wealth and lineage, wishes to rule over him; but he considers it to be worthy of him, and unnatural to submit to his wife. But those who marry a wife beneath their condition subvert the dignity and reputation of their family. One should imitate the musician, who having learned the proper tone of his voice, moderates it so as to be neither sharp nor flat, nor broken, nor strident. So wedlock should be adjusted to the tone of the soul, so that the husband and wife may accord, not only in prosperity but also in adversity. The husband should be his wife's regulator, master and preceptor. Regulator, in paying diligent attention to his wife's affairs; master, in governing, and exercising authority over her, and preceptor in teaching her such things as are fitting for her to know. This will be specially effected by him who, directing his attention to worthy parents, from their family marries a virgin in the flower of her youth. Such virgins are easily fashioned and docile; and are naturally well disposed to be instructed by, and to fear and love their husbands.

ON THE DUTIES OF A WOMAN

A woman should be a harmony of prudence and temperance. Her soul should be zealous to acquire virtue; so that she may be just, brave, prudent, frugal, and hating vain-glory. Furnished with these virtues, she will, when she become a wife act worthily towards herself, her husband, her children and her family. Frequently also such a woman will act beautifully towards cities, if she happens to rule over cities and nations, as we see is sometimes the case in a kingdom. If she subdues desire and anger, there will be produced a divine symphony. She will not be pursued by illegal loves, being devoted to her husband, children and family. Women fond of connections with outside man come to hate their families, both the free members, and the slaves. They also plot against their husbands, falsely representing them as the calumniators of all their acquaintance, so that they alone may appear benevolent; and they govern their families in a way such as may be expected from lovers of indolence.

Such conduct leads to the destruction of everything common to husband and wife.

The body should also be trained to moderation in food, clothes, baths, massage, hairdressing and jewelry adornment. Sumptuous eating, drinking, garments and keepsakes involve them in every crime, and faithlessness to their husband and everybody else. It is sufficient to satisfy hunger and thirst, and this from easily accessible things; and protect themselves from the cold by garments of the simplest description. It is quite a vice to feed on things brought from distant countries, and bought at a great price. It is also great folly to search after excessively elegant garments, made brilliant with purple or other precious colors.

The body itself demands no more than to be saved from cold and nakedness, for the sake (of) propriety, and that is all it needs. Men's opinions, combined with ignorance, demands inanities and superfluities. No woman should be decorated with gold, nor gems from India, nor any other country, nor plait her hair artistically, nor be perfumed with Arabian perfumes, nor paint her face so that it may be more white or more red, nor give a dark tinge to her eyebrows and her eyes, nor artificially dye her gray hair, nor bathe continually. A woman of this sort is hunting a spectator of female intemperance. The beauty produced by prudence, and not by these particulars, pleases women that are well born. Neither should she consider it necessary to be noble, rich

259

b--- in a great city, glory, have glory, and the friendship of renowned or royal men. The presence of such should not cause her annoyance, but should they be absent, she should not regret them; their absence will not hinder the prudent woman from living properly. Her soul should not anxiously dream about them, but ignore them. They are really more harmful than beneficial, as they mislead to misfortune; inevitable are treachery, envy and calumny, so that their possessor cannot be free from perturbation.

She should venerate the Gods, thereby hoping to achieve felicity, also by obeying the laws and sacred institutions of her country. After the gods, she should honor and venerate her parents, who cooperate with the gods in benefiting their children.

Moreover she ought to live with her husband [legally] and kindly, claiming nothing as her own property, but preserving and protecting his bed; this protection contains all. things. In a be---ring manner she should bear any stroke of fortune that may strike her husband; whether he is unfortunate in business, or makes ignorant mistakes, is sick, intoxicated, or has connection with other women. This last is a privilege granted to men, but not to women, since they are punished for this offence. She must submit to the law with equanimity, without jealousy. She should likewise patiently bear his anger, his parsimony, complaints he may make of his destiny, his jealousy, his accusations of here and whatever other faults he may inherit from his nature. All these she should cheerfully endure, conducting herself towards him with prudence and modesty. A wife who is dear to her husband, and who truly performs her duty towards him, is a domestic harmony, and loves the whole of her family, to which also she conciliates the benevolence of strangers.

If however she loves neither her husband nor her children, nor her servants, nor wishes to see any sacrifice preserved, then she becomes the herald of every kind of destruction, which she likewise prays for, as being an enemy, and also prays for the death of her husband, as being hostile to him, in order that she may be connected with other men; and in the last place she hates whatever her husband loves.

But a wife will be a domestic harmony if she is full of prudence and modesty. For then she will love not only her husband, but also her children, her kindred, her servants, and the whole of her family, among which she numbers her possessions, friends, fellow citizens, and strangers. Their bodies she will adorn without any superfluous ornaments, and will both speak and hear such things only as are beautiful and good. She should conform to her husband's opinion in respect to their common life, and be satisfied with those relatives and friends as meet his approbation. Unless she is entirely devoid of harmony she will consider pleasant or disagreeable such things which are thought so by her husband.

ON THE HARMONY OF A WOMAN

Parents ought not to be injured either in word or deed; and whatever their rank in life, small or great, they should be obeyed. Children should remain with them, and never forsake them, and almost to submit to them, even when they are insane, in every allotted condition of soul or bad body, or external circumstances, in peace, health, sickness, riches, poverty, renown, ignominy, class, or magistrate's rank. Such conduct will be wisely and cheerfully adopted by the pious. He who despises his parents will both among the living and the dead be condemned for this crime by the Gods, will be hated by men, and under earth will, together with the impious, be eternally punished in the same place by Justice, and the subterranean Gods, whose province it is to inspect things of this kind.

The aspect of parents is a thing divine and beautiful, and a diligent observance of them is attended by a delight such that neither a view of the sun, nor of all the stars which swing around the illuminated heavens, is capable of producing any spectacle greater than this. The Gods are not envious in a case like this.

We should reverence parents both while living and dead, and never oppose them in anything they say or do. If ignorant of anything through deception or disease, their children should console and instruct, but by no means hate them on this account. For no greater error or injustice can be committed by men than to act impiously towards their parents.

ARISTOXENUS OF TARENTUM
APOTHEGMS

After divinity and geniuses, the greatest respect should be paid to parents and the laws; not fictitiously, but in reality preparing ourselves to an observance of, and perseverance in, the manners and laws of our country, though they should be in a small degree worse than those of other countries.

(FROM THE FOURTH BOOK)

But after these things follow the honors which should be paid to living parents, it being right to discharge the first, the greatest, and the most ancient of all debts. Every one, likewise, should think that all which he possesses belongs to those who begot and nurtured him, in order that he may be ministrant to their want to the utmost of his ability, beginning from his property; in the second place, discharging his debt to them from things pertaining to his body; and in the third place, from things pertaining to his soul; thus with usury repaying? the cares and pains which his now very aged parents bestowed on him when he was young. Through the whole of life, likewise, he should particularly employ the most respectful language in speaking to his parents; because there is a most severe punishment for light and winged words; and Nemesis, the messenger of Justice, is appointed to be the inspector of everything of this kind.

When parents are angry therefore, we should yield to them, and appease their anger, whether it is seen in words or deeds; acknowledging that a father may reasonably be very much enraged with his son, when he thinks that he has been injured by him.

On the parents' death, the most appropriate and beautiful monuments should be raised to them; not exceeding the usual magnitude, nor yet less than those which our ancestors erected for their parents. Every year, also, attention ought to be paid to the decoration of their tombs. They should likewise be continually remembered and reverenced, and this with a moderate but appropriate expense.

By always acting and living in this manner we shall each of us be rewarded according to our deserts, both by those Gods and those natures that are superior to us, and shall pass the greatest part of our life in good hope.

EURYPHAMUS
CONCERNING HUMAN LIFE

The perfect life of man falls short indeed of the life of God, because it is not self-perfect, but surpasses that of irrational animals, participating as it does of virtue and felicity. For neither is God in want of external causes, -- as he is naturally good and happy, and is perfect from himself; -- nor any irrational animal. For brutes being destitute of reason, the are also destitute of the sciences pertaining to actions. But the nature of man partly consists of his own proper deliberate choice, and partly is in want of the assistance derived from divinity. For that which is capable of being fashioned by reason, which has an intellectual perception of things beautiful and base, can from earth erect itself and look to heaven, and with the eye of intellect can perceive the highest God, -- that which is capable of all this likewise receives assistance from the Gods.

But in consequence of possessing will, deliberate choice, and a principle of such a kind as enables it to study virtue, and to be agitated by the storms of vice, to follow, and also to apostacize from the Gods, -- it is likewise able to be moved by itself. Hence it may be praised or blamed, partly by the Gods, and partly by man, according as it applies itself zealously either to virtue or vice.

For the whole reason of the thing is as follows: Divinity introduced man into the world as a most exquisite being, to be honored reciprocally with Divinity, and as the eye of the orderly systematization of everything. Hence also man gave things names, himself becoming the character of them. He also invented letters, through these procuring a treasury of memory. He imitated the established order of the universe, by laws and judicial proceedings, organizing the communion of cities. For no human work is more honorable in the eyes of the world, nor more worthy of notice by the Gods, than proper constitution of a city governed by good laws, distributed in an orderly fashion throughout the state. For though by himself no man amounts to anything, and by himself is not able to lead a life conforming to the common concord, and to the proper organization of a state, yet he is well adapted to the perfect system of society.

Human life resembles a properly tuned and cared for lyre. Every lyre requires three things: apparatus, tuning, and musical skill of the player. By apparatus we mean preparation of all the appropriate parts; the strings, (the plectrum) and other instruments cooperating in the tuning of the instrument. By tuning we mean the adaptation of the sounds to each other. The musical skill is the motion of the player in consideration of the tuning. Human life requires the same three things. Apparatus is the preparation of the physical basis of life, riches, renown, and friends. Tuning is the organizing of these according to virtue and the laws. Musical skill is the mingling of these accord ing to virtue and the laws, virtue sailing with a prosperous wind, with no external resistance. For felicity does not consist in being driven from the purpose of voluntary intentions, but in obtaining the; nor in virtue lacking attendants and servers; but in completely possessing its own proper powers which are adapted to actions.

For man is not self-perfect; he is imperfect. He may become perfect partly from himself, and partly from some external cause. Likewise, he may be perfect either according to nature or to life. According to nature he is perfect, if he becomes a good man; as the virtue of everything is the climax and perfection of the nature of that thing. Thus the virtue of the eyes is the climax and perfection of their nature; and this is also true of the virtue of the ears. Thus too the virtue of man is the climax and perfection of the nature of man. But man is perfect according to life when he becomes happy. For felicity is the perfection and completion of human goods. Hence, again, virtue and prosperity become parts of the life of man.

Virtue, indeed is a part of him so far as he is soul; but prosperity, so far as he is connected with body; but both parts of him, so far as he is an animal. For it is the province of virtue to us in a becoming manner the goods which are conformable to nature; but of prosperity to impart the use of them. The former indeed imparts deliberate choice and right reason; but the latter, energies and actions. For to wish what is beautiful in conduct, and to endure things of a dreadful nature, is the proper business of virtue. But it is the whole of prosperity to render deliberate choice successful and to cause actions to arrive at the desired end. For a general conquers in conjunction with virtue and good fortune. The pilot sails well in conjunction with art and prosperous winds; the eye sees well in conjunction with acuteness of vision, and light. So the life of man reaches its perfection through virtue itself, and prosperity.

HIPPARCHUS
ON TRANQUILITY

Since men live but for a very short period, if their life is compared to the whole of time, they will, as it were, make a most beautiful journey, if they pass through life with tranquillity. This they will best possess if they will accurately and scientifically know themselves, namely that they are mortal and of a fleshly nature, and that they have a body which is corruptible, and can be easily injured, and which is exposed to everything most grievous and severe, even to their latest breath.

In the first place, let us observe those things which happen to the body; such as pleurisy, pneumonia, phrensy, gout, strangury, dysentery, lethargy, epilepsy, ulcers, and a thousand other diseases. But the diseases that can happen to the soul are much greater and direr. For all the iniquitous, evil, lawless and impious conduct in the life of man, originates from the passions of the soul. For through unnatural immoderate desires many have become subject to unrestrained impulses; and have not refrained from the most unholy pleasures, arising from connections with daughters and even mothers. Many have even destroyed their fathers and offspring. But what is the use to continue detailing externally impending evils, such as excessive rain, draught, violent heat, and cold; so that frequently from the anomalous state of the air, pestilence and famine arise, followed by manifold calamities making whole cities desolate. Since therefore many such calamities impend, we should neither be elated by the possession of worldly goods, which might rapidly be consumed by the irruption of some small fever, nor with what are conceived to be prosperous external circumstances, which from their own nature frequently decay quicker than they arose. For all these are uncertain and unstable, and are found to have their existence in many and various mutations; and no one of them is permanent, or immutable, or stable, or indivisible. Considering these things well, and also being persuaded that if what is present and is imparted to us, is able to remain for the smallest portion of time, it is as much as we ought to expect; we shall then live in tranquillity, and with hilarity, generously bearing whatever may befall us.

Now many people imagine that all they have and what they receive from fortune and nature is better than it is, not realizing what it is in reality; but such as it is able to become when it has arrived at its highest excellence. They then burden the soul with many and, great, and nefarious stupid evils, when they are suddenly deprived of these transitory goods. That is how they lead a most bitter and miserable life. But this takes place in the loss of riches, or the death of friends and children, or in the privation of certain other things, which by them are conceived to be possessions most honorable. Afterwards, weeping and lamenting, they assert of themselves, that they alone are most unfortunate and miserable, not remembering that these things have happened, and even now happen to many others; nor are they able to understand the life of those that are now in existence, and of those that have lived in former times, nor to see in what great calamities and waves of evils many of the present times are, and of the past have been involved. Therefore considering with ourselves that many who have lost their property have afterwards on account of this very loss been saved, since thereafter they might either have fallen into the hands of robbers, or into the power of a tyrant; that many also who have loved certain persons, and have been extremely benevolently disposed towards them, but have afterwards hated them extremely, Ñ considering all these things, of which history informs us; and learning likewise that many have been destroyed by their own children, and by those they have most dearly loved, and comparing our own life with that of those who have been more unhappy that we have been, and taking into account general human vicissitudes, that happen to others beside ourselves, we shall pass through life with greater tranquillity.

A reasonable man will not think the calamities of others easy to be born, but not his own; since he sees that the whole of life is naturally exposed to many calamities. Those however who weep and lament besides not being able to recover what they have lost, or recall to life those that are dead, impel the soul to still greater perturbations; in consequence of its being filled with much depravity. Being washed and purified, we should do our best to wipe away our inveterate stains, by the reasonings of philosophy. This we shall accomplish by adhering to prudence and tolerance, being satisfied with our present circumstances, and not aspiring after too many things. Men who gather a great abundance of external things do not consider that enjoyment of them terminates with this present life. We should therefore use the present goods; and by the assistance of the beautiful and venerable results of philosophy we shall be liberated from the insatiable desire of depraved possessions.

METOPUS
CONCERNING VIRTUE

Man's virtue is the perfection of his nature. By the proper nature of his virtue, every being becomes perfect, and arrives at the climax of its excellence. Thus the virtue of the horse is that which makes the best of the horse's nature. The same reasoning applies to details. Thus the virtue of the eyes is acuteness of vision; and this is the climax of the eyes' nature. The virtue of the ears is acuteness of hearing; and this is the [aural] nature's climax. The virtue of the feet is swiftness; and this is the pedal nature's climax.

Every virtue, however, should include these three things: reason, power, and deliberate choice. Reason indeed, judges and contemplates; power prohibits and vanquishes; and deliberate choice loves and enjoys propriety. Therefore to judge and contemplate pertain to the intellectual part of the soul; to prohibit and vanquish are the peculiarity of the irrational part of the soul; and to love and enjoy propriety includes both rational and irrational parts of the soul; for deliberate choice consists of the discursive energy of reason, and appetite. Intention therefore, pertains to the rational, but appetite to the irrational parts of the soul.

We may discern the multitude of the virtues by observing the parts of the soul; also the growth and nature of virtue. Of the soul's parts, two rank first: the rational and the irrational. It is by their rational that we judge and contemplate; by the irrational we are impelled and desire. These are either consonant or discordant, their strife and dissonance being produced be excess or defect. The rational part's victory over the irrational produces endurance and continence. When the rational leads, the irrational follows, both accord, and produce virtue. That is why endurance and continence are generally accompanied by pain; for endurance resists pain and continence pleasure. However, incontinence and effeminacy neither' resist nor vanquish pleasure. That is why men fly from good through pain, but reject it through pleasure. Likewise praise and blame, and everything beautiful in human conduct, are produced in these parts of the soul. This explains the nature, of virtue.

Let us study virtue's kinds and parts. Since the soul is divided into two parts, the rational and the irrational, the latter is also divided into two, the irascible and appetitive part. By the rational we judge and contemplate; by the irrational we are impelled and desire. The irascible part defends us, and revenges incidental molestations; the appetitive directs and preserves the body's proper constitution. So we see that the numerous virtues with all their differences and peculiarities do little more than conform to the distinctive parts of the soul.

CRITO [400 B.C.]
ON PRUDENCE AND PROSPERITY

Such is the mutual relation of prudence and prosperity. Prudence is explainable and reasonable, orderly and definite. Prosperity is unexplainable, and irrational, disorderly, and indefinite. In origination and power, prudence is prior to prosperity; the former governing and defining, the latter being governed and defined; but they are mutually adjusting, concurring in the same thing. For that which limits and adjusts must be explainable and reasonable, while that which is limited and adjusted; is naturally unexplainable and irrational. That is how the reason of the infinite's nature, and of the limiter subsists in all things. Infinites are always naturally disposed to be limited and adjusted by things possessing reason and prudence for in the relation to the latter, the former stand as matter and essence. But finites are self-adjusted and self-limited, being causal and energetic.

The mutual adjustment of these natures in different things produces a variety of adjusted substances. For in the comprehension of the whole of things, the mutual adjustment of both the moving and the passive, is the world. There is no other possible way of salvation for the whole and the universe, than by the adjustment of the things generated to the divine, and of the ever passive to the ever moved. The similar adjustment, in man, of the irrational to the rational part of the soul is virtue, for this cannot exist in case of mutual strife between the two. So also in a city, the mutual adjustment of the governors to the governed produces strength and concord. Governing is the specialty of the better nature; while being governed is more suited to the subordinate part. To both are common strength and concord. A similar mutual adjustment exists in the universe and in the family; the former being a resultance of allurements and erudition with reason, the latter of pains and pleasures, prosperity and adversity. Man's constitution is such that he needs changes, work and rest, sorrow and gladeness, prosperity and adversity.

Some things draw the intellect towards wisdom, and industry, and keep it there; others relax and delight, rendering the intellect vigorous and prompt. Should one of these elements prevail, then man's life becomes one-sided, exaggerating sorrow and difficulty, or levity and smoothness. Now all these should be mutually adjusted by prudence, which discerns and distinguishes in actions the elements of limitation and infinity. That is why prudence is the mother and leader of the other virtues. For it is prudence's reason and law which organize and harmonize all other virtues.

Summarizing: The irrational and explainable are to be found in all things; the latter defines and limits, the former is defined and bounded. The resultance of both is the proper organisation of the whole and the universe.

God fashioned man in a way such as to declare that not through the want of power or deliberate choice, that man is incapable of impulsion to beauty of conduct. In man was implanted a principle such as to combine the possible with the desirable; so that while man is the cause of power and of the possession of good, God is that of reasonable impulse and incitation. So God made man tend to heaven, gave him an intellective power, implanted in him a sight called intellect, which is capable of beholding God. For without God, it is impossible to discover what is best and most beautiful; and without intellect we cannot see God, since every mortal nature's establishment implied a progressive loss of intellect. It is not God, however, who effected this, but generation, and that impulse of the soul which lacks deliberate choice.

POLUS [ca 450 B.C.]
ON JUSTICE

I think that the justice which subsists among men may be called the mother and nurse of the other virtues. Without it no man can be temperate, brave, nor prudent. In conjunction with elegance it is the harmony and peace of the whole soul. This virtue's strength will become more manifest if we compare it to the other habits. They have a partial utility, and refer to one thing only; while this refers to a multitude, nay, to whole systems. It conducts the whole world government and is called providence, harmony, and vengeance (Dike), by the decrees of a certain kind of geniuses. In a city it is justly called peace, and equitable legislation. In a house, it is the concord between husband and wife; the kindliness of the servant towards his master, and the anxious care of the master for his servant. In the body, likewise, which to all animals is the first and dearest thing, it is the health and wholeness of each part. In the soul it is the wisdom that depends from science and justice. As therefore this virtue disciplines and saves both the whole and parts of everything, mutually tuning and familiarizing all things, it surely deserves, by universal suffrages, to be called the mother and nurse of all things.

STHENIDAS THE LOCRIAN [400 B.C.]
ON A KINGDOM

A king should be a wise man; thus will he be honored in the same manner as the supreme divinity, whose imitator he will be. As the supreme is by nature the first king and potentate, so will a king be, by birth and imitation. As the former rules in the universe, and in the whole of things, so does the latter in the earth. While the former governs all things eternally, and has a never-failing life, possessing all wisdom in himself, so the latter acquires science through time. But a king will imitate the First God in the most excellent manner, if he acquires magnanimity, gravity, and the restriction of his wants to but few things, to his subject exhibiting a paternal disposition. For it is because of this especially that the First God is called the father of both Gods and men, because he is mild to everything that is subject to him, and never ceases to govern with providential regard. Nor is he satisfied with being the Maker of all things, but he is the nourisher and preceptor of every thing beautiful, and the legislator to all things equally. Such also ought to be a king who on earth rules over men.

Nothing is beautiful, that lacks a director, or ruler. Again, no king or ruler can exist without wisdom and science. He therefore who is both a sage and a king will be an imitator and legitimate minister of God.

ECPHANTUS THE CROTONIAN [ca 400 B.C.] ON KINGS

Many arguments apparently prove that every being's nature is adapted to the world and the things it contains. Every animal thus conspiring (into union and consent) and having such an organization of its parts, it follows, through the attractive progress of the universe around it, an excellent and necessary evolution which produces the general ornamentation of the world, and the peculiar permanence of every thing it contains. Hence it is called the (ornamental) *kosmos*, and is the most perfect being.

When we study its parts, we find them many, and naturally different. First, a being who is the best, both from its native alliance to the world, and in its particular divinity (containing the stars called planets, forming the first and greatest series). Second is the nature of the geniuses, in the sublunar region, where bodies move in a right line. Third, in the earth, and with us, the best being is man, of whom the divinest is a king, surpassing other men in his general being. While his body resembles that of other men, being made of the same physical matter, he was molded by the best sculptors, who used him as the archetype. Hence, in a certain respect, a king is one and alone; being the production of the supernal king, with whom he is always familiar; being beheld by his subjects in his kingdom as a splendid light.

A kingdom has been said to resemble an eagle, the most excellent of winged animals, who undazzled, stares at the sun . A kingdom is also similar to the sun, because it is divine; and because of its exceeding splendor cannot be seen without difficulty, except by piercing eyes, that are genuine. For the numerous splendors that surround it, and the black eye-clouds it produces in those that gaze at it, as if they had ascended into some foreign altitude, demonstrates that their eyes are spurious.

Those however who can safely arrive thither, either because of their familiarity therewith, or their alliance with it can, use it properly. A kingdom, therefore, is something pure, genuine, uncorrupted and because of its preeminence, divine and difficult of access. He who is established therein should naturally be most pure and (think) clearly, that by his personal stains he may not obscure so splendid an institution; as some persons defile the most sacred places, and the impure pollute those they meet. But a king, who associates with the (best), should be undefiled, realising how much diviner than other things are both himself and his prerogatives; and from the divine exemplar of which he is an image, he should treat both himself and his subjects worthily.

When other men are delinquents, their most holy purification causes them to imitate their rulers, whether laws or king. But kings who cannot on earth find anything better than their own nature to imitate, should not waste time in seeking any model other or lower than God himself. No one would long search for the world, seeing that he exists in it, as a part of it; so the governor of others should not ignore him by whom he also is governed. Being ruled is the supreme ornament, inasmuch as there is nothing rulerless in the universe.

A king's manners should also be the inspiration of his government. Thus its beauty will immediately shine forth, since he who imitates God through virtue will surely be dear to him whom he imitates; and much more dear will he be to his subjects. No one who is beloved by the divinity will be hated by men;. since neither do the stars, nor the whole world hate God. For if they hated their ruler and leader, they would never obey him. But it is because he governs properly that human affairs are properly governed. The earthly king, therefore, should not be deficient in any of the virtues, distinctive of the heavenly ruler.

Now as an earthly king is something foreign external, inasmuch as he descends to men from the heavens, so likewise his virtues may be considered as works of God, and to descend upon him from divinity. You will find this true, if you study out the whole thing from the beginning. An earthly king obtains possession of subjects by an agreement, which is the first essential. The truth of this may be gathered from the state of affairs produced by the destruction of the unanimity among citizens, which indeed is much inferior to a divine and royal nature. Such natures are not oppressed by any such poverty; but, conforming to intellect, they supply the wants of others, assisting them in common, being perfect in virtue. But the friendship obtaining in a city, and which possesses a certain common end, imitates the concord of the universe. No city could be inhabited without an institution of magistrates. To effect this, however, and to preserve the city, there is a necessity of laws, a political domination, and a governor and the governed. All this happens for the general good, for unanimity, and the consent of the people in harmony with organic efficiency. Likewise, he who governs according to virtue, is called a king, and is so in reality; since he possesses the same friendship and communion with his subjects, as divinity possesses with the world, and its contained natures. All benevolence, however, ought to be exerted, in the first place, indeed, by the king towards his subjects; second, by the subjects towards the king; and this benevolence should be similar to that of a parent towards his child, of a shepherd towards his flock, and of the law towards the law-abiding.

For there is one virtue pertaining to the government, and to the life of men. No one should, through indigence, solicit the assistance of others, when he is able to supply himself with what nature requires. Though (in the city) there is a certain community of goods, yet every one should live so as to be self-sufficient; and the latter requires the aid of none others in his passage through life. If therefore it is necessary to lead an active life, it is evident that a king, though he should also consume other things, will nevertheless be self-sufficient. For have friends through his own virtue; and in using these, he will not use them by any virtue other than that by which he regulates his own life. For he must follow a virtue of this kind, since he cannot procure anything more excellent. God, indeed, needing neither ministers nor servants, nor employing any mandate, and neither crowning nor proclaiming those that are obedient to him, or disgracing those that are disobedient, thus administers so great an empire. In a manner to me appearing most worthy of imitation, into all things he instills a most zealous desire to participate in his nature. As he is good, the most easy possible communication thereof is his only work. Those who imitate him find that this imitation enables them to accomplish everything else better. Indeed this imitation of God is the self-sufficiency of everything else; for there is an identity, and no difference between the virtues that make things acceptable to God, and those that imitate him; and is not our earthly king, in a similar manner self-sufficient? By assimilating himself to one, and that the most excellent nature, he will beneficently endeavor to assimilate all his subjects to himself.

Such kings, however, as towards their subjects use violence and compulsion entirely destroy in every individual of the community a readiness to imitate him. Without benevolence, no assimilation is possible; since benevolence particularly effaces fear. It is indeed much to be desired that human nature should not be in want of persuasion; which is the relic of human depravity, of which the temporal being called man is not destitute. Persuasion, indeed, is akin to necessity; inasmuch as it is chiefly used on persons flying from necessity. But persuasion is needless with beings such as spontaneously seek the beautiful and good.

Again, a king alone is, capable of effecting human perfection, that through imitation of the good man may pursue propriety and loveliness; and that those who are corrupted as if by intoxication, and who have fallen into an ignorance of the good by bad education, may be strengthened by the king's eloquence, may have their diseased minds healed, and their depravity's dazedness expelled, may become mindful of an intimate associate, whose influence may persuade them. Though originating from undesirable seeds, yet (this royal influence) is the source of a certain good to humans, in which language supplies our deficiencies, in our mutual converse.

He who has a sacred and divine conception of things will in reality be a king. Persuaded by this, he will be the cause all good, but of no evil. Evidently, as he is fitted for society, he will become just. For communion or association consists in equality, and in its distribution. Justice indeed precedes, but communion participates. For it is impossible for a man to be unjust, and yet distribute equality; or that he should distribute equality, and yet not be adapted to association.

How is it possible that he who is self-sufficient should not be continent? For sumptuousness is the mother of incontinence, and this of wanton insolence, and from this an innumerable host of ills. But self-sufficiency is not mastered by sumptuousness, nor by any of its derivative evils, but itself being a principle, it leads to all things, and is not led by any. To govern is the province of God, and also of a king, (on which account indeed, he is called self-sufficient); so to both it pertains not to be governed by any one. Evidently, these things cannot be effected without prudence, and it is manifest that the world's intellectual prudence is God. For the world reveals graceful design, which would be impossible without prudence. Nor is it possible for a king without prudence to possess these virtues; I mean justice, continence, sociability and kindred virtues.

PEMPELUS [ca 400 B.C.]
ON PARENTS

Neither divinity, nor anyone possessing the least wisdom will ever advise anyone to neglect his parents. Hence we cannot have any statue or temple which will be considered by divinity as more precious than our fathers and grandfathers when grown feeble with age. For he who honors his parents by gifts will be recompensed by God; for without this, divinity will not pay any attention to the prayers of such parents for their children. Our parents' and progenitors' images should by us be considered much more venerable and divine than any inanimate images. For our parents, who are divine images that are animated, when they are continually adorned and worthily honored by us, pray for us, and implore the Gods to bestow on us the most excellent gifts; and do the contrary when we despise them; neither of which occurs with inanimate images. Hence he who behaves worthily towards his parents and progenitors, and other kindred, will possess the most worthy of all statues, and the best calculated to endear him to divinity. Every intelligent person, therefore, should honor and venerate his parents, and should dread their execrations and unfavorable prayers, knowing that many of them take effect.

Nature having disposed the matter thus, prudent and modest men will consider their living aged progenitors a treasure, to the extremity of life; and if they die before the children have arrived there, the latter will be longing for them. Moreover, progenitors will be terrible in the extreme to their depraved or stupid offspring. The profane person who is deaf to these considerations will by all intelligent persons be considered as odious to both Gods and men.

PHYNTIS, DAUGHTER OF CALLICRATES
[ca 400 B.C.]
ON WOMAN'S TEMPERANCE

Woman ought to be wholly good and modest; but she will never be a character of this kind without virtue, which renders precious whatever contains it. The eyeÕs virtue is sight; the earÕs, hearing. A horse's virtue makes it good; while the virtue of man or woman makes them worthy. A woman's principal virtue is temperance, wherethrough she will be able to honor and love her husband.

Some, perhaps may not think that it becomes a woman to philosophize, any more than it is suitable for her to ride on horseback, or to harangue in public. But I think that while there are certain employments specialized to each sex, that there are some common to both man and woman, while some belong to a sex only preferentially. Male avocations are to lead an army, to govern and to harangue in public. Female avocations are to guard the house, to stay at home, to receive and minister to her husband. Her particular virtues are fortitude, justice and prudence. Both husband and wife should achieve the virtues of the body and the soul; for as bodily health is beneficial to both, so also is health of the soul. The bodily virtues, however, are health, strength, vigor of sensation and beauty. With respect to the virtues, also some are peculiarly suitable to men, and others to women. Fortitude and prudence regard the man more than they do the women; both on account of the bodily habits, and the soul-power; but temperance peculiarly belongs to the woman.

It would be well to know the number and quality of the things through which this virtue is acquirable by women. I think that they are five. First, temperance comes through the sanctity and piety of the marriage bed. Second, through body-ornaments; thirds, through trips outside the house. Fourth, through refraining from celebrating the orgies and mysteries of Cybele. Fifth, in being cautious and moderate in sacrifices to the divinities. Of these, however, the greatest and most comprehensive cause of temperance is undefiledness in the marriage bed; and to have connexion with none but her husband.

By such lawlessness she acts unjustly towards the Gods who preside over nativities, changing them from genuine to spurious assistants to her family and kindred. In the second place, she acts unjustly towards the gods who preside over nature, by whom she and all her kindred solemnly swore that she would lawfully associate with her husband in the association of life, and the procreation of children. Third, she injures her country, in not observing its decrees. It is frivolous and unpardonable, for the sake of pleasure and wayward insolence, to offend in a matter where the crime is so great that the greatest punishment, death, is ordained. All such insolent conduct ends in death. Besides, for this offence there has been discovered no purifying remedy; which might turn such guilt into purity beloved by the divinity, for God is most averse to the pardoning of this crime. The best indication, of a woman's chastity towards her husband is her children's resemblance to their father. This suffices about the marriage bed. As to body-ornaments, a woman's garments should be white and simple and not superfluous. They will be so if they are neither transparent nor variegated, nor woven from silk, inexpensive, and white. This will prevent excessive ornamentation, luxury, and superfluity of clothes; and will avoid the imitation of depravity by others. Neither gold nor emeralds should ornament her body; for they are very expensive, and exhibit pride and arrogance toward the vulgar. Besides, a city governed by good laws, and well organized, should adjust all its interests in an equable legislation; which therefore would expel from the city the jewelers who make such things.

A woman should, besides, illuminate her face, not by powder or rouge, but by the natural glow from the towel, adorning herself with modesty, rather than by art. Thus she will reflect honor both on herself and her husband. As to gadding, women should chiefly go out of their houses to sacrifice to the municipal tutelary divinity, for the welfare of her husband and her kindred. Neither should a woman go out from her house at dawn or dusk, but openly when the forum is full of people; accompanied by one, at most two servants, to see something, or to shop.

As to sacrifices of the gods, they should be frugal, and suited to her ability; she should abstain from celebration of orgies, and the Cybelean sacred rites performed at home. For the municipal law forbids them to women. Moreover, these rites lead to intoxication and insanity. A family-mistress, presiding over domestic affairs, should be temperate and undefiled.

CLINIAS [ca 400 B.C.]

Every virtue is perfected, as was shown in the beginning, by reason, deliberate choice, and power. Each of these, however, is by itself not a part of virtue, but its cause. Such, therefore, as have the intellective and gnostic part of virtue (the theoretic virtues), are called skillful and intelligent; but such, as have its ethical and preparatory parts, are called useful and equitable. Since, however, man is naturally adapted to act unjustly from exciting causes, these are three: the love of pleasure of corporeal enjoyments, avarice in the accumulation of wealth, and ambition in surpassing equals or fellows. Now it is possible to oppose to these such things as procure fear, shame, or desire in men; fear through the laws, shame through the Gods, and desire through the energies of reason. Hence youth should be taught from the very first to honor the Gods and the laws. Following these, every human work, and every kind of human life, by the participation of sanctity and piety: will sail prosperously over the sea (of generation).

SEXTUS THE PYTHAGOREAN [ca 300 B.C.]
SELECTED SENTENCES

1. To neglect things of the smallest consequence is not the least thing in human life.

2. The sage and the contemner of wealth most resemble God.

3. Do not investigate the name of God, because you will not find it. For everything called by a name receives its appellation from that which is more worthy than itself, so that it is one person that calls, and another that hears. Who is it, therefore, who has given a name to God? The word *God* is not a name of his, but an indication of what we conceive of him.

4. God is a light incapable of receiving its opposite (darkness).

5. You have in yourself something similar to God, and therefore use yourself as the temple of God, on account of that which in you resembles God.

6. Honor God above all things, that he may rule over you.

7. Whatever you honor above all things, that which you so honor will have dominion over you. But if you give yourself to the domination of God; you will thus have the dominion over all things.

8. The greatest honor which can be paid to God is to know and imitate him.

9. There is not any thing, indeed, much wholly resembles God; nevertheless the imitation of him as much as possible by an inferior nature is grateful to him.

10. God indeed, is not in want of any thing; the wise man is in want of God alone. He, therefore who is in want of but few things, and the necessary, emulates him who is in want of nothing.

11. Endeavor to be great in the estimation of divinity; but among men avoid envy.

12. The sage whose estimation with man was but small while he was living, will be renowned when he is dead.

13. Consider lost all the time in which you do not think of divinity.

14. A good intellect is the choir of divinity.

15. A bad intellect is the choir of evil geniuses.

16. Honor that which is just, on this very account that it is just.

17. You will not be concealed from divinity when you act unjustly, nor even when you think of acting so.

18. The foundation of piety is continence, but the summit of piety is love to God.

19. Wish that what is expedient and not what is pleasing may happen to you.

20. Such as you wish your neighbor to be to you, such also be to your neighbors.

21. That which God gives you none can take away.

22. Neither do, nor even think, of that which you are unwilling. God should know.

23. Before you do anything, think of God, that his light may precede your energies.

24. The soul is illuminated by the recollection of God.

25. The use of animal food is indifferent, but it is more rational to abstain from them.

26. God is not the author of any evil.

27. You should not possess more than the use of the body requires.

28. Possess those things that no one can take away from you.

29. Bear that which is necessary, as it is necessary.

30. Ask of God things such as it is worthy of God to bestow.

31. The reason that is in you is the light of your life.

32. Ask from God those things that you cannot receive from man.

33. Wish that those things which labor ought to precede, may be possessed by you after labor.

34. Be not anxious to please the multitude.

35. It is not proper to despise those things of which we shall be in want after the dissolution of the body.

36. Do not ask of dignity that which, when you have obtained, you cannot perpetually possess.

37. Accustom your soul after (it has conceived all that is great of) divinity, to conceive something great of itself.

38. Esteem precious nothing which a bad man can take from you.

39. He is dear to divinity, who considers those things alone precious, which are to be so by divinity.

40. Everything superfluous is hostile.

41. He who loves that which is not expedient, will not love that which is expedient.

42. The intellect of the sage is always with divinity.

43. God dwells in the intellect of the wise man.

44. The wise man is always similar to himself.

45. Every desire is insatiable, and therefore is always in want.

46. The knowledge and imitation of divinity are alone sufficient to beatitude.

47. Use lying as poison.

48. Nothing is so peculiar to wisdom as truth.

49. When you preside over men, remember that divinity presides over you also.

50. Be persuaded that the end of life is to live conformably to divinity.

51. Depraved affections are the beginning of sorrows.

52. An evil disposition is the disease of the soul; but in justice and impiety is the death of it.

53. Use all men in a way such as if, after God, you were the common curator of all things.

54. He who uses badly mankind, badly uses himself.

55. Wish that you may be able to benefit your enemies.

56. Endure all things, in order that you may live conformably to God.

57. By honoring a wise man, you will honor yourself.

58. In all your actions, keep God before your eyes.

59. You may refuse matrimony, in order to live in incessant presence with God. If, however you know how to fight, and are willing to, take a wife, and beget children.

60. To live, indeed, is not in our power; but to live rightly is.

61. Be unwilling to entertain accusations against a man studious of wisdom.

62. If you wish to live successfully, you will have to avoid much, in which you will come out only second best.

63. Sweet to you should be any cup that quenches thirst.

64. Fly from intoxication as you would from insanity.

65. No good originates from the body.

66. Estimate that you are suffering a great punishment when you obtain the object of corporeal desire; for desire will never be satisfied with the attainments of any such objects.

67. Invoke God as a witness to whatever you do.

68. The bad man does not think that there is a providence.

69. Assert that your true man is he who in you possesses wisdom.

70. The wise man participates in God.

71. Wherever that which in you is wise resides, there also is your true good.

72. That which is not harmful to the soul does not harm the man.

73. He who unjustly expels from his body a wise man, by his iniquity confers a benefit on his victim; for he thus is liberated from his bonds.

74. Only through soul-ignorance is a man saddened by fear of death.

75. You will not possess intellect till you understand that you have it.

76. Realize that your body is the garment of your soul; and then you will preserve it pure.

77. Impure geniuses let not the impure soul escape them.

78. Not to every man speak of God.

79. There is danger, and no negligible one, to speak of God even the things that are true.

80. A true assertion about God is an assertion of God.

81. You should not dare to speak of God to the multitude.

82. He who does not worship God, does not know him.

83. He who is worthy of God is also a god among men.

84. It is better to have nothing, than to possess much, and impart it to no one.

85. He who thinks that there is a God and that he protects nothing, is no whit better than he who does not believe there is a God.

86. He best honors God who makes his intellect as like God as possible.

87. Who injures, none has none to fear.

88. No one who looks down to the earth is wise.

89. To lie is to deceive, and be deceived.

90. Recognize what God is, and that in you which recognizes God.

91. It is not death; but a bad life, which destroys the soul.

92. If you knew Him by whom you were made, you would know yourself.

93. It is not possible for a man to live conformably to Divinity, unless he acts modestly, well and justly.

94. Divine wisdom is true science.

95. You should not dare to speak of God to an impure soul.

96. The wise man follows God, and God follows the [soul] of the wise man.

97. A king rejoices in those he governs, and therefore God rejoices in the wise man. He who governs likewise, is inseparable from those he governs; and therefore God is inseparable from the soul of the wise man, which He defends and governs.

98. The wise man is governed by God, and on this account is blessed.

99. A scientific knowledge of God causes a man to use but few words.

100. To use many words in speaking of God obscures the subject.

101. The man who possesses a knowledge of God will not be very ambitious.

102. The erudite, chaste and wise soul is the prophet of the truth of God.

103. Accustom yourself always to look to the Divinity.

104. A wise intellect is the mirror of God.

(These sentences were preserved by Rufinus, a Christian writer, who would not have taken the trouble to do so unless indeed their intrinsic worth had been as great as it is.)

From the PROTREPTICS OF IAMBLICHUS

105. As we live through soul, it must be said that by the virtue of this we do live well; just as because we see through. the eyes, we see well through their virtues.

106. It must not be thought that gold can be injured by rust, or virtue by baseness.

107. We should betake ourselves to virtue as to an invisible temple, so that we may not be exposed to any ignoble insolence of soul, with respect to our communion with, and continuance in life.

108. We should confide in virtue as in a chaste wife; but trust to fortune as to an inconsistent mistress.

109. It is better that virtue should be received accompanied by poverty, than wealth with violence; and frugality with health, than veracity with disease.

110. An overabundance of food is harmful to the body; but the body is preserved when the soul is disposed in a becoming manner.

111. It is as dangerous to give power to a depraved man, than a sword to a madman.

112. As it is better for a part of the body that contains purulent decay to be burned, than to continue as it is, thus also is it better for a depraved man to die, than to continue to live.

113. The theorems of philosophy are to be enjoyed, as much as possible, as if they were ambrosia and nectar. For the resultant pleasure is genuine incorruptible and divine. They are also capable of producing magnanimity, and though they cannot make us eternal, yet they enable us to obtain a scientific knowledge of eternal natures.

114. If vigor of sensation is, as it is, considered to be desirable, so much more strenuously should we endeavor to obtain prudence; for it is, as it were, the sensitive vigor of the practical intellect, which we contain. And as through the former we are not deceived in sensible perceptions, so through the latter we avoid false reasonings in practical affairs.

115. We shall properly venerate Divinity if we purify our intellect from vice, as from a stain.

116. A temple should, indeed, be adorned with gifts; but our soul with disciplines.

117. As the lesser mysteries are to be delivered before the greater, thus also discipline must precede philosophy.

118. The fruits of the earth, indeed, appear annually; but the fruits of philosophy ripen at all seasons.

119. As he who wishes the best fruit must pay most attention to the land, so must the greatest attention be paid the soul, if it is to produce fruits worthy of its nature.

120. Do not even think of doing what ought not to be done.

121. Choose rather to be strong in soul, than in body.

122. Be sure that laborious thing contribute to virtue, more than do pleasurable things.

123. Every passion of the soul is most hostile to its salvation.

124. Pythagoras said that it is most difficult simultaneously to walk in many paths of life.

125. Pythagoras said that we must choose the best life; for custom will make it pleasant. Wealth is a weak anchor; glory, still weaker; and similarly with the body, dominion, and honor. Which anchors are strong? Prudence, magnanimity and fortitude; these can be shaken by no tempest. This is the law of God, that virtue is the only thing strong, all else is a trifle. (Taylor thinks that this and the next six sentences are wrongly attributed to Socrates, and are by Democrates or Demophilus).

126. All the parts of human life, just as those of a statue, should be beautiful.

127. As a statue stands immovable on its pedestal, so should a man on his deliberate choice, if he is worthy.

128. Incense is for the Gods, but praise to good men.

129. Men unjustly accused of acting unjustly should be defended, while those who excel should be praised.

130. It is not the sumptuous adornment of the horse that earns him praise, but the nature of the horse himself; nor is the man worthy merely because he owns great wealth, but he whose soul is generous.

131. When the wise man opens his mouth, the beauties of his soul present themselves to view as the statues in a temple (when the gates are opened).

132. Remind yourself that all men assert that wisdom is the greatest good, but that there are few who strenuously endeavor to obtain this greatest good. Ñ Pythagoras.

133. Be sober, and remember to be disposed to believe; for these are the nerves of wisdom. ---Epicharmus.

134. It is better to live lying on the grass, confiding in divinity and yourself, than to lie on a golden bed with perturbation.

135. You will not be in want of anything, which is in the power of Fortune to give or take away. Ñ Pythagoras.

136. Despise all those things which you will not want when liberated from the body; and exercising yourself in those things of

which you will be in want, when liberated from the body, be sure to invoke the Gods to become your helpers. Ñ Pythagoras.

137. It is as impossible to conceal fire in a garment, as a base deviation from rectitude in time. (Demophilus, rather than Socrates).

138. Wind increases fire, but custom, love. Ibidem. 139. Only those are dear to divinity who are hostile to injustice. (Democritus or Demophilus).

140. Bodily necessities are easily procured by anybody; without labor or molestation; but those things whose attainment demands effort and trouble, are objects of desire not to the body, but to depraved opinion. (Aristoxenus the Pythagorean).

141. Thus spoke Pythagoras of desire: This passion is various, laborious and very multiform. Of desires, however, some are acquired and artificial, while others are inborn. Desire is a certain tendency and impulse of the soul, and an appetite of fullness, or presence of sense, or of an emptiness and absence of it, and of non-perception. The three best known kinds of depraved desire are the improper, the unproportionate, and the unseasonable. For desire is either immediately indecorous, troublesome or illiberal; or if not absolutely so, it is improperly vehement and persistent. Or, in the third place, it is impelled at an improper time, or towards improper objects .Ñ Aristoxenus.

142. Pythagoras said: Endeavor not, to conceal your errors by words, but to remedy them by reproofs.

143. Pythagoras said: It is not so difficult to err, as not to reprove him who errs.

144. As a bodily disease cannot be healed, if it is concealed or praised, thus also can neither a remedy be applied to a diseased soul, which is badly guarded and protected. Ñ Pythagoras.

145. The grace of freedom of speech, like beauty in season, is productive of greater delight.

146. To have a blunt sword is as improper as to use ineffectual freedom of speech.

147. As little could you deprive the world of the sun, as freedom of speech from erudition.

148. As one who is clothed with a cheap robe may have a good body-habit, thus also may he whose life is poor possess freedom of speech.

149. Pythagoras said: Prefer those that reprove, to those that flatter; but avoid flatterers as much as enemies.

150. The life of the avaricious resembles a funeral banquet. For though it has all desirable elements, no one rejoices.

151. Pythagoras said: Acquire continence as the greatest strength and health.

152. ÒNot frequently man from man,Ó is one of the exhortations of Pythagoras; by which obscurely he signifies that it is not proper frequently to engage in sexual connections.

153. Pythagoras said: A slave to his passions cannot possibly be free.

154. Pythagoras said that intoxication is the preparation for insanity.

155. On being asked how a wine-lover might be cured of intoxication Pythagoras said: ÒIf he frequently considers what were his actions during intoxication."

156. Pythagoras said that unless you had something better than silence to say, you had better keep silence.

157. Pythagoras said, that rather than utter an idle word, you had better throw a stone in vain.

158. Pythagoras said: ÒSay not few things in many words, but much in few words."

159. Epicharmus said: ÒTo men genius is a divinity, either good or evil."

160. On being asked how a man ought to behave towards his country when it had acted unjustly towards him, Pythagoras said, ÒAs to a mother.Ó

161. Traveling teaches a man frugality, and self-sufficiency. The sweetest remedies for hunger and weariness are bread made of milk and floury on a bed of grass. (Democritus, probably Democrates or Demophilus; also the next one).

162. Every land is equally suitable as a residence for the wise man; the worthy soul's fatherland is the whole world.

163. Pythagoras said that into cities entered first, luxury; then being glutted; then lascivious, insolence, and last destruction.

164. Pythagoras said that was the best city which contained the worthiest men.

165. Pythagoras added to Demophilus's maxim that Òyou should do those things that you judge to be beautiful, though in doing them you should lack renown; for the rabble is a bad judge of a good thing.Ó The words, ÒTherefore despise the reprehension of those whose praise you despise.Ó

166. Pythagoras said that those who do not punish bad men, are really wishing that good men be injured.

167. Pythagoras said: ÒNot without a bridle can a horse be governed, and no less riches without prudence.Ó

168. The prosperous man who is vain is no better than the driver of a race on a slippery road. (Socrates? Probably Democrates, or Demophilus).

169. There is no gate of wealth so secure but that may open to the opportunity of Fortune. (Democritus? Probably Democrates or Demophilus).

170. The unrestrained grief of a torpid soul may be expelled by reasoning. (Democrates, not Democritus).

171. Poverty should be born with equanimity by a wise man. (Same).

172. Pythagoras: Spare your life, lest you consume it with sorrow and care.

173. Phavorinus in speaking of Old Age, said: Nor will I be silent as to this particular, that both to Plato and Pythagoras, it appeared that old age was not to be considered with reference to an egress from the present life, but to the beginning of a blessed one.

From CLEMENT OF ALEXANDRIA, Strom. 3: 415.

174. Philolaus said that the ancient theologians and priests testified that the soul is united to the body by a certain punishment, and that it is buried in this body as a sepulchre.

175. Pythagoras said that ÒWhatever we see when awake is death, and when asleep is a dream.Ó

ETHICAL FRAGMENTS
(preserved by STOBAEUS)
(His Commentary of the Golden Verses is wordy and
commonplace, and therefore is here omitted)

I
CONDUCT TOWARDS THE GODS

Concerning the Gods we should assume that they are immutable,
and do not change their decrees, from the very beginning they never
vary their conceptions of propriety. The immutability and firmness of
the virtues we know, and reason suggests that it must transcendently
obtain with the Gods, and be the element which to their conception
imparts a never-failing stability. Evidently no punishment which
divinity thinks proper to inflict is likely to be remitted. For if, the Gods
changed their decisions, and omitted to punish someone whom they
had designed to punish, for the world could be neither beautifully nor
justly governed; nor can we assign any probable reason for repentance
(on their part). Rashly, indeed, and without any reason, have poets
written words such as the following:
ÒMen bend the Gods, by incense and libation,
By gentle vows, and sacrifice and prayer,
When they transgress and stray from what is right.Ó
(Homer, Iliad, ix:495-7)
And:
"Flexible are e'en the Gods themselves!"
Ibidem. (493).
Nor is this the only such expression in poetry.
Nor must we omit to observe, that though the Gods are not the
causes of evil, yet they connect certain persons with things of this kind,
and surround those who deserve to be afflicted with corporeal and
external hindrances; not through any malignity, or because they think it
advisable that men should struggle with difficulties, but for the sake of
punishment. For as in general, pestilence and draught, rains-torms,
earthquakes and the like, are indeed for the most part produced by
natural causes, and yet are sometimes caused by the Gods, when the
times are such that the multitude's, iniquity needs to be punished
publicly, and in common, likewise in particular the Gods sometimes
afflict an individual with corporeal and external difficulties, in order to

punish him, and convert others to what is right. The belief that the Gods are never the cause of any evil, it seems to me, contributes greatly to proper conduct towards the Gods. For evils proceed from vice alone, while the Gods are of themselves the causes of good, and of any advantage; though in the meantime we slight their beneficence, and surround ourselves with voluntary evils. That is why I agree with the poet who says:

ÒThat mortals blame the Gods.....
as if they were the causes of their evils!
Though not from fate, But for their crimes they suffer woe!Ó
   (Homer, Odyssey, i.32-34)

Many arguments prove that God is never in anyway the cause of evil; but will suffice to read (in the first book of the Republic) the words of Plato, Òthat as it [is] not the nature of heat to refrigerate, so the beneficent cannot harm; but the contrary.Ó Moreover, God being good, and from the beginning replete with every virtue, cannot harm nor cause evil to any one; on the contrary imparting good to all willing to receive it; bestowing on us also such indifferent things as flow from nature, and which result in accordance with nature. But there is only one cause of evil.

II
PROPER CONDUCT TOWARDS OUR COUNTRY

After speaking of the Gods, it is most reasonable, in the second place, to show how we should conduct ourselves towards our country. For God is my witness that our country is a sort of secondary divinity, and our first and greatest parent. That is why its name is, for good reason, *patris*, derived from *pater*, a father; but taking a feminine termination, to be as it were a mixture of father and mother. This also explains that our country should be honored equally with our parents; preferring it to either of them separately, and not even to it preferring both our parents; preferring it besides to our wife, children and friends; and in short to all things, under the Gods. He who would esteem, one finger more than five would be considered stupid; inasmuch as it is reasonable to prefer five to one; the former despising the most desirable, while the latter, among the five preserves also the one finger. Likewise, he who prefers to save himself rather than his country, in addition to acting unlawfully, desires an impossibility. On the contrary, he who to himself prefers his country is dear to divinity, and reasons properly and irrefutably. Moreover it has been observed that though someone should not be a member of an organised society, remaining apart therefrom, yet is it proper that he should prefer the safety of society to his own; for the city's destruction would demonstrate that on its existence depended that of the individual citizen, just as the amputation of the hand involves the destruction of the finger, as an integral part. We may therefore draw the general conclusion that general utility cannot be separated from private welfare, both at bottom being identical. For whatever is beneficial to the whole country is common to every single part, inasmuch as without the parts the whole is nothing. Vice versa, whatever redounds to the benefit of the citizen extends also to the city; the nature of which is to extend benefits to the citizen. For example, whatever is beneficial to a dancer, must, in so far as he is a dancer, be so also to the whole choric ballet. Applying this reasoning to the discursive power of the soul, it will shed light on every particular duty, and we shall never omit to perform whatever may by us be due to our country.

That is the reason why a man who proposes to act honorably by his country should from his soul remove every passion and disease. The laws of his country should, by a citizen, be observed as (precepts of) a secondary divinity, conforming himself entirely to their mandates. He who endeavors to transgress or make any innovation in these laws should be opposed in every way, and be prevented therefrom in every possible way. By no means beneficial to a city, is contempt of existing laws, and preference for the new. Incurable innovators, therefore, should be restrained from giving their votes, and making precipitate innovations. I therefore commend the Locrian legislator Zaleucus, who ordained that he who intended to introduce a new law should do it with a rope around his neck, in order that he might be immediately strangled unless he succeeded in changing the ancient constitution of the state, to the very great advantage of the community. But customs which are truly those of the country, and which, perhaps are more ancient than the laws themselves, are, no less than the laws, to be preserved. However, the customs of the present, which are but of yesterday, and which, have been everywhere introduced only so very recently are not to be dignified as the institutes of our ancestors, and perhaps they are not even to be considered customs. Moreover, because, custom is an unwritten law, it has as sanction the authority of a very good legislator, namely, common consent of all that use it; and perhaps on this account its authority is next to that of justice itself.

III
PROPER CONDUCT TOWARDS THE PARENTS

After considering the Gods and our parents, what person deserves to be mentioned more than, or prior to our parents? That is why we turn towards them. No mistake, therefore, will be made by him who says that they are as it were secondary or terrestrial divinities, since, on account of their proximity, they should, in a certain not blasphemous sense, be by us more honored than the Gods themselves. To begin with, the only gratitude worthy of the name is a perpetual and unremitting promptness to repay the benefits received from them; since, though we do our very utmost, this would yet fall short of what they deserve. Moreover, we might also say that in one sense our deeds are to be counted as theirs, because we who perform them were once produced by them. If, for instance, the works of Phidias and other artists should themselves produce other works of art, we should not hesitate to attribute these latter deeds also to the original artists; that is why we may justly say that our performances are the deeds of our parents, through whom we originally derived our existence.

In order that we may the more easily apprehend the duties we owe them, we should keep in mind the underlying principle, that our parents should by us be considered as the images of the Gods; and, so help [to] heaven, images of the Gods; domestic?, who are our benefactors, our relatives, our creditors, our lords, and our most stable friends. They are indeed most stable images of the gods, possessing a likeness to them which no artist could possibly surpass. They are the guardian divinities of the home, and live with us; they are our greatest benefactors, endowing us with benefits of the greatest consequence, and indeed bestowing on us not only all we possess, but also such things as they wish to give us, and for which they themselves pray. Further, they are our nearest kindred, and the causes of our alliance with others. They are also creditors of things of the most honorable nature, and repay themselves only by taking what we shall be benefited by returning. For to a child what benefit can be so great as piety and gratitude to his parents? Most justly, too, are they our lords, for of what can we be the possession in a degree greater than of those through whom we exist? Moreover, they are perpetual and spontaneous friends and auxiliaries, affording, us assistance at all times and in every circumstance. Since, besides, the name of parent is the most excellent of names, which we apply even to the divinities, we may add something further to this conception; namely, that children should be persuaded that they dwell in their father's house, as if they were ministers and priests in a temple, appointed and consecrated for this purpose by nature herself, who entrusted to their care a reverential attention to their parents. If we are willing to carry out the dictates of reason, we shall readily attend to both kinds of affective regard, that regarding the, body and the soul. Yet reason will show us that to the body is to be paid less regard than to the soul, although we shall not neglect the former very necessary duties. For our parents, therefore, we should obtain liberal food, and such as is adapted to the weakness of old age; besides this, a bed, sleep, massage, a bath, and proper garments; in short, the necessaries of the body, that they may at no time experience the want of any of these, by this, imitating their care for the nurture of ourselves, when we were infants. Our attention to them should partake of the prophetic nature, whereby we may discover what special bodily necessity they may be longing, without pressing it to us. Respecting us, indeed, they divined many things, when our desires could be expressed by no more than inarticulate and distressful cries, unable to express the objects of our wants clearly. By the benefits they formerly conferred upon us, our parents became to us the preceptors or what we ought to bestow upon them.

With respect to our parents' souls, we should in the first place, procure for them diversion, which will be obtained especially if we associate with them by night and day, taking walks, being massaged, and living by their side, unless some thing necessary interferes. For just as those who are undertaking a long journey desire the presence of their families and friends to see them off, as if accompanying a solemn procession, so also parents, verging on the grave, enjoy most of all the sedulous and unremitting attention of their children. Moreover, should our parents at any time, as happens often, especially with those whose education was deficient, their conduct should be reprehensible, they should indeed be corrected but not as we are accustomed to do with our inferiors or equals, but as it were with suggestiveness; not as if they had erred through ignorance, but as if they had committed an oversight through inattention, as if they would not have erred, had they considered the matter. For reproof, especially if personal, is to the old bitter. That is why their oversights should be supplemented by mild exhortation, as by an elegant artifice.

Children, besides, rejoice their parents by performing for them servile offices such as washing their feet, making their bed, or ministering to their wants. These necessary servile attentions are all the more precious when performed by the dear hands of their children, accepting their ministrations. Parents will be especially gratified when their children publicly show their honor to those whom they love and very much esteem.

That is why children should affectionately love their parents' kindred, and pay them proper attention, as also to their parents' friends and acquaintances. These general principles will aid us to deduce many other smaller filial duties, which are neither unimportant nor accidental. For since our parents are gratified by the attention we pay to those they love, it will be evident that as we are in a most eminent degree beloved by parents, we shall surely much please them by a proper attention to ourselves.

IV
ON FRATERNAL LOVE

The first admonition therefore, is very [clear] and convincing, and obligatory generally, being [sane] and self-evident. Here it is: Act by everyone, in the same manner as if you supposed yourself to be him, and him to be you. A servant will be well treated by one who considers how he would like to be treated by him, if he was the master, and himself the servant. The same principle might be applied between parents and children, and vice versa; and in short, between all men. This principle, however, is peculiarly adapted to the mutual relation of brothers; since no other preliminary considerations are necessary, in the matter of conduct towards one's brother, than promptly to assume that equable mutual relation. This therefore is the first precept, to act towards one's brother in the same manner in which he would think it proper for his brother to act towards him.

But someone will say, I do not transgress propriety, and am equitable; but my brother's manners are rough and brusque. This is not right; for, in the first place, he may not be speaking the truth; as excessive vanity might lead a man to extol and magnify his own manners, and diminish and vilify what pertains to others. It frequently happens indeed, that men of inferior worth prefer themselves to others who are far more excellent characters. Second, though the brother should indeed be of the rough character mentioned above, the course to take would be to prove oneself the better by vanquishing his boorishness by [your worthiness] Those who conduct themselves worthily towards moderate, benignant men are entitled to no great thanks; but transform to graciousness the stupid vulgar man, he deserves the greatest applause.

It must not be thought impossible for exhortation to take marked effect; for in men of the moat impossible manners there are possibilities of improvement, and of love and honor for their benefactors. Not even animals, and such as naturally are the most hostile to our race, who are captured and dragged off in chains, and confined in cages, -- are not beyond being tamed by appropriate treatment, and daily food. Will not then the man who is a brother, or even the first man you meet, who deserves attention far greater than a brute, be rendered gentle by proper treatment even though he should never entirely lose his boorishness. In our behavior, therefore, toward every man, and in much greater degree towards a brother, we should imitate Socrates who to a person who cried out against him, ÒMay I die, unless I am revenged on you,Ó answered, ÒMay I die, if I do not make you my friend!Ó So much then for external fraternal relations. Further, a man should consider that in a certain sense his brothers are part of him, just as my [eyes] are part of me; also my legs, my hands, and other parts of me. For the relation of brothers to a family social organism (are the same as members a body). If then the eyes and the hands should receive a particular soul and intellect, they would because of the above mentioned communion, and because they could not all perform their proper offices without the presence of the other members watch over the interests of the other members [with] the interest of a guardian genius. So also, we who are men, and who acknowledge that we have a soul, should, towards our brothers, omit no proper offices. Indeed, more naturally adapted for [mutual] assistance than parts of the body; are brothers. The eyes, being mutually adjusted, do see what [is] before them, and one hand cooperates with the other; but the mutual adaptation of brothers is far more various. For they accomplish things which are mutually profitable, though at the greatest intervening distance; and they will greatly benefit each other though their mutual difference be immeasurable. In short, it must be considered [that] our life resembles nothing so much as a prolonged conflict, which arises partly from the strife in the nature of things, and partly through the sudden unexpected blows of fortune; but most of all through vice itself, which abstains neither from violence, fraud, or evil stratagems. Hence nature, as being not ignorant of the purpose for which she generated us, produced each of us as it were accompanied by an auxiliary.

No one, therefore, is alone, nor does he derive his origin from an oak or a rock, but from parents, in conjunction or with brothers, relatives, and other intimates. Here reason for us performs a great work, conciliating to us strangers, who are no relatives of ours, furnishing us with many assistants. That is the very reason why we naturally endeavor to allure and make every one our friend. How insane a thing it therefore is to wish to be united to those who naturally have nothing suitable to procure our love, and become as familiar as possible with them, voluntarily; and yet neglect those willing helpers and associates supplied by nature herself, who are called brothers!

V
ON MARRIAGE

The discussion of marriage is most necessary, as the whole of our race is naturally social; and the most fundamental social association is that effected by marriage. Without a household, there could exist no cities; and households of the unmarried are most imperfect, while on the contrary those of the married are most complete. That is why in our treatise *on Families*, we have shown that the married state is to be preferred by the sage; while a single life is not to be chosen except under peculiar circumstances. (Pythagoras and Socrates were married, while Plato, Plotinus and Proclus were not). Therefore, inasmuch as we should imitate the man of intellect, so far as possible, and as for him marriage is preferable, it is evident it will be so also for us, except if hindered by some exceptional circumstance. This is the first reason for marriage.

Entirely apart from the model of the sage, Nature herself seems to incite us thereto. Not only did she make us gregarious, but adapted us to sexual intercourse, and proposed the procreation of children and stability of life as the one and universal work of wedlock. Now Nature justly teaches us that a choice of such things as are fit should be made so as to accord with what she has procured for us. Every animal, therefore, lives in conformity to its natural constitution, and so also every plant in harmony with its laws of life. But there obtains this difference: that the latter do not employ any reasoning or calculation, in the selection of the things on which they lay hold, using alone nature, without participating in soul. Animals are drawn to investigate what may be proper for them by imaginations and desires. To us, however, Nature gave reason, to survey everything else, and, together with all things, nay, prior to all things, to direct its attention to Nature itself, so as to tend towards her, as a glorious aim, in an orderly manner, that by choosing everything consonant with her, we might live in a becoming manner. Following this line of argument, he will not err in saying that a family without wedlock is imperfect; for (nature) does not conceive of the governor without the governed, nor the governed without a governor. Nature therefore seems to me to shame those who are averse to marriage. In the next place, marriage is beneficial. First, because it produces a truly divine fruit, the procreation of children, who are, as partaking of our nature, to assist us in all our undertakings, while our strength is yet undiminished; and when we shall be worn out, oppressed with old age, they will be our assistants. In prosperity they will be the associates of our joy, and in adversity, the sympathetic diminishers of our sorrows.

Marriage is beneficial not only because of procreation of children, but for the association of a wife. When we are wearied with our labors outside of the home, she receives us with officious kindness, and refreshes us by her solicitous attentions. Next, she induces a forgetfulness of molestations outside of the house. The annoyances in the forum, the gymnasium or the country, and in short all the vicissitudes of our intercourse with friends and acquaintances, do not disturb us so obviously, being obscured by necessary occupations; but when released from these, we return home, and our mind has time to reflect, then, availing themselves of this opportunity these cares and anxieties rush in upon us, to torment us, at the very moment when life seems cheerless and lonely. Then comes the wife as a great solace, and by making some inquiry about external affairs, or by referring to, and together considering some domestic problem, she, by her sincere vivacity inspires him with pleasure and delight. It is needless to enumerate all the help a wife can be in festivals, when sacrificing victims; or during her husband's journeys, she can keep the household running smoothly, and direct at times of urgency; in managing the domestics, and in nursing her husband when sick.

Summarizing, in order to pass through life properly, all men need two things; the aid of relatives, and kindly sympathy. But nothing can be more sympathetic then a wife; nor anything more kindred, than children. Both of these are afforded by marriage; how therefore could we find anything more beneficial?

Also beautiful is a married life, it seems to me. What relation can be more ornamental to a family, than that between husband and wife? Not sumptuous edifices, not walls covered with marble plaster, not piazzas adorned with stones, which are indeed admired by those ignorant of true goods; not paintings and arched myrtle walks, nor anything else which is the subject of astonishment to the stupid, is the ornament of a family. The beauty of a household consists in the conjunction of man and wife, united to each other by destiny, and consecrated to the gods presiding over nuptial births, and [---]es, and who harmonize, and use all things in [common] for their bodies, or even their very souls; likewise exercise a becoming authority over their house and servants; who are properly solicitous [-----]t the education of their children; and to the necessaries of life pay an attention which is neither excessive or negligent, but moderate and appropriate. For, as the most admirable Homer says, what can be better and more excellent,

"Than when at home the husband and wife,
Live in entire unanimity!" (Odyssey, 7:183).

That is the reason why I have frequently wondered at those who conceive that life in common with a woman must be burdensome and grievous. Though to them she appears to be a burden and molestation, she is not so; on the contrary, she is something light and easy to be borne, or rather, she possesses the power of charming away from her husband things burdensome and grievous. No trouble so great is there which cannot easily be borne by a husband and wife who harmonize, and are willing to endure it in common. But what is truly burdensome and unbearable is imprudence, for through it things naturally light, and among others a wife, become heavy. To many, indeed, marriage is intolerable, in reality not from itself, or because such an association as this with a woman is naturally insufferable, but when we marry the wrong person, and, in addition to this, are ourselves entirely ignorant of life, and unprepared to take a wife in a way such as a free-born woman ought to be taken, than indeed it happens that this association with her becomes difficult and intolerable. Vulgar people do marry in this way; taking a wife neither for the procreation of children, nor for harmonious association; being attracted to the union by the magnitude of the dower, or through physical attractiveness, or the like; and by following these bad counselors, they pay no attention to the bride's disposition and. manners, celebrating nuptials to their own destruction, and with crowned doors introduce to themselves instead of a wife, a tyrant, whom they cannot resist, and with whom they are unable to contend for chief authority.

Evidently, therefore, marriage becomes burdensome and intolerable to many, not through itself, but through these causes. But it is not wise to blame things which are not harmful, nor to make our own deficient use of these things the cause of our complaint against them. Most absurd, besides, is it feverishly to seek the auxiliaries of friendship, and achieve certain friends and associates, to aid and defend us in the vicissitudes of life, without seeking and endeavoring to obtain the relief, defence and assistance afforded us by Nature, the gods, and the laws, through a wife and children. As to a numerous offspring, it is generally suitable to nature and marriage that all, or the majority of the offspring be nurtured. Many dissent from this, for a not very beautiful reason, avariciousness, and the fear of poverty as the greatest evil. To begin with, in procreating children, we are not only begetting assistants, nurses for our old age, and associates in every vicissitude of life; Ñ we do not however beget them for ourselves alone, but in many ways also for our parents. To them our procreation of children is gratifying; because, if we should suffer anything calamitous prior to their decease, we shall, instead of ourselves, leave our children as the support of their old age. Then for a grandfather it is a beautiful thing to be conducted by the hands of his grandchildren, and by them to be considered as worthy of every attention. Hence, in the first place, we shall gratify our own parents by paying attention to the procreation of children. In the next, we shall be cooperating with the ardent wishes and fervent prayers of those who begot us. They were solicitous about our birth from the first, there through looking for an extended succession of themselves, that they should leave behind them children of children, therefore paying attention to our marriage, procreation, and nurture. Hence, by marrying and begetting children we shall be, as it were, fulfilling a part of their prayers; while, acting contrariwise, we shall be destroying the object of their deliberate choice.

Moreover, it would seem that everyone who voluntarily, and without some prohibiting circumstance avoids marriage and the procreation of children, accuses his parents of madness, as having engaged in wedlock without the right conception of things. Here we see an unavoidable contradiction. How could that man live without dissension, who finds a pleasure in living, and willingly continues in life as one who was properly brought into existence by his parents, and yet conceives that for him procreation of offspring is something to be rejected?

We must remember that we beget children not only for our own sake, but, as we have already stated, for our parents; but further also for the sake of our friends and kindred. It is gratifying to see children which are our offspring on account of human kindness, relatives, and security. Like ships which, though greatly agitated by the waves, are firmly secured by many anchors, so do those who have children, or whose friends or relatives have them, ride at anchor in port, in absolute security. For this reason, then, will a man who is a lover of his kindred, and associates, earnestly desire to marry and beget children.

Our country also loudly calls upon us to do so. For after all we do not beget children so much for ourselves, as for our country, procuring a race that may follow us, and supplying the community with successors to ourselves. Hence the priest should realize that to the city he owes priests; the ruler, that he owes rulers; the orator, that he owes orators; and in short, the citizen, that he owes citizens. So it is gratifying to a choric ballet that those who compose it should continue perennially; and as an army looks to the continuance of its soldiers, so the perpetuation of its citizens is a matter of concern to a city. A city would not need succession were it only a temporary grouping, of duration commensurate with the life-time of any one man; but as it extends to many generations, and if it invokes a fortunate genius may endure for many ages, it evidently necessary to direct its attention not only to its present, but also to its future, not despising our natal soil, nor leaving it desolate, but establishing it in good hopes for our posterity.

VI
CONDUCT TOWARDS OUR RELATIVES

Duties to relatives depend on duties to our immediate families, the arguments for which apply also to the former. Each of us is, indeed, as it were circumscribed by many circles, larger and smaller, comprehending and comprehended, according to various mutual circumstances.

The first and nearest circle is that which every one describes about the centre of his own mind, wherein is comprehended the body, and all its interests: this is the smallest circle nearly touching the centre itself. The second and further circle which comprehends the first, is that which includes parents, brethren, wife, and children. The third greater circle is the one containing uncles, aunts, grandfathers, and grandmothers and the children of brothers and sisters. Beyond this is the circle containing the remaining relatives. Next to this is the circle containing the common people, then that which comprehends our tribe, then that of all the citizens; then follow two further circles; that of the neighboring suburbs, and those of the province. The outermost and greatest circle is that which comprehends the whole human race (as repeated Pope, in his Essay on Man).

In view of this, he who strives to conduct himself properly in each of these connections should, in a certain respect, gather together the circles into one centre, and always endeavor to transfer himself from the comprehending circles to the several particulars which they comprehend.

The lover of his kindred, therefore, should conduct himself in a becoming manner towards his parents and brothers; also, according to the same analogy, towards the more elderly of his relatives of both sexes, such as grandfathers, uncles and aunts; towards those of the same age as himself, as his cousins; and towards his juniors, as the children of his cousins. This summarizes his conduct towards his kindred, having already shown how he should act towards himself, his parents and brothers; and besides these, towards wife and children. To which must be added that those who belong to the third circle should be honored similarly to these; and again, kindred similarly to those that belong to the third circle. For benevolence must somehow fade way from those who are more distant from us by blood; though at the same time we should endeavor, to effect a mutual assimilation. This distance will moderate if through the diligent attention which we pay to them we shorten the bond connecting us with each. Such then are the most comprehensive duties towards our kindred.

It might be well to say a word about the general names of kindred, such as the calling of cousins, uncles and aunts by the names of brothers, fathers and mothers; while of the other kindred, to call some uncle, others the children of brother and sisters, and others cousins, according to the difference in age, for the sake of the emotional extension derivable from names. Such name-extension will manifest our sedulous attention to these relatives, and at the same time will incite and extend us in a greater degree to the contraction of the above circles.

We should however remember the distinction between parents that we made above. Comparing parents, we said that to mother was due more love, but to the father more honor. Similarly, we should show more love to those connected with us by a maternal alliance, but more honor to those connected with us by an alliance that is paternal.

VII
ON ECONOMICS

To begin with, we must mention the kind of labor which preserves the union of the family. To the husband are usually assigned rural, forensic and political activities; while to the mother belong spinning of wool, making of bread, cooking, and in short, everything of a domestic nature. Nevertheless, neither should be entirely exempt from the labors of the other. For sometimes it will be proper, when the wife is in the country, that she should superintend the laborers, and act as major-domo; and that the husband should sometimes attend to domestic affairs, inquiring about, and inspecting what is doing in the house. This joint participation of necessary cares will more firmly unite their mutual association.

We should not fail to mention the manual operations, which are associated with the spheres of occupations. Why should the man meddle with agricultural labors? This is generally admitted; and though men of the present day spend much time in idleness and luxury, yet it is rare to find any unwilling to engage in the labor of sowing and planting, and other agricultural pursuits. Much less persuasive perhaps, will be the arguments which invite the man to engage in those other occupations that belong to the woman. For such men as pay great attention to neatness and cleanliness will not conceive wool-spinning to be their business; since, for the most part vile, diminutive men, delicate and effeminate apply themselves to the elaboration of wool, through an emulation of feminine softness. But it does not become a man, who is manly, to apply himself to things of this kind: so that perhaps neither shall I advise such employments to those who have not unmistakably demonstrated their modesty and virility. What therefore should hinder the man from sharing in the labors pertaining to a woman, whose past life has been such as to free him from all suspicion of absurd and effeminate conduct? For is it not thought that more domestic labors pertain to man than to women in other fields? For they are more laborious, and require corporeal strength, such as to grind, to knead meal, to cut wood, to draw water from a well, to carry large vessels from one place to another, to shake coverlets and carpets, and such like. It will be quite proper for men to engage in such occupations.

But it would be well if the legitimate work of a woman be enlarged in other directions, so that she may not only engage with her maid-servants in the spinning of wool, but may also apply herself to other more virile occupations. It seems to me that breadmaking, drawing water from a well, the lighting of fires, the making of beds, and such like, are labors suited to a free-born woman.

But to her husband a wife will seem much more beautiful, especially if she is young, and not yet worn out by the bearing of children, if she becomes his associate in the gathering of grapes, and collecting the olives; and if he is verging toward old age, she will render herself more pleasing to him by sharing with him the labor of sowing and plowing, and while he is digging or planting, extending to him the instruments he needs for his work. For when by the husband and wife a family is governed thus, in respect to necessary labors, it seems to me that it will be conducted in the best manner.

TIMAEUS LOCRIUS, The Teacher of Plato, on THE SOUL AND THE WORLD

I
MIND, NECESSITY, FORM & MATTER

Timaeus the Locrian asserted this: Ñ that of all the things in the Universe, there are, two causes, (one) Mind, (the cause) of things existing according to reason; (the other) Necessity, (the cause) of things (existing) by (some) force, according to the power of the bodies; and that the former of these is the nature of the good and is called God, and the principle of things that are best; but what accessory causes follow, are referred to Necessity. As regards the things in the Universe, there are Form, Matter, and the perceptible; which is, as it were, a resistance of the two others; and that Form is unproduced, and unmoved, and stationary and of the nature of the same, and perceptible by the mind, and a pattern of such things produced, as exist by a state of change; for that some such thing as this is Form, spoken of and conceived to be.

Matter, however, is a mold, and a mother and a nurse, and procreative of the third kind of being; for receiving upon itself the resemblances, and as it were remolding them, it perfects these productions. He asserted moreover that Matter, though eternal is not unmoved; and though of itself it is formless and shapeless, yet it receives every kind of form; and that what is around bodies, is divisible, and partakes of the nature of the different; and that Matter is called by the twin names of Plane and Space. These two principles, then, are opposite to each, other; of which Form relates to a male power, and a father; while matter relates to a female, and a mother. Being three, they are recognisable by three marks: Form, by mind, according to knowledge; Matter by a spurious kind of reasoning, because of its not being mentally perceived directly, but by analogy and their productions by sensation and opinion.

II
CREATION OF THE WORLD

Before the heavens, then, there existed through reason, Form and Matter, and the God who develops the best. But since the older surpasses the younger and the ordered surpasses the orderless, the deity being good, on seeing that Matter receives Form, and is altered in every way, but without order, the necessity of organizing it, altering the undefined to the defined, so that the differences between bodies might be similarly related, not receiving various turns at hap-hazard. He therefore made this world out of the whole of Matter, laying it down as a limit to the nature of being, through its containing in itself all the rest of things, being one, only-begotten, perfect, endued with soul and reason, for these qualities are superior to the soul-lees and the irrational, Ñ and of a sphere like body; for this is more perfect than the rest of forms.

Desirous then of making a very good production, he made it a deity, created and never to be destroyed by any cause other than the God, who had put it in order, if indeed he should ever wish to dissolve it. But on the part of the good there is no rushing forward to the destruction of a very beautiful production. Such therefore being the world, it continues without corruption and destruction, being blessed. It is the best of things ordered; since it has been produced by the best cause, that looks not to patterns made by hand, but to Form in the abstract, and to Existence, perceived by the mind to which the created thing, having been carefully adjusted, has become the most beautiful, and to be not wrongly undertaken. It is [ever]perfect according to the things perceived by sense because the pattern perceived by mind contains [in] itself all the living things perceived by mind; he left out of itself nothing, as being the limit [of]the things perceived by mind, as this world is [of] those perceived by sense.

As being solid, and perceptible by touch and sight, it has a share of earth and fire, and of the things between them, air and water; and it is composed of bodies all perfect, which are in it as wholes so that no part might ever be left out of it, in order that the body of the Universe might be altogether self-sufficient, uninjured by corruption without or within; for apart from these there is nothing else, for the things combined according the best proportions and with equal powers, neither rule over, nor are ruled by each other in turn, so that some receive an increase, others a decrease, remaining indissolubly united according to the very best proportions.

III
PROPORTIONS OF THE WORLD-COMBINATION

For whenever there are any three terms, with mutually equal intervals, that are proportionate, we then perceive that, after the manner of an extended string, the middle is to the first, as is the third to it; and this holds true inversely and alternately, interchanging places and order; so that it is impossible to arrange them numerically without producing an equivalence of results. Likewise the world's shape and movement are well arranged; the shape is a sphere self similar on all sides, able to contain all shapes that are similar; the movement endlessly exhibits the change dependent on a circle.

Now as the sphere is on every side equidistant from the centre, it is able to retain its poise whether in movement or at rest; neither leaving its poise, nor assuming another. Its external appearance being exactly smooth, it needs no mortal organs such as are fitted to, and present in all other living beings, because of their wants. The world-soul's element of divinity radiates out from the centre, entirely penetrating the whole world, forming a single mixture of divided substance with undivided form; and this mixture of two forces, the same and the different, became the origin of motion; which indeed was not accomplished in the easiest way, being extremely difficult.

Now all these proportions are combined harmonically according to numbers; which proportions were scientifically divided according to scale which reveals the elements and the means of the soul's combination. Now seeing that the earlier is more powerful in power and time than the later, the deity did not rank the soul after the substance of the body, but made it older, by taking the first of unities, 384 (12 x 16)[x 2?]. Knowing this first, we can easily reckon the double and the triple and all the terms together, with the complements and eighths, must amount to 114,69 and likewise the divisions (sum of the tone sequences of 36 tones, amounting to 384 x 27, the perfect cube).

IV
PLANETARY REVOLUTIONS AND TIME

God the eternal, the chief ruler of the Universe, and its creator is beheld alone by the mind; but we may behold by sight all that is produced this world and its parts, how many soever they [----] in heaven; which as being ethereal, must be [divided] into kinds, some relating to sameness, others to difference. Sameness draws inward all that is without, along the general eastward movement from the West. Difference draws from within all self-moved portions from West to East, fortuitously rolling around and along by the superior power of sameness.

The different's movement being divided in harmonical proportion, assumes the order of [seven] circles Nearest to the earth, ,the Moon revolves in a month; while beyond her the Sun completes his revolution in a year. Two planets run a [co---]equal with that of the Sun: Mercury, and Juno, also called Venus and Lucifer, because shepherds and people generally are not skillful in sacred astronomy, confusing the western and eastern rise. The same star may shine in the West when following the Sun at a distance great enough to be visible in spite of solar splendor; and at another time in the East, when, as herald of the day it rises before the Sun, leading it. Because of its [running] together with the sun, Venus is Lucifer frequently but not always; for there are planet and stars of any magnitude seen above the horizon before sunrise, herald the day. But the three other planets, Mars, Jupiter and Saturn have their peculiar velocities and different years, completing their course while making their periods of effulgence, of visibility, of obscuration and eclipse, causing accurate rising and settings. Moreover they complete their appearances conspicuously in East or West according to their position relative to the Sun, who during the day speeds westward, which during the night it reverses, under the influence of sameness; while its annual revolution is due to its inherent motion. In resultance of these two kinds of motion it rolls out a spiral, creeping according to one portion, in the time of a day, but, whirled around under the sphere of the fixed stars, according to each revolution of darkness and day.

Now these revolutions are by men called portions of time, which the deity arranged together with the world. For before the world the stars did not exist; and hence there was neither year, nor periods of seasons, by which this generated time is measured, and which is the representation of the ungenerated time called eternity. For as this heaven has been produced according to an eternal pattern, (the world of ideas), Ñ so according to the pattern of eternity was our world-time created simultaneously with the world.

V
THE EARTH'S CREATION BY GEOMETRIC
FIGURES

The Earth, fixed at the centre, becomes the hearth of the gods, and the boundary of darkness and day, producing both settings and risings, according to the occultations produced by the things that form the boundary, just as we im prove our sight by making a tube with our closed hand, to exclude refraction. The Earth is the oldest body in the heavens. Water was not produced without Earth, nor air without moisture; nor could fire continue without moisture and the materials that are inflammable; so that the Earth is fixed upon its balance as the root and base of all other substances. Of produced things, the substratum is Matter, while the reason of each shape is abstract Form; of these two the resultance is Earth, and Water, Air and Fire.

This is how they were created. Every body is composed of surfaces, whose elements are triangles; of which one is right-angled, and the other has all unequal sides, with the greater angle thrice the size of the lesser; while its least angle is the third of a right angle, and the middle [one] is double of the least; for it is two parts out of three; while the greatest is a right angle, being one and a half greater than the middle one, and the triple of the least. Now this unequal [sided] triangle is the half of a equilateral triangle, out into two equal parts by a line let down from apex to that base. Now in each of these triangles there is a right angle; but in the one, the two sides about the right angle are equal, and in the other, all the sides are unequal. Now let this be called a scalene triangle; while the other, the half of the square, is the principle of the constitution the Earth. For the square produced from this scalene triangle is composed of four half squares and from such a square is produced the cube, a [body] the most stationary and steady in every way; having six sides and eight angles, and on this account [the]Earth is a body the heaviest and most difficult [to] be moved and its substance is inconvertible because it has no affinity with a triangle of any kind. Only the Earth has as peculiar element [the--] square and this is the element of the three other substances, Fire, Air and Water. For when the half triangle is put together six times, it produces a solid equilateral triangle; the exemplar of the [pyramid], which has four faces with equal angles, which is the form of Fire, as the easiest to be moved and composed of the finest particles. After this ranks the octohedron, with

318

eight faces and six angles, the element of Air, and the third is the icosahedron, with twenty faces and twelve angles, the element of Water, composed of the most numerous and heaviest particles.

These then, as being composed of the same element, are transmuted. But the deity has made the dodecahedron, as being the nearest to the sphere, the image of the Universe. Fire then, by the fineness of its particles, passes through all things; and Air through the rest of things, with the exception of Fire; and Water through the Earth. All things are therefore full, and have no vacuum. They cohere by the revolving movement of the Universe, and are pressed against, and rubbed by, each other in turn, and produce the never-failing change from production to destruction.

VI
CONCRETION OF THE ELEMENTS

By making use of these the deity put together this world, sensible to touch through the particles of Earth, and to sight through those of Fire; which two are the extremes. Through the particles of Air and Water he has conjoined the world by the strongest chain, namely, proportion; which restrains not only itself but all its subjects. Now if the conjoined object is a plane surface, one middle term is sufficient; but if a solid, there will be need of two. With two middle terms, therefore, he combined two extremes; so that as Fire is to Air, Air might be to Water, and Water to Earth; and by alternation, as Fire is to Water, Air might be to Earth; and by inversion as Earth is to Water, Water might be to Air, and Air to Fire; and by alternation, as Earth is to Air, so Water might be to Fire. Now since all are equal in power, their ratios are in a state of equality. This world is then one, through the bond of the deity, made according to proportion.

How each of these substances possesses many forms; Fire, those of Flame, and Burning and Luminousness, through the inequality of the triangles in each of them. In the same manner, Air is partly clear and dry, and partly turbid and foggy; and Water partly flowing and partly congealed, according as it is Snow, Hoar-frost, Hail or Ice; and that which is Moist, is in one respect flowing as honey and oil; but in another is compact, as pitch and wax; and of compact-forms there are some fusible, as gold, silver, copper, tin, lead and steel; and some friable, as sulphur, pitch, nitre, salt, alum, and similar metals.

VII
COMPOSITION OF THE SOUL

After putting together the world, the deity planned the creation of living beings, subject to death, so that, himself being perfect, he might perfectly work it out according to his image. Therefore he mixed up the soul of man out of the same proportions and powers, and after taking the particles and distributing them, he delivered them? over to Nature, whose office is to effect change. She then took up the task of working out mortal and ephemeral living beings, whose souls ware drawn in from different sources, some from the Moon, others from the Sun, and others from various planets, that cycle within the Difference, -- with the exception of one single power which was derived from Sameness, which she mixed up in the rational portion of the soul, as the image of wisdom in those of a happy fate.

Now of the soul of man one portion is rational and intellectual; and another irrational and unintellectual. Of the logical part, the best portion is derived from Sameness, while the worse comes from Difference; and each is situated around the head, so that the other portions of the soul and body may minister to it, as the uppermost of the whole tabernacle. Of the irrational portion, that which represents passion hangs around the heart, while desire inhabits the liver. The principle of the body, and root of the marrow is the brain, wherein inheres leadership; and from this, like an effusion, through the back-bone flows what remains, from which are separated the particles for seed and reason; while the marrow's surrounding defences are the bones, of which the flesh is the covering and concealment. To the nerves he united joints by ligatures, suitable for their movement. Of the internal organs, some exist for the sake of nourishment, and others for safety; of communications, some convey outside movements to the interior intelligent places of perception, while others, not falling under the power of apprehension, are unperceived, either because the affected bodies are too earthlike, or because the movements are too feeble; the painful movements tend to arouse Nature, while the pleasurable lull Nature into remaining within itself.

VIII
SENSATIONS

Amongst the senses, the deity has in us lit sight to view the objects in the heavens, and for the reception of knowledge; while to make us capable to receive speech and melody, he has in us implanted hearing, of which he who is deprived thereof from birth will become dumb, nor be able to utter any speech, and that is why this sense is said to be related closest to speech. .As many affections of the body as have a name are so called with reference to touch; and others from relation to their seat. Touch judges of the properties connected with life, such as warmth, coldness, dryness, moisture, smoothness, roughness, and of things, that they are yielding, opposing, hard, or soft. Touch also decides of heaviness or lightness. Reason defines these affections as being centripetal and centrifugal; which men mean to express when they say below, and middle. For the centre of a sphere is below, and that part lying above it and stretching to the circumference, is called upwardness.

Now what is warm appears to consist of fine particles, causing bodies to separate; while coldness consists of the grossness of the particles, causing a tendency to condense.

The circumstances connected with the sense of taste are similar to those of touch. For substances grow either smooth or rough by concretion and secretion, by entering the pores, and assuming shapes. For those that cause the tongue to melt away, or that scrape it, appear to be rough; while those that act moderately in scraping appear brackish; while those that inflame or separate the skin are acrid; while their opposites, the smooth sweet, are reduced to a juicy state.

Of smelling, the kinds have not been defined; for, because of their percolating through narrow pores, that are too stiff to be closed or separated, things seem to be sweet-smelling or bad-smelling from the putrefaction or concoction of the earth and similar substances.

A vocal sound is a percussion in the air, arriving at the soul through the ears; the pores (or communications) of which reach to the liver; and among them is breath, by the movement of which hearing exists. Now of the voice and hearing, that portion which is quick is acute; while that which is slow, is grave; the medium being the most harmonious. What is much and diffused, is great; what is little and compressed, is small; what is arranged according to musical proportions is in tune, while that which is unarranged, and unproportionate, is out of tune, and not properly adjusted.

The fourth kind of things relating to the senses is the most multiform and various, and they are called objects of sight, in which are all kinds of colors, and an infinity of colored substances. The principle are four: white, black, brilliant (blue) and red, out of a mixture of which all other colors are prepared. What is white causes the vision to expand, and what is black causes it to contract; just as warmth expands, and cold contracts, and what is rough contracts the tasting, and what is sharp dilates it.

IX
RESPIRATION

It is natural for the covering of animals that live in the air to be nourished and kept together by the food being distributed by the veins through the whole mass, in the manner of a stream, conveyed as it were by channels, and moistened by the breath, which diffuses it, and carries it to the extremities. Respiration is produced through there being no vacuum in nature; while the air, as it flows in, is inhaled in place of that which is exhaled, through unseen pores such as those through which perspiration -drops appear on the skin; but a portion is excreted by the natural warmth of the body. Then it becomes necessary for an equivalent portion to be reintroduced, to avoid a vacuum, which is impossible, for the animal would no longer be concentrating, and single, when the covering had been separated by the vacuum.

Now in lifeless substances, according to the analogy of respiration, the same organization occurs. The gourd, and the amber, for instance, bear resemblance to respiration.

Now the breath flows through the body to an orifice outwards, and is in turn introduced through respiration by the mouth and nostrils, and again after the manner of the Euripus, is in turn carried to the body, which is expended according to the expiration. Also the gourd, when the air within is expelled by fire, attracts moisture to itself; and amber, when the air is separated from it, receives an equal substance. Now all nourishment comes as from a root from the heart; and from the stomach; as a fountain; and is conveyed to the body, to which, if it be moistened by more than what flows out, there is said to be an increase; but if less, by a decay; but the point of perfection is the boundary between these two, and is considered to exist in an equality of efflux and influx; but when the joints of the system are broken, should there no longer exist any passage for the breath, or the nourishment not be distributed, then the animal dies.

X
DISORDERS

There are many things hurtful to life, which are causes of death. One kind is disease. Its beginning is disharmony of the functions, when the simple powers, such as heat, cold, moisture or dryness are excessive or deficient. Then come turns and alterations in the blood, from corruption, and the deterioration of the flesh, when wasting away, should the turns take place according to the changes, to what is acid, or brackish, or bitter, in the blood, or wasting away of the flesh. Hence arise the production of bile, and of phlegm, diseased juices, and the rottenness of liquids weak indeed, unless deeply seated; but difficult to cure, when their commencement is generated from the bones, and painful, if in a state of inflammation of the marrow. The last of disorders are those of the breath, bile and phlegm, when they increase and flow into situations foreign to them, or into places inappropriate for them, by laying hold, of the situation, belonging to what is better, and be driving away what is congenial they fix themselves there, injuring the bodies, and resolving them into the very things.

These then are the sufferings of the body; and hence arise many diseases of the soul; some from one faculty, and some from another. Of the perceptive soul the disease is a difficulty of perception, of the recollecting, a forgetfulness of the appetitive part, a deficiency of desire and eagerness; of the affective, a violent suffering and excited madness; of the rational, an indisposition to learn and think.

But of wickedness the beginnings are pleasure and pains; desires and fears, inflamed by the body, mingled with the wind and called by different names. For there loves and regrets, desires let loose, and passions on the stretch, heavy resentments, and appetites of various kinds, and pleasures immoderate. Plainly, to be unreasonably disposed towards the affections is the limit of virtue, and to be under their rule is that of vice; for to abound in them, or to be superior to them, places us in a good or bad position. Against such impulses the temperaments of our bodies is greatly able to cooperate, whether quick or hot, or various, by leading us to melancholy or violent lewdness; and certain parts, when affected by a catarrh, produce itchings and forms of body more similar to a state of inflammation than one of health; through which a sinking of the spirits and a forgetfulness, a stillness and a state of fear are witnessed.

XI
DISCIPLINE

Important, too, are the habits in which persons are trained, in the city or at home, and their daily food, by luxury enervating the soul, or fortifying it for strength. For the living out of doors, and single fare, and gymnastic exercises, and the morals of companions, produce the greatest effect in the way of vice and virtue. These causes are derived from our parents and the elements, rather than ourselves, provided that on our part there be no remissness, by keeping aloof from acts of duty. The animal cannot be in good condition unless the body possesses the better properties under its control; namely, health and correct perception, and strength and beauty.

Now the principles of beauty are a symmetry as regards its parts, and as regards the soul. For nature has arranged the body, like an instrument to be subservient to, and in harmony with, the subjects of life. The soul must likewise be brought into harmony with its analogous good qualities, namely, in the case of temperance, as the body is in the case of health; and in that of prudence, as in the case of correct perception; and in that of fortitude, as in the case of vigor and strength; and in that of justice, as in the case of beauty.

Nature, of course, furnishes their beginnings; but their continuation and maturation result from carefulness; those relating to the body, through the gymnastic and medical arts, those to the soul through instruction and philosophy. For these are the powers that nourish and give a tone to the body and soul by means of labor and gymnastic exercise, and pureness of diet; some through drug medication applied to the body, and others through discipline applied to the soul by means of punishments and reproaches; for by the encouragement they give strength and excite to an onward, movement, and exhort to beneficial deeds. The art of the gymnasium trainer, and its nearest approach, that of the medical man, do, on application to the body, reduce their powers to the utmost symmetry, purifying the blood, and equalizing the breath, so that, if there were there any diseased virulence, the powers of blood and breath may be vigorous; but music, and its leader, philosophy, which the laws and the gods ordained as regulators for the soul, accustom, persuade and partly compel the irrational to obey reason, and the two irrational, passion and desire, to become, the one mild, and the other quiet, so as not to be moved without reason, nor to be unmoved when the mind incites either to desire or enjoy something; for this is the definition of temperance, namely, docility and firmness. Intelligence and philosophy the highest in honor, after cleansing the soul from false opinions, have introduced knowledge, recalling the mind from excessive ignorance, and setting it free for the contemplation of divine things; in which to occupy oneself with self-sufficiency, as regards the affairs of a man, and with an abundance, for the commensurate period of life, is a happy state.

XII
HUMAN DESTINY

Now he to whom the deity has happened to assign some what of a good fate, is, through opinion, led to the happiest life. But if he be morose and indocile, let the punishment that comes from law and reason follow him; bringing with it the fears ever on the stretch, both those that originate in heaven or Hades; how that punishments inexorable, are below laid up for the unhappy, as well as those ancient Homeric threats of retaliation for the wickedness of those defiled by crime (Odyssey, xii 571-599). For as we sometimes restore bodies to health by means of diseased substances, if they will not yield to the more healthy, so if the soul will not be led by true reasoning, we restrain it by false. Strange indeed would those punishments be called since, by a change, the souls of cowards enter into bodies of women, who are inclined to insulting conduct; and those of the blood-stained would be punished by being introduced into the bodies of wild beasts; of the lascivious, into the bodies of sows and boars; of the light-minded and frivolous into shaper and aeronautic birds; and of those who neither do learn or think of nothing, into the bodies of idle fish.

On all these matters, however, there has, at a second period, been delivered a judgment by Nemesis, or Fate, together with the avenging deities that preside over murderers, and those under the earth in Hades, and the inspectors of human affairs, to whom God, the leader of all, has entrusted the administration of the world which is filled with gods and men, and the rest of the living beings which by the demiurgic creator according to the best model of an unbegotten, eternal and mentally-perceived form.

FINIS.

CPSIA information can be obtained
at www.ICGtesting.com
Printed in the USA
BVHW041118020221
599225BV00045B/1686